Modern Rock

From the 1960s On

First Edition

Scott D. Bacon

Drexel University

Bassim Hamadeh, CEO and Publisher
John Remington, Executive Editor
Gem Rabanera, Project Editor
Christian Berk, Production Editor
Emely Villavicencio, Senior Graphic Designer
Trey Soto, Licensing Coordinator
Jennifer Redding, Interior Designer
Natalie Piccotti, Senior Marketing Manager
Kassie Graves, Vice President of Editorial
Jamie Giganti, Director of Academic Publishing

Printed in the United States of America.

www.cognella.com 800-200-3908

ACTIVE LEARNING

This book has interactive activities available to complement your reading.

Your instructor may have customized the selection of activities available for your unique course. Please check with your professor to verify whether your class will access this content through the Cognella Active Learning portal (http://active.cognella.com) or through your home learning management system.

Dedication

I dedicate this book to my wife, Tammy, and my children, Matthew and Sarah, who have tolerated and supported me through the countless hours of work on this project. Love you!

The author wishes to thank those who have helped this text become a reality, including Gem Rabanera, Arielle Lewis, Jamie Giganti, Faye Delosreyes, Christian Berk, John Remington, and the entire staff at Cognella Academic Publishing. I also want to thank my students and colleagues at Drexel University, who provided me with critical input for the preliminary edition of the text. I am also grateful for the support of friends and colleagues at LCOB, who still roll their eyes at me quite often. Also, my deepest thanks to those music teachers and professors who cultivated my love for music from a young age and still inspire me every day.

To all of the fans of rock music—may this book introduce you to a new musician or style of music that inspires you in the way I was inspired as a teenager, leading you to a life as a fan, discerning consumer, and future rock geek.

Contents

Preface

This preface was completed on the eve of the 50th anniversary of the Woodstock Music and Art Fair, one of the most celebrated events in the history of rock music. Far from just a concert, Woodstock was a musical, social, and political event that made headlines around the world and defined a generation of young adults. Older generations actively rejected the growing counterculture that spawned Woodstock. Younger generations know it only as a historical event. This example of the Woodstock festival demonstrates how each generation identifies with the popular music of its youth. Older people will dislike and distrust newer music, while younger people view the music of their older siblings and parents as "old." Each generation, then, has what is essentially its very own rock and roll soundtrack: just as a movie would fall flat without the background music that heightens the story on the screen, the years of adolescence through high school are scored by each era's popular musicians expressing the feelings and attitudes of that time. In later years, hearing a song from that soundtrack will instantly take us back to our teens again.

For most people, then, their experience and enjoyment of music ends up being relatively constrained to the familiar period in which they grew up. The result is often ignorance of the history of even their own generation's music and a hesitation to engage with unfamiliar music. In other words, most casual music fans like what they like and dismiss all other music and those fans who like it. I can attest to this by recalling my own early tastes. I cannot remember a time when I did not love rock. My teenage years coincided with the first decade of MTV, the rise of hair bands, and Michael Jackson's greatest success. Like those of most fans, my musical tastes, knowledge of rock music history, and opinion were narrow in scope. When I became a classically trained musician, my two seemingly separate musical worlds collided. Only at that point did I begin to view rock music with a different, broader perspective. There seemed to be a common belief among rock fans that too much knowledge would somehow lessen the love for the music, that passion and scholarship cannot coexist. In more than 40 years as a fan and 25 years of study, my passion for rock has only grown. When I became a card-carrying rock geek, I found myself needing to understand how this music came to be. That exploration, followed by a quarter century of love for the teaching of rock and roll, culminated in the creation of this book.

It has been my privilege for many years to be an educator. That I get to teach what truly inspires me is one of the great blessings of my life. My wish for this book is for you to gain enjoyment while learning something new. May your passion for rock and roll continue throughout your life.

Introduction

Purpose of this Book

This book provides a succinct history of rock and roll. My goal was to create a text that I would not have minded reading as a student but also one that would also adequately cover the styles and musicians. My objective, both in writing this book and in teaching rock and roll courses, is to help students realize that rock and roll is linear. Nothing lives in a bubble: all styles are related, and the similarities far outweigh the differences among seemingly disparate musical styles. While this book's audience is college and high school students, it is also a great resource for anyone who wants to connect the dots on rock. It will inspire a greater appreciation for rock music as a whole, expose readers to many styles and artists they may not have previously known, and, hopefully, motivate readers to expand their personal playlists.

How to Read This Book

Organized chronologically by chapter, the book focuses on rock as a developed style, emphasizing the 1960s and beyond. The creation of rock and its early success in the 1950s is briefly covered, but rock's biggest growth occurred later, so greater emphasis is placed on the 1960s and the decades that followed.

Each chapter begins with an overview of the historical context of the era covered, as the text focuses on the musicians, the music, and the place of that music in society. The reader must understand the social, political, and economic environment during each period, as music is a reflection of all of these. Rather than using listening guides, this book focuses on giving the reader a greater number of **listening examples**, thus fostering greater familiarity with the artists who have made rock and roll great. The reader can access these examples, marked in the text with the below logo directly through the Active Learning Component or through online research."

Rock&Roll

The Development of Rock Through the Mid-1960s

Rock. Pop. Country. Rap. Rock and roll. Whatever name you prefer, it is America's greatest artistic contribution to the world. It exists and thrives in almost every corner of the globe, eclipsing most traditional music forms on every continent. It is a uniquely American creation, rising out of a combination of styles and circumstances that could not have occurred elsewhere.

While our primary goal in this text is to cover the second and third generations of these genres (circa 1965 through 2015), this introductory chapter will quickly cover the history of the creation of rock and roll. We need to cover this early era, as no art can exist in a bubble. It is always influenced by what comes before it and will always influence what occurs later.

The Streams of Influence

European Stream of Influence

The birth of American popular music really begins with the Emancipation Proclamation and the end of the American Civil War. To study this properly, we must discuss these streams of influence through the study of race in the United States. Although it would be simplistic to call the European stream "white" and the African stream "black," only once these two distinct musical styles began to mix did true American music exist. Music written and published before this time was created based on the European tradition. The **European stream** brought to the Unites States the music of the European classical tradition: the music of Mozart, Beethoven, and Tchaikovsky, including the musical elements of strong melodies, a keen sense of harmonization, and advanced composition. Composers were the "gods" of their creations, dictating to the musicians nearly every direction needed to perform a piece of music. The ability of musicians to follow all these directions showed their skill. Opera, ballet, symphonies, and choral church hymns were all derived from the European stream.

African Stream of Influence

The African musical tradition, or **African stream,** brought to this country through the 300-year practice of slavery and later subdued through forced segregation, added very different ingredients to what would become American music. The African tradition favored a strong rhythmic drive and thrived on the individuality of musicians. Rather than notating music on paper with detailed musical instructions, African musicians believed that once a song was committed to memory, it became the property of the musicians, who could alter the music in any way they desired. The style of a voice or instrument was determined by the performer rather than based on long-standing rules adhered to by the European musician. The African tradition involved **improvisation**, which is to create music as you play, not relying on music previously put on paper. **Call and response**—a question-and-answer motif whereby a leader plays a musical passage and is answered by another musician or group of musicians—was an important part of the African musical tradition.

These two styles and the traditions that birthed each one were so different that combining these styles was both difficult and controversial. Once the institution of slavery ended in the United States, the African tradition began to gradually become part of the mainstream American musical scene. This process, which occurred slowly due to resistance from much of the white public, eventually would develop over the remainder of the nineteenth century and throughout the twentieth century. While we are still living through this process, and while we have failed to achieve complete equality, mainstream society has for the most part accepted and embraced African American music.

Jazz and the Three Styles That Most Influenced Rock

As stated earlier, for music to be "American," there must be an integration of the European and African music styles. The first great contribution of American music to the world was jazz.

Jazz is an incredibly diverse collection of subgenres that includes a large contribution of African styles with additions from the European stream. First performed by African Americans and thus derided by much of the white American public, jazz eventually would be accepted by people of all cultures in every corner of the globe. There are many styles of jazz performed by differing ensembles and utilizing an extremely wide variety of musical traits. The three jazz styles that were most important to the formation of rock and roll in the middle of the twentieth century were the blues, gospel, and swing.

The Blues

The blues, developed in the late 1800s in the deep South, incorporated much of the traditions of enslaved African Americans. This music was derived from work songs, spirituals, and, to a degree, the European music that plantation owners taught slaves. This music form utilized patterns, the most well-known of which is 12-bar blues. Twelve-bar blues consists of 12 bars or measures of four beats each. These 48 total beats occur through a specific chord progression. This musical form was adapted by most of the music that would become rock and roll by the mid-1950s. One of the most famous and mysterious bluesmen was Robert Johnson.

FIGURE 1.1 Robert Johnson

Robert Johnson (1911–1938) is considered an early master of the blues. His early death at age 27, after he'd recorded only 29 songs, has helped to fan the flames of the crossroad myth. The legend states that Johnson met the devil at a crossroads in Mississippi and sold his soul for the ability to play the guitar. Rock guitar great Eric Clapton has called Johnson "the most important blues musician who ever lived" (LaVere 1990).

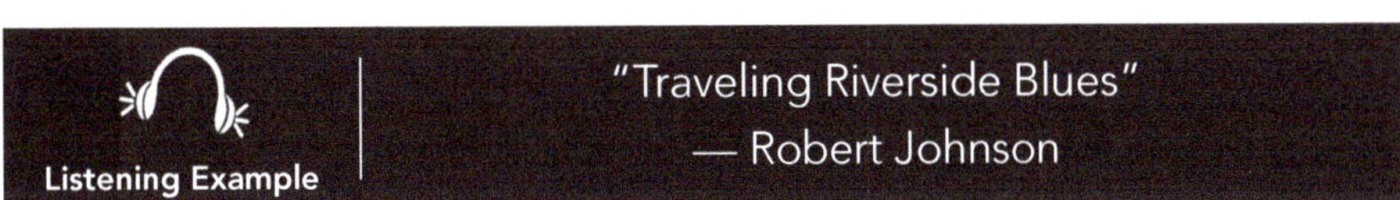

Gospel

The second jazz form to have an enormous impact on what would become rock and roll was gospel. Gospel provided the vocal energy injected into rhythm and blues (R&B) following the swing era (1935–1945). A soloist, accompanied by a choir and/or band, marks this singing style with an unrestrained vocal technique. The gospel singing style, derived from the traditional Southern African American church service (with a minister preaching the sermon with increasing intensity) was designed specifically to increase the excitement levels of the congregation. This style could include a backup band and choir. The soloist would also act as a sort of preacher, with vocals increasing in intensity throughout the song or service. Gospel soloists are known for their raw power, vocal gymnastics, and emotional sound. Although gospel directly influenced some rock musicians (Ray Charles, Little Richard, Aretha Franklin, Whitney Houston, and others), all rock and roll musicians would be influenced by the gospel vocal creed: if you feel it, sing it. We hear this sound from Mahalia Jackson, the "Queen of Gospel" (1911–1972) when she sings "Great Gettin' Up Morning."

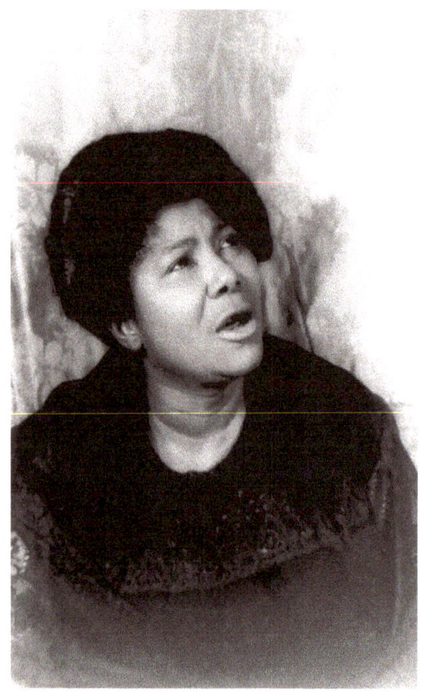

FIGURE 1.2 Mahalia Jackson

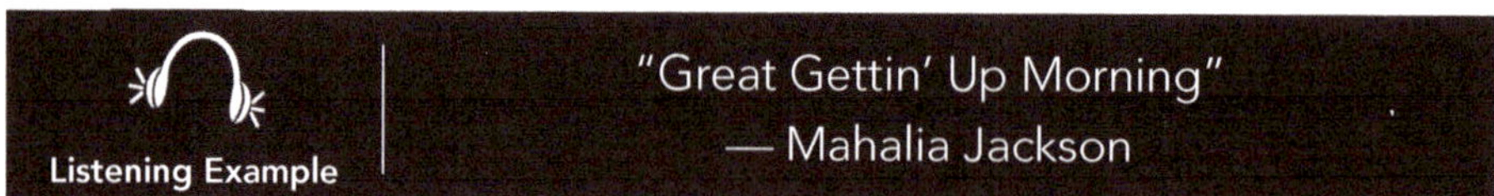

Swing

The third style of jazz that directly influenced rock and roll was swing. Swing was unique as a jazz style in that it became mainstream popular music for about a decade (1935–1945). Swing has always been linked with World War II and the "Greatest Generation." Swing was much more than just a style of music. The term was used to describe a culture that stretched across racial, economic, generational, and geographic lines. It included particular styles of dress, dance, architecture, and language. Primarily, it was music for dancing. Swing bands consisted of three sections and numbered anywhere from 12 to 40 members. The brass section had trumpets and trombones, the woodwind section had clarinets and a variety of saxophones, and the rhythm section had a drum set, a bass violin (plucked rather than bowed), a piano, and a rhythm guitar. The syncopated **call and response** among the sections of the swing band created a new rhythmic intensity not found in previous musical styles. Society was looking for a new form of entertainment following the Great Depression, and swing dancing became the new way to party on a weekend night.

The great swing bands toured constantly, and huge numbers of young people would dress up for a night of dining and dancing. The swing era made international stars of performers such as Benny Goodman, Glenn Miller, and Tommy Dorsey. Swing crossed cultural and ethnic divides, even though the success of the performers was largely based on race. The white swing performers dominated the radio airwaves, while African American swing performers were relegated to black radio stations, as radio was still segregated. Although there was some rare integration of performers in swing bands, most audiences were necessarily segregated according to which clubs allowed African American patrons. Two of the most famous performers of the swing era were Glenn Miller (1904–1944 [MIA]) and Duke Ellington (1899–1974). Glenn Miller was the undisputed "King of Swing." His white swing bands dominated the charts from 1939–1943, compiling 23 number one hits. The best known of all of Miller's hits (and the best known of any swing era hit) was "In the Mood." Although Miller's music is no longer considered the best of the era, it was the most popular of that time.

FIGURE 1.3 Glenn Miller

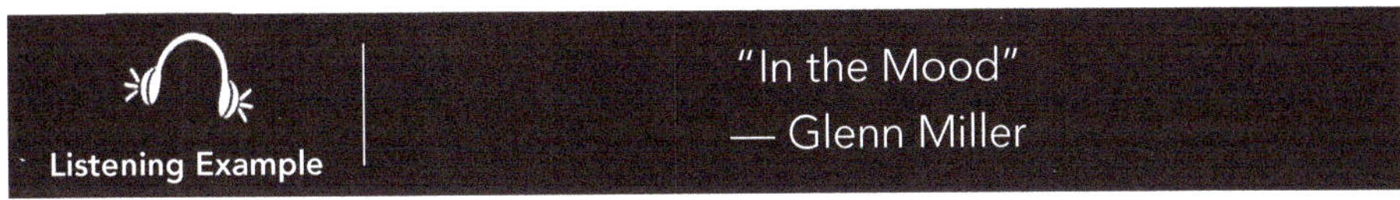

FIGURE 1.4 Duke Ellington

Edward "Duke" Ellington grew up in Washington, DC, the son of upper-middle-class parents. From an early age, his demeanor and personality earned him the nickname "Duke." Ellington would have a career of more than 50 years and eventually be considered one of the greatest American musicians of the 20th century. His rhythmic and harmonic innovations are now considered genius, but during the swing era, his music, although viewed live by some white audiences, was nevertheless banned from white radio. As we listen to "Crescendo and Diminuendo in Blue," listen for the new, dense tone colors and rhythmic vitality. This truly was the innovative music of its day.

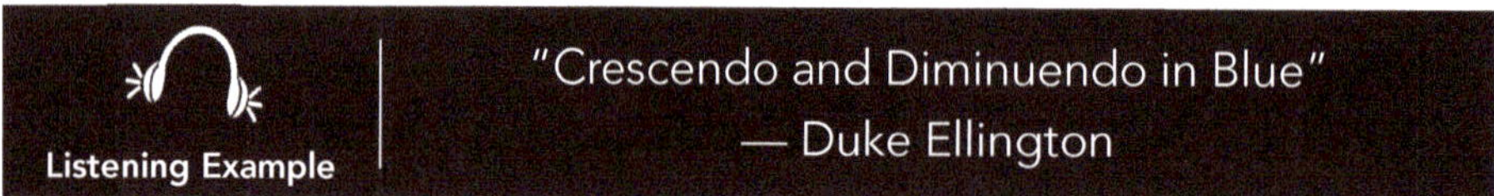

The Decline of Swing

When World War II ended in 1945, the swing era was already in decline. There were multitudes of reasons for this, both aesthetic and practical in nature. During the war, it had become increasingly impractical and unaffordable for swing bands to continue. There had been rationing and taxes on many everyday activities and commodities to help finance the war effort. These included rationed tires and gasoline as well as a 20 percent entertainment tax. Therefore, for a 30-piece swing band to tour, these restrictions made it increasingly expensive.

The attitudes of the listening public also changed during the war. Those living on the home front were less likely to go out and party while siblings, parents, and friends were on different continents fighting for the very survival of the country. It was also likely that most Americans would know someone close to them who had become a casualty of the war. It affected almost everyone.

During this difficult time, people were increasingly drawn toward the sentimental music of the crooner, a singer who sang sweet songs about love and loss, songs about what everyone was experiencing at the time. As swing bands went into decline, they began to become more economical: that is, the number of musicians in the bands began to shrink. The first instruments to go were the brass instruments, followed by the clarinets and some of the saxophones. What was left would go on to become the basis for the rock and roll band—a guitar, a bass, a drum set, a piano, and a saxophone or two. This is how the rock band came into existence.

As the swing era ended and adult swing fans moved on to the sentimental music of the crooners, we started to see the beginnings of a generational split. The youngest of the swing fans, who were far less likely to be emotionally affected by World War II, wanted music that would continue to allow them to dance: music that was fast, energetic, and had a strong beat. This brings us to a transitional form that existed between swing and rock and roll—not quite either but comprised of elements of both forms. This music was called **jump**.

Jump: The Transition to Rhythm and Blues/Rock and Roll

A great example of this style is the music of Louis Jordan (1908–1975). Jordan came out of the swing era, but he was always a bit too enigmatic to be a swing singer. Jordan combined elements of the 12-bar blues, boogie-woogie piano, and a smaller version of a swing band that became so influential to what would become rock and roll that he was inducted into the Rock and Roll Hall of Fame in 1987. His A-type personality, humor, and crazy saxophone solos would become the best examples of "pre–rock and roll." Listen to "Choo Choo Ch' Boogie." You will hear elements of both swing music and early rock and roll. While we hear the harmonies of swing brass and woodwinds, we also hear the strong bass line of the 12-bar blues. We also hear a saxophone solo that would not fit in a traditional swing song and provides a great example of the way in which the saxophone became the first solo instrument of rock and roll.

FIGURE 1.5 Louis Jordan

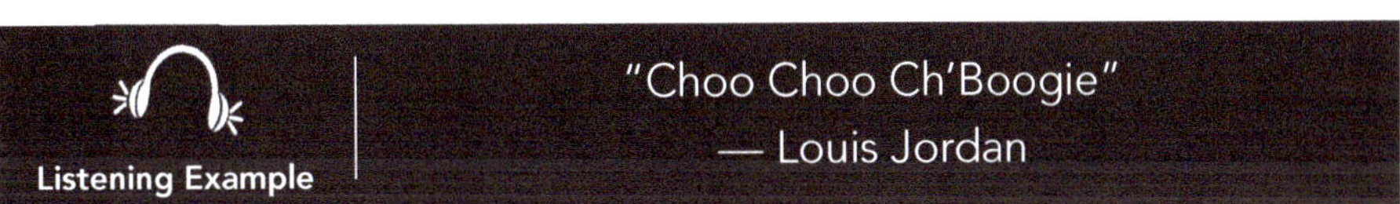

Rhythm and Blues

By the late 1940s, the term "rhythm and blues" was used to describe African American music that developed out of the transition from swing to jump. While the style was varied, it almost always included the danceable intensity of swing with up-tempo blues patterns. What would cause this style to become very popular in the 1950s would be the increasing number of white teenagers who loved this music. As you will read later, this would also cause many controversies.

FIGURE 1.6 Fats Domino

One of the first R&B performers was Antoine "Fats" Domino (1928–2017). Fats Domino was born and raised in New Orleans and sold tens of millions of records in the 1950s. Domino's music and personality were a great first step for white kids to get into rock and roll. His presentation was contained, which meant that it was not too bluesy or gospel based for white teenagers to understand. His song "The Fat Man" (released in 1949) is widely considered one of the first rock and roll records and is the first rock and roll record to sell one million copies (Pareles 2017). Other great hits for Fats were "Ain't That a Shame," "Blueberry Hill," and "I'm Walkin'."

Cover Tunes and the 1950s

FIGURE 1.7A Little Richard

Cover tunes were a tool record companies used in the 1950s to promote R&B to white kids. Today we use the terms "cover band" or "cover tune" to describe any band or musician who re-records music originally performed by another musician, but in the 1950s, cover tunes were the means to recast black R&B songs with a white singer. It was believed that white teenagers, and the parents of white teenagers in particular, would be more willing to accept a great song if it was sung by a white performer. Ultimately, it became a money-making tool for record companies. One of the most famous cover song singers was Pat Boone (born 1934). Boone sold more than 45 million records in the late 1950s and early 1960s, surpassed in popularity only by Elvis Presley. According to *Billboard*, Boone ranks ninth all-time in chart success from 1955–1995 (Whitburn 1996, 806). Boone's covers were antiseptic, removing most blues and gospel influences from the original African American versions.

FIGURE 1.7B Pat Boone

One great example of a cover song from the 1950s is "Tutti Frutti." Originally written and recorded by Little Richard in 1955 and released as a single in 1956, it was covered by Boone the same year. Boone's version scored better on the pop charts, as white America was still very concerned and perplexed about black music and musicians. Although Little Richard was resentful of Boone's success at the time, he has more recently stated that he believes his music became more accepted through cover tunes. As you listen to both versions, ask yourself these questions:

1. How are they different? (You can include instrumentation, lyric content, tempo, etc.)
2. Which do you prefer, and why?
3. How do you feel about cover songs that are created today?

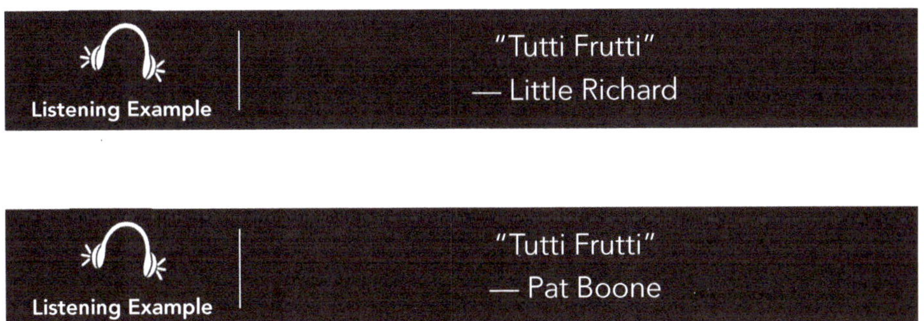

Chuck, Elvis, and Racial Identity in 1956

In 1955, just as rock and roll was becoming a greater influence on teen audiences, Chuck Berry (1926–2017) and Elvis Presley (1935–1977) began careers that would dominate rock and roll and influence scores of future musicians. Aside from their great success on the charts and their iconic status, they both inadvertently became producers of social change. They were performers who broke stereotypes, and radio play of their early hits confused a listening public. Was the performer white or black?

Was he singing country and western or rhythm and blues? This confusion, based on the style of the individual performer, caused a greater number of young white listeners to ignore race when choosing music they loved. In today's society, with the 24-hour news cycle and instant information on our phones and televisions, it seems as if all information is immediately available to us on almost any given subject. In 1955, only about a half of homes in the United States had televisions (Genova 2013), and most of those homes were in urban and suburban areas on the East Coast. Most television shows were not airing performances of this new teen music, preferring to satisfy the viewing requirements of parents, who were the ones buying the expensive televisions.

Chuck Berry

Chuck Berry (1926–2017) was the first rock and roller to make the electric guitar, rather than the piano or saxophone, the primary solo instrument of rock and roll. Berry, who was born in St. Louis, Missouri, was influenced by white singers, such as Frank Sinatra and Gene Autry ("The Singing Cowboy"). He was not from the South and did not sing with a Southern accent. His first hit, "Maybellene," provoked racial questioning when it first played on the radio. Listeners called radio stations demanding to know if Berry was white or black. Even as Berry played live in concert, he would hear people in the audience say to one another, "I thought he was white." Although the concern was paramount to older white America, it seemed that by the time teens found out Berry was an African American, they already loved the songs and did not seem to care as much about Berry's skin color. This failure to adhere to the stereotype of white music versus black music is one of the great moments of the beginnings of social change, both in music and society.

FIGURE 1.8 Chuck Berry

Berry was very cognizant of his audience. He realized that to gain a large audience, he needed to create music that would be accepted by all teenagers, regardless of race. His songs were about the major thoughts and concerns of all teenagers, such as love, cars, and school. What was most unusual about Berry was that he was nearly 30 years old when he began his career in rock and roll. He was far removed from those angst-filled teen years. It may have been this age difference that allowed him to aim his message directly at the teen market.

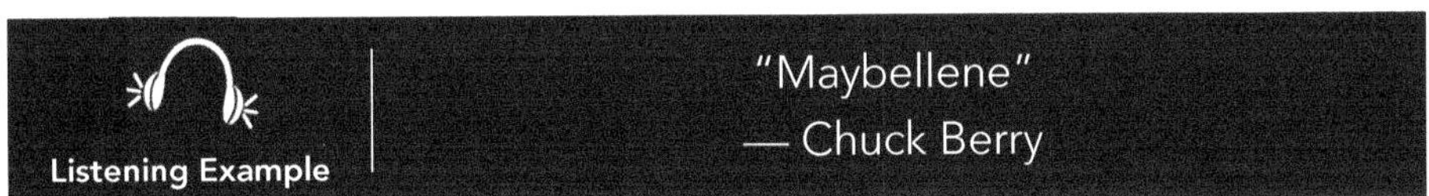

"Maybellene," Berry's first hit song, is a fascinating record. While it does include the 12-bar blues, it is not considered a blues song. It has a meter grouping of two rather than four beats, which was usually used for blues and R&B songs. The two-beat meter was used primarily for country and western music. Combined with Chuck's Midwest vocal performance, the song was often perceived to be a country and western song. Berry's lyrics were often overlooked at the time (as most rock lyrics were) as being shallow. However, Berry's lyrics often added a deeper meaning that has earned him respect from musicians he has influenced. With "Maybellene," we hear a song about the narrator in a car race with a girl named Maybellene. Therefore, we hear a boy both literally and figuratively chasing a girl. He is in love with her as he sings, "Maybellene, why can't you be true?" We also hear that he has a blue-collar background and is driving a V8 Ford, and she is wealthier and driving a Cadillac. Therefore, this song is about class. He is chasing a girl who is "out of his league." The song avoids any reference to race, however.

Elvis Presley

Elvis Presley (1935–1977) became the first mass-marketed rock and roll star, a performer who, though white, defied stereotypes by singing with influences of the blues, gospel, and country and western music. Presley became known as "The King of Rock and Roll" or "The King." He dominated the pop charts from 1956 until 1958, and he continued to be a celebrated performer until his death from heart failure in 1977 at the age of 42. Presley grew up in Tupelo, Mississippi, surrounded by black gospel music. As a teenager, he moved to Memphis with his family. Presley was the perfect face of rock and roll in 1956. He was white, so he was less susceptible to dismissal based purely on race, but he was dangerous enough to drive teenage girls into screaming fits. His singing ability was incredible. He could sing blues-based rock and sweet sentimental ballads with equal brilliance. Sam Phillips, owner of Sun Records in Memphis, signed Presley to a contract after Elvis showed up at Sun Studio to make a record for his mother for her birthday. Immediately, Phillips saw what he was looking for: "A white Southern boy who could sing like a black man" (Deane, Thomson, and Espar 1995). Although politically incorrect today, Phillips recognized

FIGURE 1.9 Elvis Presley

that it would take a white singer to get this music accepted by the greater public. While white teens were getting into rock and roll, the adult public was resistant. When Presley was first broadcast on radio, the same confusion that beset Berry occurred. Was Presley black or white? Was he a country singer or a blues singer? Just as had occurred with Berry, this temporary confusion assisted with broadening the base of rock music fans at a time when it was difficult to do so. Here are two great examples that show Presley's versatility as a singer:

In 1958, Presley was drafted into the Army. While the draft was an accepted part of society, the author believes this occurred as part of a conspiracy to stop Presley's domination of the music charts and thus end the new domination of rock and roll. Many forces within the U.S. government and society did not like the influence of this new music. Whereas some certainly were against this music based on its African American roots, many would publicly use other reasoning to debase it. Although Presley did not choose to fight his draft notice, it seems more than coincidence that his draft occurred at the exact apex of his career. After Presley returned from his Army service, he continued to create hit songs, act in very popular movies, and sing to sold-out concert audiences. However, his reign as the wild, dangerous teen heartthrob had ended. In just the two years that he was out of the public eye, music had begun to rapidly change, and, for the rest of his career, he would constantly chase the ever-changing new styles of music.

Buddy Holly, the Day the Music Died, and the End of Rock and Roll

Buddy Holly (1936–1959), born in Lubbock, Texas, would be the last great rock and roll star of the 1950s and the last of the original rock and rollers. He was the heir apparent to the fans of Presley and Little Richard and was preferred by the younger brothers and sisters of those fans. Holly was different from Presley and Richard, however. Part of the popularity of Presley and Richard was that they were so incredibly different from the fans who loved their music. Kids did not relate to Presley or Richard, but they loved them for their personalities and stage presence. Holly, however, was perceived by many teens to be more approachable and like a normal person. His black-rimmed glasses and calmer stage style brought some of the sincerity of country music into rock and roll. Holly's career would be brief, however. On February 3, 1959, Holly, J. P. "The Big Bopper" Richardson, and Richie Valens, were killed in a plane crash along with the pilot in Clear Lake, Iowa, while on tour. This crash became the subject matter of the 1970 Don McLean song "American Pie" and is known in rock music history as "The Day the Music Died."

FIGURE 1.10 Buddy Holly

The Payola Scandal

The payola scandal occurred in the late 1950s due to an increasing backlash from those who were hoping to curb the rising success of rock and roll. Payola, by definition, is the illegal practice of giving money or benefits to radio disc jockeys for preferential or repeated playing of an individual song or group of songs. This practice had existed long before the success of rock and roll, but many during the 1950s attempted to link payola with rock. Rock disc jockeys (DJs) were incredibly influential, sometimes having as much or more influence on listeners than artists, so record company executives knew that to have hit records, they had to have DJs at big radio stations play them. Often, record company executives would personally bring stacks

FIGURE 1.11 Alan Freed

of singles to the most popular DJs, and often the executives would include a pile of cash with those records. This practice existed from the beginning of radio and was overlooked by the police and the government, but in the late 1950s it was used as a way to hurt this new music. Alan Freed, the famous DJ who originated the term "rock and roll," was forced to testify about the practice in front of the U.S. Congress in 1959. While this scandal brought to the public's attention the fact that the DJs did not pay taxes on the income paid by the record companies, the true motivation was to discredit the new music form attributed to African Americans.

This scandal, along with Presley's Army service, Little Richard's decision to return to gospel music, a Berry run-in with the law, and the deaths of Holly, Valens, and The Big Bopper, seemed to bring the initial era of rock and roll to an end. It left a void, and many were not sure what might fill that void. As the 1950s ended, no one seemed sure if rock would survive or, if it did, how it would move forward. In Chapter 2, we will move on to the 1960s, when big changes would dominate the landscape of rock music moving forward.

References

Deane, Elizabeth, Hugh Thomson, and David Espar, prods. *Rock and Roll: Renegades and In the Groove.* Featuring Fats Domino, Little Richard, Chuck Berry, Elvis Presley, Jerry Lee Lewis, Muddy Waters, etc. WGBH, Boston and British Broadcasting Corporation, 1995. VHS.

Genova, Tom. *Television History—The First 75 Years.* Accessed June 20, 2019. http://www.tvhistory.tv/.

LaVere, Stephen. Booklet accompanying Robert Johnson, *The Complete Recordings*, 26. Sony Music Entertainment, 1990.

Pareles, Jon, and William Grimes. "Fats Domino, Early Rock 'n' Roller with a Boogie-Woogie Piano, Is Dead at 89." October 25, 2017. Accessed October 26, 2017. https://www.nytimes.com/2017/10/25/obituaries/fats-domino-89-one-of-rock-n-rolls-first-stars-is-dead.html.

Whitburn, Joel. *The Billboard Book of Top 40 Hits.* New York: Billboard, 1996.

Figure Credits

IMG. 1.1: Copyright © 2010 Depositphotos/wetnose.

Fig. 1.1: Copyright © by Joe Mazzola (CC BY-SA 2.0) at https://commons.wikimedia.org/wiki/File:ClarksdaleMS_Crossroads.jpg.

Fig. 1.2: Source: https://commons.wikimedia.org/wiki/File:Mahalia_Jackson_1962,_van_Vechten,_LC-USZ62-91314.jpg.

Fig. 1.3: Source: https://commons.wikimedia.org/wiki/File:Glenn_Miller_Billboard.jpg.

Fig. 1.4: Source: https://commons.wikimedia.org/wiki/File:Duke_Ellington_-_publicity.JPG.

Fig. 1.5: Source: https://commons.wikimedia.org/wiki/File:Louis_Jordan,_New_York,_N.Y.,_ca._July_1946_(William_P._Gottlieb_04721).jpg.

Fig. 1.6: Source: https://commons.wikimedia.org/wiki/File:Fats_Domino_in_Amsterdam,_Fats_tijdens_zijn_optreden_in_het_Concertgebouw,_Bestanddeelnr_914-4777.jpg.

Fig. 1.7a: Source: https://commons.wikimedia.org/wiki/File:Little_Richard_in_2007.jpg.

Fig. 1.7b: Source: https://commons.wikimedia.org/wiki/File:Pat_Boone,_Pic,_10.jpg.

Fig. 1.8: Source: https://commons.wikimedia.org/wiki/File:Chuck_Berry_1957.jpg.

Fig. 1.9: Source: https://en.wikipedia.org/wiki/File:Elvis_Presley_promoting_Jailhouse_Rock.jpg.

Fig. 1.10: Source: https://commons.wikimedia.org/wiki/File:Buddy_Holly_cropped.JPG.

Fig. 1.11: Source: https://commons.wikimedia.org/wiki/File:Alan_Freed_disk_jockey.jpg.

CHAPTER 2

The Early 1960s: Between Elvis and the Beatles

Historical Context for the Decade

The 1960s was a decade of intense social and musical change. Most casual rock fans know about the dominance of Elvis in the 1950s and the Beatles a decade later but do not understand the important changes that occurred between the heydays of these groundbreaking artists. In the early 1960s, there were four important new developments in rock: (1) the "Wall of Sound" recording technique of Phil Spector; (2) the Brill Building assembly line of songwriting; (3) the new dominance of surf pop and the influence of surf rock; and (4) the emergence of Motown. These developments would set the scene for the rapid change that would occur in music during the remainder of the decade. Music is always a reflection of society as a whole, and in the 1960s, American society underwent a rapid transformation. The best way to begin discussing this decade is to talk about the culture of the United States in the 1960s.

FIGURE 2.1 Vietnam War Protest

The 1960s was a time of rapid development and change in the United States. While most think of the 1960s as the era of the "hippy" counterculture and the Vietnam War protests, these events occurred during the last half of the decade and were not representative of society or the decade as a whole. For American society, the 1960s began as the 1950s had ended, as a time of conformity. The post–World War II norms included the stability of President Dwight D. Eisenhower (1953–1961), relative economic prosperity, and the perceived blessings of suburbia. This conformity made perfect sense, as those who were parents of young children had experienced the hardships and loss of World War II. This sense of normalcy often meant leaving the city in favor of sprawling suburban subdivisions with cookie-cutter homes. The dream of many World War II veterans (often called the "Greatest Generation") was to earn a college degree through the GI Bill, get married, start a family, and own a home. While this lifestyle seemed the ideal for those who lived through World War II, it would later be the foundation from which the 1960s youth counterculture would emerge. The 1950s would also begin the advancements of the modern-day civil rights movement. In 1954, the Supreme Court heard the arguments in the case of *Brown v. Board of Education*, which ended the legal practice of segregating schools based on race.

In 1955, Rosa Parks refused to give up her bus seat to a white rider. Upon her arrest, a boycott of the Montgomery, Alabama, bus system by African American riders continued for more than a year. The leader of that boycott was a 26-year-old minister named Martin Luther King Jr. Most mark this protest as the beginning of the modern civil rights movement (Branch 1988). The emergence of rock and roll in the 1950s coincided with many of these new changes in societal norms. While our society today continues to move forward and strive for equality as an accepted norm, this was not the case at the time. Rock and roll, perceived to be black music, became the target of many white Americans' fear based on these changes.

The 1960s Explode

While great social advances were made in the 1950s, the process was slow and cumbersome. By the 1960s, most white teenagers had accepted black music, though many of their parents were not fans. In 1961, John F. Kennedy was elected president (1961–1963). This was regarded as a new era in American life. Kennedy was young (43 at the time of his election), glamorous, and focused on advancing civil rights in a way no previous president had attempted. This progressive president was particularly popular with younger voters who were looking for a change from the policies of the 1950s. The record industry, while generally accepting African American music and realizing its popularity with teenagers, would sometimes refuse to show the faces of black singers on album or single record covers. The popularity of rock continued to grow, and the first second-generation rock and rollers became popular. Whenever a new style of music arises and has limited appeal, that style will eventually move toward the populist center. Rock and roll in the 1960s would soften the edges of Little Richard's unrestrained, gospel-derived vocal techniques in favor of a smoother, contained sound that often included string instruments and orchestral percussion. The music producer would become someone who, for the first time in rock, had great artistic control over the music. One producer who epitomized this control was Phil Spector.

Phil Spector and the Wall of Sound

Phil Spector born 1939 (dec 26 1939) began his career in music as a member of the 1950s group the Teddy Bears. He would begin his producing career as an intern for Jerry Leiber and Mike Stoller (successful songwriting and record producing partners), but he would become better known as the producer for many early 1960s girl groups, including the Crystals, the Ronettes, and Darlene Love. By the age of 21, he had started Philles Records, usually working out of Gold Star Studios in Los Angeles, California. His influence over these recordings was complete. He often wrote or cowrote the songs, hired and fired the players, and applied his Wall of Sound recording technique to the songs. Also known for his intense personality, he was convicted of second-degree murder in 2009 and sentenced to 19 years in prison.

FIGURE 2.2 Phil Spector

The Wall of Sound

The Wall of Sound was a production technique that revolutionized the sound of recorded music in the early 1960s. Spector's idea was to create "little teen symphonies" that had the musical power of opera and the symphonic works of the late 19th century. The process was simple: double or triple the number of instruments in the recording studio and use microphones on all the instruments in that small space. The effect of having so many musicians in a small space created echo, and each microphone picked up not only the instrument to which it was assigned but also sounds from surrounding instruments. This provided a very thick sound, which would hit you like a "wall." This huge, seemingly unending sound was new in the world of rock and roll. Whereas recordings today tend to isolate instruments, allowing the recording of each particular instrument to be altered, rock and roll was usually recorded using the

FIGURE 2.3 The Ronettes

entire group and requiring multiple takes, if necessary. Spector's technique, while new and revolutionary then, is now considered antiquated. The style became so popular so quickly that the new norm of music in the early 1960s was a female vocal group backed by a dense instrumental sound. Two great examples of this sound are "Da Doo Ron Ron" as performed by the Crystals and "Be My Baby" as performed by the Ronettes. As you listen to these two examples, take in the dense sound of the backing instruments. Spector's goal was that the listener would never hear even a split second of silence. He wanted you to be overcome by a rolling wave of sound that never stops.

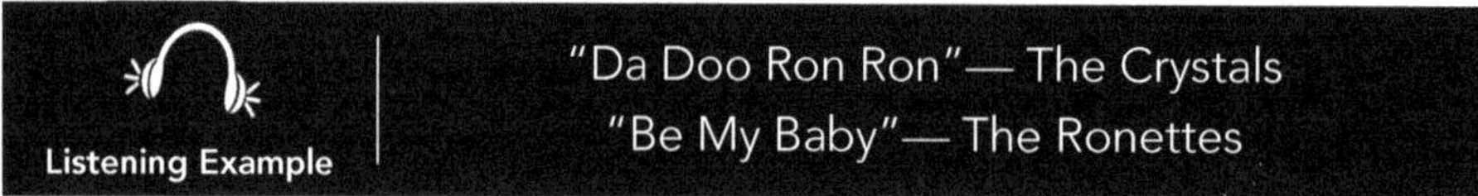

Brill Building Pop: Legendary Composers

From circa 1959 until the British Invasion began in 1964, songs written by "Brill Building" composers dominated pop music. The Brill Building is located at 1619 Broadway at 49th Street in Midtown Manhattan. This building, and several others in the vicinity, became home to many songwriters, publishing companies, and artists' representatives during this period. Brill Building songs were known for their simple lyrics that continued the pop music tradition of the time with a new emphasis on adding instrumentation that was more complex. Phil Spector used Brill Building composers for much of his success with his girl groups. Brill Building composers and producers often used string instruments and orchestral percussion, such as the timpani, to "elevate" or enhance rock and roll, which up to that point had been stereotyped as inferior music. Brill Building popular music was often called the New Tin Pan Alley, which was the location in New York City (about 20 blocks south) where much of the popular music in the United States from the late 19th century through the stock market crash of 1929 had been composed (Fontenot 2015). Although Tin Pan Alley existed past that time, the emergence of radio and the phonograph diluted its influence. Married songwriting teams wrote many of the Brill Building songs that dominated the charts in the 1960s. Three of the most successful of these teams are highlighted below.

Gerry Goffin and Carole King

Gerry Goffin (1939–2014) and Carole King (born 1942) wrote dozens of successful hits during the 1960s for the Drifters ("Up on the Roof"), the Shirelles ("Will You Still Love Me Tomorrow"), Little Eva ("The Loca-Motion"), Aretha Franklin ("You Make Me Feel Like a Natural Woman"), and the Monkees ("Pleasant Valley Sunday"). Their great success with songwriting ultimately delayed King's own career as a singer. Her career exploded with the release of her album *Tapestry* in 1971, which sold more than 25 million records. King's great tune writing, paired with Goffin's simple yet elevated lyrics, provided inspiration for many great songwriters who would follow. Paul McCartney once said that he wished he could write music as well as Goffin and King, and the Beatles covered the Goffin and King song "Chains" on their 1963 *Please Please Me* album (Johnston 2016).

The Shirelles recorded the first hit Goffin and King had as songwriters in 1960. "Will You Love Me Tomorrow" was a perfect song to begin a new decade with great changes coming. The song was the first number one song recorded by an African American female group (Bronson 1992). The lyric content of the song was controversial. In the song, the female singer is asking her boyfriend if he will still love her tomorrow if they have sex. In the pre–sexual revolution era of 1960, with the birth control pill having recently been approved for use, the question of whether to remain a virgin became something teenage girls were, for the first time, considering as a choice rather than holding to the norms of society. This song addresses that issue and includes wonderful instrumentation, including a solo section in the middle of the song dominated by string instruments. The use of strings in rock and roll was a new concept. It helped rock to be more mainstream, as orchestral instrumentation seemed to elevate rock to a more acceptable level of music for older listeners.

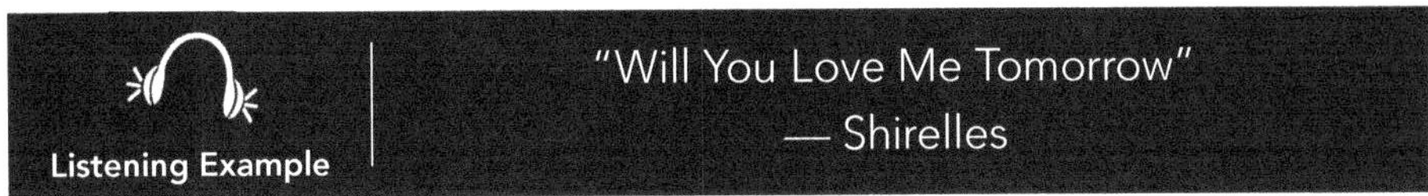

Jeff Barry and Ellie Greenwich

Jeff Barry (Joel Adelberg, born 1938) met Ellie Greenwich (1940–2009) at the Brill Building while waiting for an audition. Jerry Lieber and Mike Stoller also overheard her playing the piano between auditions, and they immediately signed her to work for them. Barry and Greenwich were married in 1963 (until 1965) but continued to work together writing songs throughout much of the remainder of the 1960s. Their biggest successes were songs they wrote for Phil Spector. While Spector's input in the songwriting process may have been minimal, he often demanded and received songwriting credits for songs he would accept for his girl groups. These songs included "Be My Baby" and "Da Doo Ron Ron" as well as "Leader of the Pack," recorded by the Shangri-Las, "Do-Wah-Diddy," a number one hit for the British Invasion group Manfred Mann, and "Christmas (Baby Please Come Home)," a perennial Christmas favorite recorded by Darlene Love ("Ellie Greenwich" 2009).

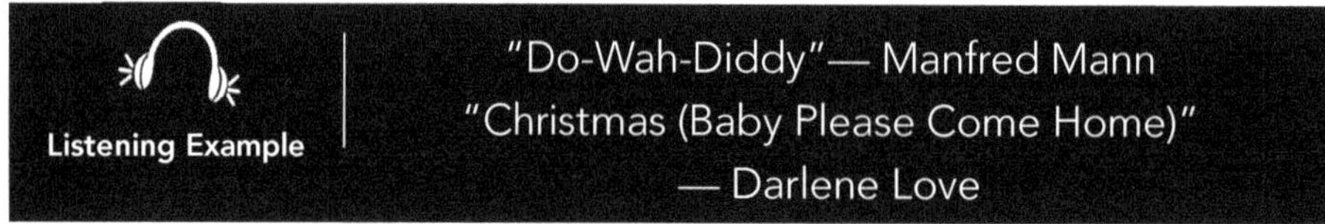

Barry Mann and Cynthia Weil

Barry Mann (born 1939) and Cynthia Weil (born 1940) met near the Brill Building at Aldon Music, where they were both staff writers. They married in 1961 and have had a very successful career cowriting songs, including "On Broadway" for the Drifters (with cowriting credits for Leiber and Stoller) and the Righteous Brothers number one hit "You've Lost that Lovin' Feeling." What distinguishes Mann and Weil from most other Brill Building composers is the continued success they had as songwriters long after the initial success of Brill Building rock. They had great success in the 1980s with "Just Once," recorded by Quincy Jones featuring James Ingram, and "Don't Know Much" by Linda Ronstadt and Aaron Neville. Their 1986 song "Somewhere Out There" from the Disney movie *An American Tail* won two Grammy Awards. They even cowrote a top ten hit with pop group Hanson in 1997.

Listen to "You've Lost that Lovin' Feeling" by the Righteous Brothers. This song, produced by Phil Spector in 1964, is considered one of the most often-played songs of the 20th century. It was, at the time, a recording masterpiece. The slow tempo, low pitch, and symphonic bombast that builds throughout the song were another brand-new sound from Phil Spector.

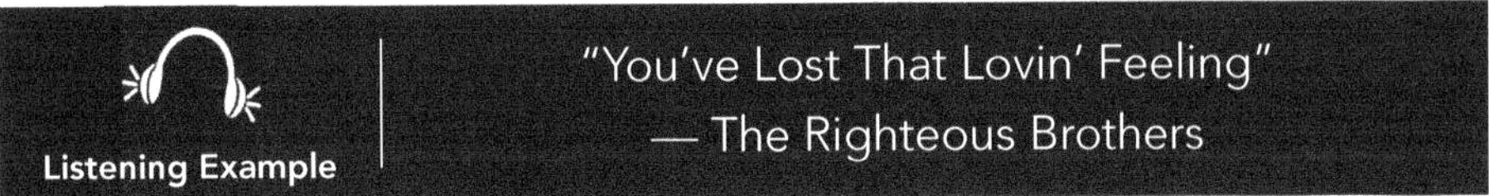

Surf Pop and Surf Rock

By the late 1950s, the growing scene in Southern California around surfing was beginning to influence young people around the country. This surf culture had its own language, dress, and music. There were two particular types of surf music. Surf rock was created by and performed for surfers in California and would influence guitar players of future generations. Its counterpart, surf pop, would become one of the most successful forms of 1960s rock and roll.

Surf Rock and Dick Dale

Dick Dale (1937–2019), known as "The King of the Surf Guitar" was one of the most influential guitarists of the 20th century. His guitar sound, influenced by his Lebanese ancestry, incorporated fast alternating picking and Middle Eastern melodies. He was born in Boston, Massachusetts, but moved with his family to El Segundo, California, as a teenager. He immediately became a surfer and began to incorporate the sounds he heard when he was riding waves (Huey 2019). He also began keeping lions and tigers as pets and added the sounds of their roars into his playing. These three unusual influences provided a base for a guitar sound not heard before but one that would later influence Jimi Hendrix and Eddie Van Halen. While the surf pop sounds of the Beach Boys would top the charts throughout the 1960s, Dale would, without national hit records, become an innovator in electric guitar playing. Dale is also credited as the one of the fathers of heavy metal music for his guitar technique and for

FIGURE 2.4 Dick Dale

being the first guitarist to play using a 15-inch, 100-watt amplifier. Although his success was short-lived in the 1960s, many musicians and music fans have continued to play and listen to his music. In 1994, director Quentin Tarantino used Dale's song "Miserlou" in his film *Pulp Fiction*. Listen for the staccato picking technique, the Middle Eastern–influenced melody, and the lion's roars in "Miserlou."

Surf Pop

While not as authentic to surfing as Dick Dale's surf rock, surf pop became an international sensation and the musical canvas for a true genius in rock—Brian Wilson.

FIGURE 2.5 The Beach Boys

In 1961, Brian Wilson (born 1942) formed the Pendletones in Hawthorne, California, with his two younger brothers, Dennis (1944–1983) and Carl (1946–1998), his cousin, Mike Love (born 1941), and high school friend Al Jardine (born 1942). This group, renamed the Beach Boys upon the release of their first album, would be the template for Brian Wilson's musical ideas for the remainder of the 1960s and beyond (Bush 2019). Wilson grew up listening to vocal harmony groups like the Four Freshmen. These types of vocal groups and the new Wall of Sound from Phil Spector had an enormous influence on Brian Wilson, who ultimately created the Beach Boys sound. Wilson once remarked that he was riding in a car with his girlfriend when he heard "Be My Baby" by the Ronettes on the radio, which forced him to pull over to the side of the road. He said from that point, his mind had been "re-set." (Deane, Thomson, and Espar 1995). Wilson made the decision to create his own Wall of Sound using voices rather than instruments. While the songs that became popular early in their career would be about surfing, only one of the Beach Boys (Dennis Wilson) was a surfer. Dennis suggested that Brian write songs that would capitalize on the rising surf scene in Southern California. In 1961, they released the song "Surfin'," which was a local success that hit number 75 on the *Billboard* Top

100 (Schinder 2007). The next year, their first album, *Surfin' Safari*, hit number 32 on the *Billboard* charts. In 1963, the Beach Boys released *Surfin' USA*, which reached number two on the *Billboard* top album chart (Badman 2004). The success of this album and the related publicity were the predominant forces that pushed the surfing lifestyle to national prominence.

By 1963, Brian had become increasingly dissatisfied with touring and wanted to spend his time working in the studio. This change marked the end of the Beach Boys as a rock and roll band and began a transformation to a more complex sound that moved away from songs about sand, surf, bikinis, and high school. Wilson wanted to create music that he felt was too difficult for the Beach Boys to play, so he brought in a group of studio musicians nicknamed "The Wrecking Crew." These talented session musicians were immediately impressed with Wilson's musicianship. From that point forward, Wilson would write or cowrite all The Beach Boys songs, record his vocals and bass guitar, have session musicians record the other instrumental parts, complete much of the production of the album, and then bring in the remaining members of the Beach Boys from the touring circuit to provide backing vocal harmonies and some lead vocals. This change marked the first time anyone in rock and roll simultaneously wrote, produced, and performed music, and Brian Wilson became the first second-generation rock and roller.

Just as the Beach Boys were dominating the charts, 1964 brought the British Invasion, a new foe for American rock and roll. Wilson was perplexed at how American kids went crazy for the Beatles, because he didn't think their songs were very good. He believed that early in their career, the Beatles were getting by on being cute and different. This challenge led Wilson to greater innovation, and in 1966, Wilson composed and released (with the Beach Boys) what is considered by many to be one of the greatest albums in rock music history. *Pet Sounds* ranked number two in the top 500 albums of all time as selected by *Rolling Stone* magazine ("500 Greatest Albums" 2012). *Pet Sounds* is an early example in rock music of the **concept album,** an album of songs that share a particular concept or theme. *Pet Sounds* utilized new sounds not previously heard in rock and roll, including sleigh bells, barking dogs, silverware, and plucked piano strings. The concept revolves around the composer's growing isolation and quest for security in an increasingly complex world. Wilson's point of view grows increasingly negative as the album unfolds, shifting from the positivity of "Wouldn't It Be Nice" to the insecurity of "I Just Wasn't Made for These Times" and "Caroline, No." This isolation reflected Wilson's personal downward spiral into mental illness and drug abuse. He would spend much of the next 25 years fighting these demons, emerging in the 1990s to resurrect his career and life. *Pet Sounds,* though considered a masterpiece today, received mixed reviews from critics and fans in 1966. Beach Boys fans, who loved "Surfin' USA," "I Get Around," and party songs about surf, sun, and sand, did not seem quite ready to deal with songs reflecting insecurity and isolation. Rock and roll was supposed to be simple and fun, not complex and adult. While *Pet Sounds* did have hit singles, it was a bit ahead of its time in both concept and complexity. While the Beatles would have unprecedented success the next year with *Sgt. Pepper's Lonely Hearts Club Band,* an album Paul McCartney attributed to his love of *Pet Sounds*, Wilson and the Beach Boys seemed somewhat out of touch and passé. Although they would continue to have success, they would forever after be in the shadow of the British Invasion. These four songs best reflect the genius that is Brian Wilson.

- **"Surfin' USA"** (1963): This song, with music borrowed from Chuck Berry, introduced the surf music craze. The lyrics introduced the listener to many different surfing locales while showering them with the vocal "Wall of Sound" not heard previously in rock and roll.
- **"In My Room"** (1964): Wilson began his journey into introspection with this hit. While still in line with teen thoughts, this song is no longer just party music. Rather, Wilson shows a depth of thought normally not found in teen pop songs when he talks about his room as a place to "do my dreaming and my scheming, lie awake and pray, do my crying and my sighing, laugh at yesterday." The harmonies are some of the most celebrated in pop history.
- **"Wouldn't It Be Nice"** (1966): Written by Brian Wilson with Tony Asher and Mike Love, this song opened the *Pet Sounds* album. This song moves away from glorifying teen life and toward wishing for adulthood. The young lovers in the song want to be older so that they can get married and be together forever. Musically, it includes tempo changes and instrumentation not common up to that point in rock music. The song also utilizes a ritardando (gradual slowing of the tempo), which was not often utilized in rock because it removes the possibility for listeners to dance to the song.
- **"Good Vibrations"** (1966): This masterpiece of rock and roll was recorded during the sessions for *Pet Sounds*, but it was not on the album. Instead, it was released as a single in October 1966. The lyrics were about the cosmic

vibrations that Wilson believed each person "gave off" and written to express a kinship with those who were part of the new counterculture movement. It is considered one of the greatest compositions of the rock music era, utilizing a more dense sound and having multiple shifts in key, tempo, instrumentation, and mood. It included instruments such as the theremin, which you will hear as a sliding whine several times in the song.

Although "Good Vibrations" was a massive hit record, the Beach Boys failed to become part of the counterculture. They were considered a part of the old guard, the pre-counterculture 1960s. The hippies often said that no one over the age of 25 was to be trusted, and it seemed the Beach Boys were part of this older generation (even though the members were barely past that age range, if at all). Although Wilson's genius remained a force in music and the Beach Boys continue to be one of the quintessential American rock bands, their influence as a driving force in music has greatly waned in the past three decades. One musical entity, however, remained a force throughout the 1960s and beyond, based on adapting African American music so it appealed to a large market.

FIGURE 2.6 Hitsville USA

Motown

The greatest success in American rock music throughout the 1960s came from Motown. Motown Records, named after Detroit, Michigan (a.k.a. "The Motor City"), was formed by Berry Gordy Jr. (born 1929) in 1959 as Tamla Records but was renamed Motown Records in 1960. Not only did Motown continue to have success throughout the 1960s—even in the face of the British Invasion—but it was also incredibly important in the greater integration and acceptance of African American music during that decade. This was made possible by Gordy's desire to create music that, while performed by African Americans, would be accepted by both white and black America. While most of the other great African American music of the 1960s was negatively affected by the sudden success of the Beatles, the Rolling Stones, and other British Invasion groups, Motown thrived during this era. The success of the vocal groups Smokey Robinson and the Miracles, Diana Ross and the Supremes, the Temptations, the Four Tops, Martha and the Vandellas, and solo artists Stevie Wonder and Marvin Gaye would bring African American music to the forefront of the pop scene, giving it a mainstream acceptance thought impossible just a few years earlier.

Gordy's plan began with his love of jazz music. After a brief time in the military and a short career as a professional boxer, Gordy opened a jazz record store in his hometown of Detroit. The store failed, but Gordy realized the music people wanted in Detroit was rhythm and blues (R&B), not jazz. He also realized R&B music had a difficult time being accepted by the mainstream white public, as its main components, the blues and gospel, were not well understood by a white public that had limited exposure to these black music forms. Gordy believed he could make this music acceptable to most white people by softening the unrestrained gospel vocals and polishing the blues-derived instrumentals with arrangements that included string instruments. To achieve this vision, he exercised complete control of every step of the process, from songwriting to recording and live performances. Gordy had his own in-house songwriters, producers, arrangers, instrumentalists, choreographers, and artist representatives. This vision and process made Motown an assembly line, similar to the automakers throughout the city. Three important parts of this process were Maxine Powell, Cholly Atkins, and the Funk Brothers.

Maxine Powell

Maxine Powell (1915–2013) owned a finishing school and was hired by Gordy to run what would become International Talent Management Inc., or ITM. Finishing schools were much more common in the 1950s and 1960s. These schools were usually attended by upper-middle-class and wealthy teenage girls who were taught how to be ladylike and act mature. The singers at Motown called ITM the "charm school." Powell taught Motown's singers social graces, such as making eye contact, proper speech patterns, grooming, and posture, and the use of makeup and best practices for performing in front of audiences. Powell always instructed her students to perform as if they were in front of royalty. These practices were necessary for Motown's performers, who most often came from poor backgrounds with very little education and worldliness.

Cholly Atkins

Charles "Cholly" Atkins (1913–2003) was brought to Motown in 1964 by Berry Gordy as the principle choreographer for acts such as Diana Ross and the Supremes, the Temptations, and many other Motown performers. His background in tap dancing as well as influences from ballet created a style that set Motown dance moves apart from the do-it-yourself dance styles that had been associated with African American vaudeville and the church. Atkins wanted artists to keep their bodies elevated, keeping their eyes and heads forward while using the posture techniques they were learning from Powell. This would be much more acceptable to a white audience not familiar with previous African American dance styles while also helping with proper singing technique.

The Funk Brothers

The Funk Brothers was a name eventually given to the house band that played the instrumental tracks on many Motown recordings from 1958 until Motown left Detroit in 1972. This band included incredibly talented jazz musicians. The jazz background of these musicians was thought to be a benefit to the singers involved, as the musicians knew when to bring themselves to the forefront and when to back away so the singers could be featured. Although there were dozens of musicians who played on Motown tracks, 13 of those musicians were considered permanent members of the band. The Funk Brothers received a Lifetime Achievement Grammy Award in 2004, and two members, James Jamerson and Benny Benjamin, were inducted into the Rock and Roll Hall of Fame. According to the book *Standing in the Shadows of Motown: The Life and Music of Legendary Bassist James Jamerson* by Allan Slutsky (a.k.a. Dr. Licks), these members played on more number one hits than the Beatles, the Rolling Stones, and the Beach Boys combined, and we can throw in all the number one hits by Elvis Presley as well (1989). Let us explore some of the most important artists and recordings from Motown during the 1960s.

Smokey Robinson and the Miracles

The Miracles, later called Smokey Robinson and the Miracles, were the first successful group for Motown. The group was led by William (Smokey) Robinson and included Claudette Robinson, "Pete" Moore, Ronnie White, Bobby Rogers, and Marv Tarplin. Gordy brought the Miracles to Tamla Records when he formed the company in 1959, and they produced Motown's first million-selling record in 1960 with "Shop Around." Throughout the 1960s, they had great success with hit singles: "Ooo Baby Baby,"

"You've Really Got a Hold on Me," "The Tracks of My Tears," "I Second That Emotion," and "The Tears of a Clown." Overall, the Miracles had 26 Top 40 hits. Their first single with Motown, "Shop Around," which reached number two on the *Billboard* charts, gave Gordy the funding to not only keep Motown operating but also expand ("Miracles" 2019).

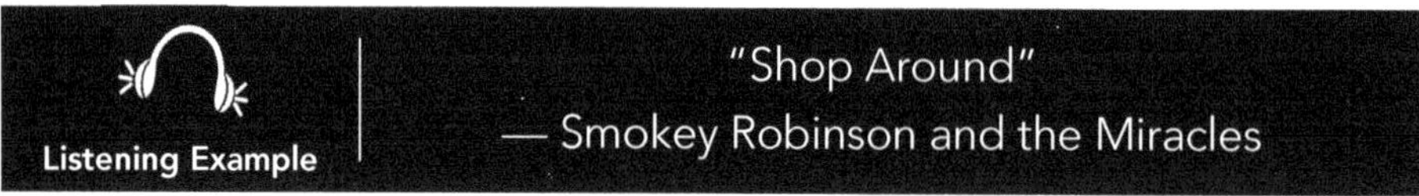

Martha and the Vandellas

Martha and the Vandellas included lead singer Martha Reeves, who began as a secretary at Motown Records. After the trio recorded background vocals for other acts at Motown, Gordy awarded them a recording contract of their own in 1962. At that time, they named themselves after their favorite singer, Della Reese. Their biggest hit, "Heat Wave," became the first million seller by a female vocal group at Motown in 1963. The Motown composing trio of Brian Holland, Lamont Dozier, and Eddie Holland—who would later become the primary songwriters for Diana Ross and the Supremes—wrote the song.

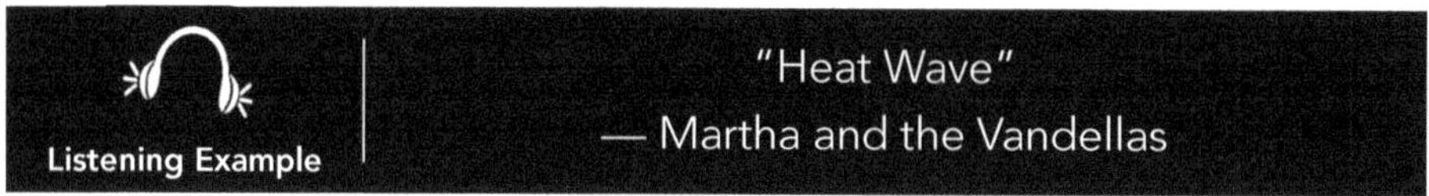

Diana Ross and the Supremes

Diana Ross and the Supremes, also called the Supremes, were the most successful act at Motown Records in the 1960s and the most successful female vocal group in U.S. pop music history (Bronson 2003). They had 12 number one singles on the *Billboard* charts. The members of the Supremes grew up in the Brewster-Douglass housing project in Detroit. They formed a quartet called the Primettes in 1959 but were signed to Motown in 1961 as the Supremes. Success, however, was not immediate. The first few singles released by the Supremes failed to chart. In 1964, the Holland-Dozier-Holland song "Where Did Our Love Go" was offered to the group only after it was rejected by the Marvelettes. The Supremes did not like the song but recorded it anyway, and it became their first hit, topping the *Billboard* charts and hitting number three on the British charts in August 1964, all during Beatlemania and the British Invasion craze. The Supremes were able to continue successfully at a time when most African American R&B acts were kept off the charts by British pop. Some of the Supremes' success was due to their polished, glamorous, high-class look, which included wearing ball gowns, fancy makeup, and wigs. The Supremes would go on to record huge Motown hits, such as "Come See About Me," "Baby Love," "Stop! In the Name of Love," and "Back in My Arms Again." Diana Ross left the group in 1970 to pursue a solo career, and the Supremes continued as an act with several other singers until 1977.

FIGURE 2.7 Diana Ross and the Supremes

The Temptations

The Temptations were formed in 1960 from two competing vocal groups in Detroit, and Gordy signed them to Motown in 1961. In 1964, they would have success, teaming up with Motown singer/producer Smokey Robinson, who wrote "My Girl" with Miracles member Ronald White. It became a number one *Billboard* pop hit in March 1965. "My Girl" has a sweeter sound, utilizing strings for a bigger sound. In 1966, Motown producer/composer Norman Whitfield took over producing the Temptations. Their first hit together was "Ain't Too Proud to Beg." Whitfield began moving the Temptations away from sweet love songs and more toward what would later be known as funk music.

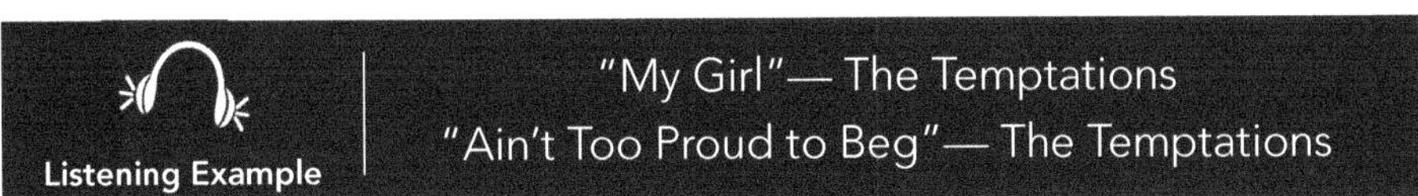

Marvin Gaye

Marvin Gaye (1939–1984) grew up the son of a Pentecostal minister in Washington, D.C. As a boy, he joined musical groups to escape a terrible home life. Marvin ended up at Motown after a brief period in the Air Force and singing in vocal groups in Washington and Chicago. He was signed to Motown Records after performing at a holiday party for Gordy. He would become known for "I Heard It Through the Grapevine" and duets with Tammi Terrell. Her death in 1970 from cancer caused Gaye to create the album that would make him a legend. After Terrell's death, Gaye had an epiphany. He felt the need to create an album of music that would cause people to ask questions, think, and challenge authority. This was controversial, as Gordy did not want Motown artists to create any music that was politically edgy. After Gaye recorded "What's Going On," Gordy refused to release it. Gaye responded by refusing to work for Motown until the situation was resolved. That strike lasted for nearly a year. When Gordy finally did release the song, it immediately went to the top of the charts, selling more than two million copies. Gaye came back to Motown and recorded the album *What's Going On*, which was released in 1971 and was an immediate success. *What's Going On* is a concept album, speaking to what Gaye believed to be the most relevant social issues of that time. It spoke of crime in the inner city, bigotry in the United States, poverty, drug abuse, the Vietnam War, and global warming.

> In 1969 or 1970, I began to reevaluate my whole concept of what I wanted my music to say. … I was very much affected by letters my brother was sending me from Vietnam as well as the social situation here at home. I realized that I had to put my own fantasies behind me if I wanted to write songs that would reach the souls of people. I wanted them to take a look at what was happening in the world (*Rolling Stone* 2012).

What's Going On, considered one of the greatest albums in rock music history, ranks sixth on *Rolling Stone's* "500 Greatest Albums of All Time" list. It also marked an important change in Motown's process. For this album, Gaye bypassed the Motown assembly line, taking control of every aspect of the album's creation. It also marked the first time in Motown's history when the album, rather than the single, was the focus of the artistry. Until that point, Motown's albums had just been packages for quality single songs rather than a complete album of music. Though *What's Going On* was very successful at the time, the album realized greater critical praise following

Gaye's death in 1984. In a strange, tragic twist of irony, Gaye was murdered by his own father following an argument. This tragedy prompted a rediscovery of an album promoting peace, brotherhood, and love for one's fellow men.

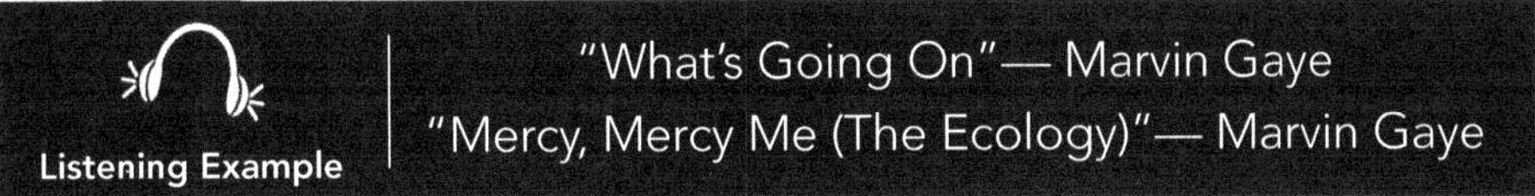

The Jackson 5

One of the last great acts to emerge from Motown Records was the Jackson 5. The group was formed in 1964 in Gary, Indiana (a Chicago suburb), with brothers Jackie (born 1951), Tito (born 1953), Jermaine (born 1954), Marlon (born 1957), and Michael (1958–2009). After the group won several vocal group contests, including one at the prized Apollo Theater in New York, singer Gladys Knight sent a tape of the Jackson 5 to Berry Gordy. In 1968, Gordy rejected the tape but signed them to Motown Records a year later. They immediately began touring as an opening act for Diana Ross and the Supremes. By the beginning of 1970, the Jackson 5 had a number one hit, had performed live on the *Ed Sullivan Show*, and were the first group to have their first four singles reach number one (Huey 2019). Part of the appeal was 11-year-old lead singer Michael, whose stage personality and vocals headlined an act composed of his older brothers. During this time, Motown Records moved its base of operations to Hollywood, California, to get more involved with movies and other media. The Jackson 5 were the first Motown group to spend most of their time there rather than at the Detroit studios. Throughout the 1970s, the Jackson 5 continued to record, eventually leaving Motown in 1975 for a better contract at Epic Records. Jermaine, who had married Gordy's daughter, decided to stay with Motown as a solo artist and was replaced by younger brother Randy (born 1961). At that point, the group changed their name to the Jacksons and continued to record for Epic Records for the remainder of the 1970s. In 1979, Michael

FIGURE 2.8 Michael Jackson and the Jackson 5

Jackson released *Off the Wall*, a hugely successful solo album that began his monumental solo career, which we will discuss at greater length in the section on the music of the 1980s.

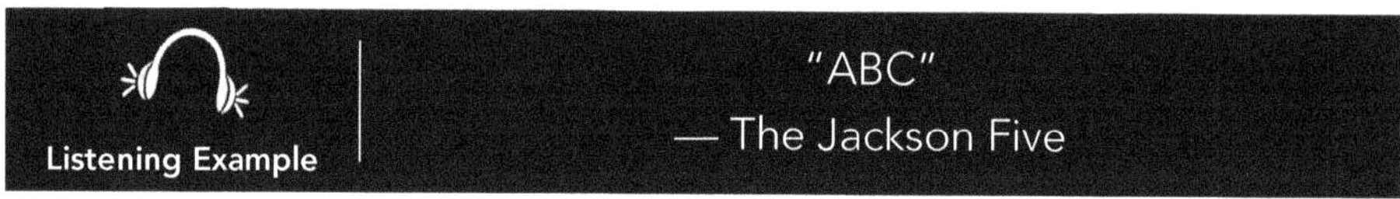

Stevie Wonder

Stevie Wonder (born 1950) was initially signed as "Little Stevie Wonder" to Motown Records as a novelty act in 1961. Blind since shortly after birth, Wonder was discovered by Ronald White of the Miracles and signed to Motown after an audition with Berry Gordy. While his first two albums failed to produce hits, he toured with the Motortown Revue, the touring arm of Motown Records. It was 20 minutes of live performance that was taped and released as *Recorded Live: The 12-Year-Old Genius*, that made Wonder a star. The song "Fingertips" became the first number one song recorded live and made Wonder the youngest artist to have a number one song (he was 12 years old). It also was the first song that occupied both the *Billboard* pop and R&B charts.

Wonder's greatest contribution to pop music came in the 1970s. When he turned 21 in 1971, he renegotiated his contract with Motown to receive greater royalties and gain complete independence over creating his music. Wonder released *Music of My Mind* and *Talking Book* (both in 1972), *Innervisions* (1973), *Fulfillingness' First Finale* (1974), and *Songs in the Key of Life* (1975).

During his career, Stevie Wonder has had more than 30 top ten hits and won 25 Grammy Awards—more than any other solo performer—and is considered one of the greatest composers and artists of the 20th century. Wonder's albums released between 1972 and 1977 are looked upon as the products of one of the greatest creative periods experienced by any musician, rivaling what the Beatles accomplished between 1965 and 1967.

Let us listen to two very different recordings by Stevie Wonder. We will begin with his first Motown hit as Little Stevie Wonder in 1963 with the live recording of "Fingertips, Part Two" and then listen to "Superstition" from the 1972 album *Talking Book.* You will hear how very different these songs are, from the improvisation-based R&B sound of the live recording to the new funk sounds that became big in the 1970s.

Listening Example

"Fingertips, Part 2"— Stevie Wonder
"Superstition"— Stevie Wonder

What we have explored in this chapter has hopefully opened your eyes to an extremely dynamic time in music that is often overlooked by those who view the period solely in terms of Elvis and the British Invasion. Without the Wall of Sound, Brill Building, surf rock and pop, and Motown, we would have never heard the new sounds created in the mid-1960s and beyond. Although all these styles continued through the 1960s and beyond, the events of 1963 and 1964 would forever change the face of rock music. In the next chapter, the British Invasion will build upon these styles and achieve even greater success, ultimately negatively affecting African American chart success.

References

"500 Greatest Albums of All Time." *Rolling Stone*, May 31, 2012. https://www.rollingstone.com/music/music-lists/500-greatest-albums-of-all-time-156826/.

Badman, Keith. *The Beach Boys: The Definitive Diary of America's Greatest Band, on Stage and in the Studio.* New York: Backbeat Books, 2004.

Branch, Taylor. *Parting the Waters: America in the King Years.* New York: Simon & Schuster, 1988.

"Brill Building Sound, The." The History of Rock 'n' Roll. Accessed December 15, 2017. https://www.history-of-rock.com/brill_building.htm.

Bronson, Fred. *The Billboard Book of Number One Hits.* New York: Billboard, 1992.

Bush, John. "The Beach Boys." AllMusic, 2019. https://www.allmusic.com/artist/the-beach-boys-mn0000041874/biography

"Carole King and Gerry Goffin." The History of Rock 'n' Roll. Accessed December 15, 2017. https://www.history-of-rock.com/carole_king_and_gerry_goffin.htm.

Deane, Elizabeth, Hugh Thomson, and David Espar, prods. *Rock and Roll: Renegades and In the Groove.* Featuring Fats Domino, Little Richard, Chuck Berry, Elvis Presley, Jerry Lee Lewis, Muddy Waters, etc. WGBH, Boston and British Broadcasting Corporation, 1995. VHS.

Dr. Licks. *Standing in the Shadows of Motown: The Life and Music of Legendary Bassist James Jamerson.* Montclair, New Jersey: Hal Leonard, 1989.

"Ellie Greenwich." *The Telegraph*. August 27, 2009.

Fontenot, Robert. "What Is Brill Building Music?" LiveAbout. Accessed December 15, 2017. https://www.thoughtco.com/overview-of-brill-building-music-2522601.

Huey, Steve. "Dick Dale." AllMusic, 2019. https://www.allmusic.com/artist/dick-dale-mn0000820232/biography.

———"The Jackson 5." AllMusic. Accessed December 17, 2017. https://www.allmusic.com/artist/the-jackson-5-mn0000083013/biography.

Johnston, Alex. "How Did Carole King and Gerry Goffin Influence Lennon/McCartney's Style of Songwriting?" *Quora*. September 28, 2016. Accessed June 20, 2019. https://www.quora.com/How-did-Carole-King-and-Gerry-Goffin-influence-Lennon-McCartneys-style-of-songwriting.

Motown Museum. "Miracles." Accessed December 16, 2017. https://www.motownmuseum.org/motown-sound/the-artists/miracles/.

Nero, Mark Edward. "Greatest 20 R&B and Soul Artists of All-Time." LiveAbout. Accessed July 23, 2019. https://www.liveabout.com/greatest-randb-singers-of-all-time-2851645.

Schinder, Scott. "The Beach Boys." In *Icons of Rock: An Encyclopedia of the Legends Who Changed Music Forever*, edited by Scott Schinder and Andy Schwartz. Westport, CT: Greenwood Press, 2007.

Figure Credits

IMG. 2.1: Source: https://commons.wikimedia.org/wiki/File:JFK_White_House_portrait_looking_up_lighting_corrected.jpg.

Fig. 2.1: Source: https://commons.wikimedia.org/wiki/File:Vietnamdem.jpg.

Fig. 2.2: Source: https://en.wikipedia.org/wiki/File:Phil_Spector.jpg.

Fig. 2.3: Source: https://commons.wikimedia.org/wiki/File:The_Ronettes.JPG.

Fig. 2.4: Copyright © by Mike Burns (CC BY-SA 2.0) at https://commons.wikimedia.org/wiki/File:Dick_Dale.jpg.

Fig. 2.5: Source: https://commons.wikimedia.org/wiki/File:The_Beach_Boys_(1965).png.

Fig. 2.6: Source: https://commons.wikimedia.org/wiki/File:Hitsville_USA.jpg.

Fig. 2.7: Source: https://commons.wikimedia.org/wiki/File:1966_The_Supremes.JPG.

Fig. 2.8: Source: https://commons.wikimedia.org/wiki/File:Jackson_5_1969.jpg.

CHAPTER

3 The British Invasion

Historical Context

In 1964, the rock music scene in the United States changed, fueled by the same rhythm and blues–based homegrown music that dominated in the 1950s and early 1960s. This music was different, though. It had been exported to England in the late 1950s and reinterpreted by young British teenagers, and it was now being reintroduced to American teenagers through the "British Invasion."

During World War II, Great Britain suffered devastation at the hands of the Nazis. Though not invaded, England was bombed mercilessly by Hitler's Luftwaffe in an attempt to force the British to surrender. Many kids born during this time would grow up to become some of the most influential musicians of the 20th century, both at home and throughout the rest of the world. The music scene in Britain was similar to that in the United States during World War II. Swing music, as discussed in Chapter 1, dominated the British music scene. Many of the great American swing musicians, such as Glenn Miller and Tommy Dorsey, had great followings in England. After World War II, Great Britain had to rebuild, which took many years. As we discussed earlier, the music scene in the United States rapidly changed after the war, but the change was much slower in England, as swing music continued to flourish throughout the remainder of the 1940s and into the 1950s. While rock and roll was quickly growing as the music of the young in the United States, access to rock and roll was much more limited in the British Isles. British kids were exposed to swing and other American jazz forms such as the blues, boogie woogie, and its offspring—rhythm and blues (R&B).

In 1955, British music would adopt some of these styles into a form called skiffle. **Skiffle** was a combination of British and American folk styles combined with jazz and

R&B. The musician who would make it most famous was Anthony James "Lonnie" Donegan. Donegan was a jazz musician at heart who interpreted American songs such as "Rock Island Line," which would become a number two hit in Britain. During his British Army service, Donegan was stationed in Vienna, Austria, where he was able to hear American Forces Radio. It was the music on these stations that made Donegan grow a great love for American R&B. When performing in England, Donegan would add stripped-down versions of blues and folk songs to his concerts. These simplified versions could be played on a washboard and broom handle bass. By the late 1950s, skiffle had taken over as the new music of the British teenager. It was simple to play and cheap to acquire the necessary instruments. This unique combination of American folk and blues played by a jazz band–trained Brit would be the catalyst for British teens in the 1950s. In a few years, these teenagers would take over the world of rock and roll.

The Beatles

The Beatles are considered to be the most successful, respected, and influential band in rock music history. Although they ended up together as a band for nearly 12 years, they were only famous in the United States from 1964 through their dissolution in 1970. In that six-year period, they revolutionized rock music, taking it from "dumb music for kids to dance to" to a form of music that became respected as art. Their rapid transformation as composers and performers is unprecedented in popular music history. While many bands have lasted longer (for example, the Rolling Stones, from 1962 to present), each of the six years that the Beatles were famous showed new and groundbreaking advances in tone colors, instrumentation, technology, and subject matter. Their effect on pop culture in general, including hairstyles and fashion, set trends in the 1960s. To begin our study of the Beatles, we need to begin in Liverpool.

The Beatles and Liverpool

Liverpool was a city known for its shipbuilding, and it was the home base of the *Titanic*. Looked down upon as blue-collar and working-class, it did have one huge advantage over other British cities when it came to rock and roll. As a port city, Liverpool had the greatest exchange of goods between England and the United States. Following World War II and through the 1950s, the port of Liverpool was incredibly busy bringing in goods from the United States to rebuild Britain. The merchant marines who worked these ships also had a second income: British teenagers would come to the docks when the ships arrived and buy American rock and roll and R&B singles from these sailors. Therefore, kids in Liverpool had greater access to records by Elvis Presley, Fats Domino, Little Richard, and Chuck Berry than teens in London.

One teen would form a skiffle group called the Quarrymen in 1957 in Liverpool. John Lennon (1940–1980) was a huge fan of Elvis Presley and Chuck Berry and bought many of these single records at the Liverpool docks. He spent his time attempting to copy these records with a cheap guitar. By 1956, American rock and roll had begun to get some airplay on British radio, and acts such as Bill Haley and His Comets, toured the U.K. to mass appeal. In July of that year, while playing a gig at a local church social, Lennon was introduced to Paul McCartney (born 1942). Lennon was impressed that McCartney could tune a guitar and had a natural ease with singing. Two weeks later, McCartney became a member of the Quarrymen. McCartney soon introduced Lennon to a schoolmate named George Harrison (1943–2001). They would also be joined by an art school friend of Lennon's named Stu Sutcliffe (1940–1962) on bass guitar. Through many name changes, including Johnny and the Moondogs, the Silver Beetles, and finally, the Beatles, the group continued to struggle.

In 1960, the Beatles were given the opportunity to play in Hamburg, Germany. Needing a drummer at the last minute, they chose Pete Best (born 1941), whose mother operated a club in the basement of their home. The grueling Hamburg sets, sometimes lasting seven hours and played seven days a week, helped the band become better players. When the Beatles returned to Liverpool, it was without Sutcliffe, who elected to stay (and never really wanted to be a musician). Sutcliffe would die at 21 from a brain hemorrhage the next year. The four-piece group, with McCartney switching to bass guitar, would begin playing gigs at the Cavern Club. It was there that the Beatles began to gain a following in Liverpool. One fan asked Brian Epstein, who managed a record shop in Liverpool, if he had an obscure recording that included the Beatles. Interested, he checked out the band at the Cavern Club and offered to be their manager.

Epstein began shopping the Beatles around to record companies in England with little success. Finally, in 1962, he succeeded with EMI records and producer George Martin (1926–2016). Martin was not known for pop or rock and roll; rather, he was experienced in producing comedy records and orchestral recordings. He was not impressed with the band's sound but thought they were charming, funny people. He signed them with the idea that they would record songs provided by a professional songwriter. He also decided that he would not use their drummer in his studio recordings. Based on this decision, the remaining members of the band fired Pete

Best and hired veteran Liverpool drummer Richard (Ringo Starr) Starkey (born 1940). The recordings that followed would begin to take over England, and the phenomenon known as Beatlemania would begin. For the next year, the Beatles would grow increasingly popular in England, and the fans' reaction and obsession with the band would hit levels not seen before in rock and roll. Epstein wanted to get the band involved in the more lucrative American pop market, but rarely had this been successful for British musicians in the past.

The Beatles in America

The meteoric rise of Beatlemania in the United States was based to a large degree on lucky timing rather than great songs. In late November 1963, U.S. TV news programs began to report, in a mocking manner, about the silly phenomenon in England called the Beatles. They reported that the band may try to come to America in the near future. They also reported that the music was not good, the haircuts made the band members look like sheepdogs, and the fans were ridiculous and silly. The Beatles were set up to fail.

FIGURE 3.1 Photo of the Beatles with Ed Sullivan from their first appearance on Sullivan's US variety television program in February 1964. From left: Ringo Starr, George Harrison, Ed Sullivan, John Lennon, Paul McCartney.

On November 22, President John F. Kennedy was assassinated in Dallas, Texas. This tragedy, made more impactful because of previous television coverage of the young, handsome president, his glamorous wife, and their young children, sent the country into an emotional depression. Kennedy was the voice of young America, the first pop culture president. Previously, presidents had been older men, revered for their military past (Dwight Eisenhower) or ability to lead during war (Harry Truman). Kennedy was the first president embraced by the young, post-World War II baby boomer generation, even though most were too young to vote.

A little more than two months after Kennedy's death, on February 9, 1964, the Beatles performed live on *The Ed Sullivan Show,* America's most-watched television show. Nearly 73 million people, or 60 percent of U.S. homes, watched that performance, making it the largest single TV viewing audience in U.S. history up to that point ("Beatles' First Ed Sullivan Show" 2019). The Kennedy assassination set the United States up for Beatlemania. Americans needed something to take their minds off the tragedy that had struck the country. This different, foreign group was the perfect antidote. They were funny, looked and spoke differently than any American, and sang fun pop songs that were looked upon as harmless but not brilliant. Beatlemania's rise in the United States would not have been as meteoric had the country not needed cheering up. By April 1964, the Beatles owned the top five spots on the US *Billboard* charts, a feat not achieved before or since ("The Beatles Occupy the *Billboard* Hot 100 Top Five" 2019).

Beatlemania would hit its stride during summer 1964 with the release of the film *A Hard Day's Night.* This was not the first time popular musicians had taken their talents to film and successfully used the medium to promote their music and personalities. What separates *A Hard Day's Night* is that it was critically praised as a film. *A Hard Day's Night* not only served to promote the Beatles by giving a defining characteristic to each member; it is still considered by many to be one of the 100 best films ever made (Corliss 2010). Filmed in black and white to give it the look of a documentary, it shows the Beatles as young rebels, fighting the old folks and the establishment, cheerfully defying their managers and a TV producer. It was the perfect film to express teens' growing frustration with the mores of their parents' generation. It also was revolutionary in that it hinted at the changing pop culture landscape of the 1960s and the emerging, soon-to-explode counterculture. While there are no psychedelic references, it embraced the new absurdist humor that would dominate pop culture in the later 1960s and 1970s. Like the Beatles themselves, it used humor to conceal a disrespect for authority. It also served to differentiate each member of the group and thus allow teens to immediately connect with each separate Beatle. John Lennon became the leader—the rude instigator. Paul McCartney became the "cute" one. George Harrison became the quiet, thoughtful one, and Ringo Starr became the everyman, the normal guy who is picked on by the other members of the band. What began with *A Hard Day's Night* continued forward as one of the greatest marketing plans ever conceived. Suddenly you could buy anything with "The Beatles" printed on it.

Although the music created by the Beatles in 1964 was hugely successful, it was not considered groundbreaking or brilliant. Early Beatles music was danceable, catchy teen rock that was based largely on American rock and roll. On their early albums in 1964, the Beatles performed covers of American rock songs, from Chuck Berry and Little Richard to Motown and Brill Building pop. One important distinction from American cover music of the 1950s is that the British Invasion groups did not perform covers with the idea of "putting a white face on African American music." Rather, the Beatles, and later, the Rolling Stones and others, performed black American music because they loved it and wanted to show respect for the music and those who created it. The Beatles wanted to meet Elvis, Little Richard, the Brill Building writers, and many other American rock icons, as they idolized these musicians.

While all the fame and hype of Beatlemania makes sense (musical fads have come and gone throughout our history), what differentiates the Beatles is what would begin to occur in their songwriting and performances. Their final five years as a band are considered the most groundbreaking era of rock music and of any single entity within the genre. The growth of their songwriting, lyric content, instrumentation, and utilization of recording technology, coupled with their influence on popular culture, was unprecedented in rock. The best way to show this influence is by listening to several tracks by the Beatles in chronological order. These tracks were chosen to show how quickly the Beatles progressed from writing simple dance songs about love to complex compositions that changed the landscape of rock.

1964: Beatlemania!

"I Want to Hold Your Hand"

This song is a great example of the music that created Beatlemania. The lyrics are a simple request from a boy to a girl. Parents accepted the song, as it was not suggestive. After the initial stage of rock and roll, this clean-cut music ends up being a relief for parents, even if the Beatles' hairstyles are less than acceptable. While the group bemuses parents, teenage girls go crazy, screaming at their TV sets.

1965: The Change Begins

In late 1964, the Beatles were able to meet with Bob Dylan, the great American urban folk musician. While Dylan expressed his respect for the crowd appeal of the Beatles, he also thought their lyrics were shallow. This insult, possibly coupled with the first reported use of marijuana by the Beatles, led Lennon and McCartney to write more personal songs rather than songs specifically aimed at their teen audiences. In 1965, it became evident that the Dylan insult and the changing times influenced great change in the Beatles. The highlights of 1965 include the release of "Yesterday," the first acoustic Beatles song, the filming and release of *Help!*, the second Beatles feature film, and *Rubber Soul,* the first album of what Lennon would call "our self-conscious period" of music. All three of these highlights would feature Dylan's influence. The Beatles would also break into new live performance territory. They would become the first rock band to begin performing in outdoor sports stadiums. The highlight of this new concert norm would be a performance at New York's Shea Stadium in August 1965 ("Beatles Live at Shea Stadium" 2019).

"Yesterday" Written by Paul McCartney

"Yesterday" is a song written with two meanings. It comes across as a song about a lost love, a girlfriend who has left the singer. The second meaning behind the song involves the loss of McCartney's mother, who died when he was 14. The song was written on a six-string guitar and presented to producer Martin in early 1965. Martin's response was that the song needed strings. McCartney was concerned, but Martin convinced him to add a string quartet rather than the bigger string sounds used by Phil Spector and some Brill Building writers (Runtaugh 2016). The result was a rock song with one voice, an acoustic guitar, and a string quartet that gave the song a sound not heard before in rock music. The strings add to the emotion of the song, leading the listener to share the grief and loss of the singer.

Beatles Albums and Their Influence on Music Genres

Rubber Soul

This album became the first of the truly groundbreaking Beatles albums and opened one of the most productive and genre-changing eras in music. Songs on the album deal with the pain of an on again/off again relationship ("You Won't See Me," "I'm Looking Through You") to songs about varying versions of love ("The Word" and "If I Needed Someone") and even a jealous threat to a girlfriend ("Run for Your Life"). As Rob Sheffield from *Rolling Stone* magazine stated, "As soon as it dropped in December 1965, *Rubber Soul* cut the story of pop music in half—we're all living in the future this album invented. Now as then, every pop artist wants to make a *Rubber Soul* of their own" (Sheffield 2015). A few highlights of this album include:

- **"In My Life"**: One of the most respected songs on the album is "In My Life," a song Lennon wrote about the people and places he knew in Liverpool that compared them to a current love. It represents the introspection Dylan wanted to hear from the Beatles. Songs like "In My Life" began to show music critics and fans alike that the Beatles were not a simple boy band but a musical force.
- **"Norwegian Wood (This Bird Has Flown)"**: This song, which utilizes Harrison's new interest in the Indian sitar, speaks to Lennon's disinterest in his own marriage and an affair with a strange ending.
- **"Nowhere Man"**: Lennon wrote of himself as the "Nowhere Man," someone unconfident and bound by his circumstances rather than someone who is self-assured. This type of self-doubt, previously lacking in popular music, opened up a new realm of emotional possibilities in rock and roll.
- **"The Word"**: "The Word" is love, and this version of love is universal. Rather than a love between a boy and a girl, which dominated pop music up until this time, this love speaks to the growing counterculture's use of love as a theme for all people, nationalities, and, indeed, the world. While this "love" would become well recognized in the hippie subculture in the next few years, this piece advertises "love" as a global commodity, and the Beatles begin to use love as an advertising tool or political currency.

The success of *Rubber Soul* would garner praise that was not previously given to rock and roll. Up until that time, rock had been a style of music not thought of in the same vein as "art." The praise given to Mozart, Beethoven, or Tchaikovsky for their great musical works of art had not been extended to rock music, which was considered "bad music for teenagers." The new sounds explored by the Beatles on *Rubber Soul* caused many who criticized rock music to take notice. Over the next two years and albums, the Beatles would expand upon this new musical territory, moving beyond the previous ranks of pop musicians and joining the list of true composers and musical idols of the 20th century.

Revolver

In 1966, the Beatles stopped performing live concerts, mostly because of crowds that were becoming more unruly, the inability of either the band or audience to hear the music, and the increasingly complex instrumentation required by Beatles songs. They also followed up their 1965 *Rubber Soul* release with *Revolver*. This album would further increase the critical appeal of the Beatles. *Revolver* utilized greater studio technology, including tape loops and backward recordings. It expanded, both musically and lyrically, what was previously accepted as "normal" for a rock album. It included "Taxman," the George Harrison song protesting the 95% tax rate paid by the highest earners; "Yellow Submarine," a children's song written by Paul McCartney and sung by Ringo Starr; "Eleanor Rigby," a song about loneliness and death accompanied only by a string octet; "Love You To," Harrison's song utilizing Indian musicians; "Got To Get You Into My Life," a love song about marijuana; and ended with "Tomorrow Never Knows," with lyrics based on *The Tibetan Book of the Dead* and fueled by Lennon's increasing use of LSD. The release of this album in August 1966 gave further credibility to the exploding counterculture movement. Richard Goldstein of the *Village Voice* commented, "It seems now that we will view this album in retrospect as a key work in the development of rock and roll into an artistic pursuit" (Reising 2002). The members of the Grateful Dead, upon hearing "Tomorrow Never Knows," realized that the Beatles had now joined the ranks of the hippie counterculture.

Revolver Listening Examples

- **"Taxman":** Harrison wrote the song as a protest of the tax rate in England. Harrison also sang it on the album.
- **"Eleanor Rigby"**: McCartney's song of loneliness, unfulfilled love, and, ultimately, death. McCartney later said that "All the lonely people, where do they all come from?" was a comment about Beatles fans who were consumed with the group rather than trying to live their own lives.
- **"Yellow Submarine"**: Written by McCartney and sung by Starr. It was specifically written as a children's song, which was unheard of on previous rock albums. The sound effects and echo put the listener into the middle of this underwater fantasy world.
- **"Tomorrow Never Knows"**: This psychedelic piece used sitar solos that were sped up and backward as well as a very insistent, chant-like beat from Starr on the drums. Lennon wanted his voice altered to sound like the "Dalai Lama on a mountaintop."

Sgt. Pepper's Lonely Hearts Club Band

In 1967, the Beatles had perhaps the most influential year in rock's history. That summer, known as "The Summer of Love," represented the apex of the hippy counterculture movement, and the Beatles provided the soundtrack with their June release of *Sgt. Pepper's Lonely Hearts Club Band*. Listed by *Rolling Stone* as the greatest album in rock history (*Rolling Stone* 2012), *Sgt. Pepper's* elevated the Beatles from rock icons to musical gods, now considered great composers in the realm of Bach and Mozart. The album was named after a McCartney concept: that the Beatles should release an entire album representing a performance by a fictional band. This would allow the Beatles to "be something else." This album, considered a masterpiece of rock music, expands on *Revolver*'s complexity of both instrumentation and lyric subject matter. It incorporates a wide range of musical styles, including circus music, vaudeville, Indian classical music, and psychedelic pop.

The first songs recorded for the album, "Strawberry Fields Forever" and "Penny Lane," were both about the original album concept, which was to write about childhood memories of Liverpool. Although the songs were released as singles and have the distinction of being early examples of music videos, they never ended up on the album. The Beatles took seven months to record *Sgt. Pepper's*. This extended period allowed them to create using the full technology available in the studio. As the songs were never meant to be live performances, any necessity for creating tour music was removed, so for the first time, a rock band was creating an album as a studio performance. The album begins with the noise of a band warming up and follows with "Sgt. Pepper's Lonely Hearts Club Band," which introduces the concert, the band, and the singer (the fictional Billy Shears). It immediately proceeds into "With a Little Help from My Friends," sung by Ringo and banned on radio in the United States for its phrase "I get high with a little help from my friends." "Lucy in the Sky with Diamonds," which follows, was inspired by a picture that four-year-old Julian Lennon brought home to his father. It was a picture of his friend Lucy flying through the sky. The song will forever be associated with LSD for the lyric content and the **L**ucy **S**ky **D**iamonds reference, which in 1967 was considered more than coincidence. At the end of the album, two studio tricks were played on fans by the Beatles. First, Lennon had a 15-kilohertz tone inserted for several seconds to "annoy your dog," and then side two of the record ends with a nonexistent run-out groove filled with nonsense sounds that would continue to play forever unless you physically turned off the phonograph (Giles 2017).

Sgt. Pepper's Lonely Hearts Club Band Listening Examples

- **"Sgt. Pepper's Lonely Hearts Club Band," "With a Little Help from My Friends," and "Lucy in the Sky with Diamonds":** With these three songs, you hear the introduction of the album, which leads directly into two pieces with psychedelic references.
- **"She's Leaving Home":** A narrator and parents who lament that their daughter has "run away from home" sing this song. We hear the story and the parents' response to the note left by their daughter. This piece represented a year in which millions of teens ran away from home to join the counterculture.
- **"Being for the Benefit of Mr. Kite":** Lennon wrote this song based on a circus poster from 1843. Lennon then wanted to create a psychedelic circus, which was achieved by cutting up a tape of carousel music and taping it back together in whatever order it was found, thus creating music that was sometimes backward.
- **"Within You, Without You":** Harrison's song inspired by Hindustani classical music. The Beatles' interest in Indian music helped to popularize this style of music in the United States and England.
- **"When I'm Sixty-Four":** Written by McCartney with his father, who had turned 64 that year, in mind. The song is styled on Tin Pan Alley and vaudeville styles yet makes good-natured fun of old people, stereotyping the age group as those who "Dig in the garden … Sunday morning, go for a ride … and grandchildren on your knee …"
- **"Sgt. Pepper's Lonely Hearts Club Band" (Reprise) and "A Day in the Life":** The reprise has the band saying goodbye to their fans at the end of the concert and immediately transitions to "A Day in the Life," a song with parts written and sung by both Lennon and McCartney. This song borrows subjects from headlines in the newspaper, including a traffic accident death, footage of war images, and a story about 4,000 potholes in a British town.

While this 38-minute album has received unbelievable adulation since its release, it is a picture postcard of its time (1967) yet is often looked upon as timeless. The Beatles, who would continue as a band until 1970, would not again find the cohesiveness achieved on *Rubber Soul, Revolver,* and *Sgt. Pepper's Lonely Hearts Club Band.* These three years and albums represent the greatest growth of creativity and expression in rock music's life span.

The Beatles also known as "The White Album"

In 1968, the Beatles took time off to travel to India to study with the Maharishi Mahesh Yogi. While this time proved to be very fruitful for songwriting, it also served to lead the members of the band in differing directions, which would ultimately lead to the breakup of the group in 1970 (Swanson 2016). The album that was created from this songwriting was called *The Beatles*. Often referred to as "The White Album" for its plain white cover, this double album is primarily represented by the four individual members of the band and is the least collaborative of any Beatles album. This album also backs away from the studio tricks found on *Sgt. Pepper's*, so the songs tend to be simpler. Its plain white cover also is in direct contrast to the bright, fancy covers made famous by their previous albums. The recording sessions were punctuated by disagreements among the members of the band and included the constant presence of artist Yoko Ono, Lennon's new love. It includes love songs, such as McCartney's "I Will" and Lennon's "Julia" as well as political songs, such as McCartney's "Blackbird" and Harrison's "Piggies." There are compositional contributions from all four members of the band. The four songs that follow represent the album well and are required listening for the album.

FIGURE 3.2 A later picture of the Beatles

"The White Album" Listening Examples

- **"Back in the USSR"**: Beach Boy Mike Love, while in India with the Beatles, dared McCartney to write a song about something as "not pop" as the Soviet Union. McCartney responded with a parody of a Beach Boys/Chuck Berry song. The song became an underground hit in the Soviet Union, where Beatles music was banned.
- **"Helter Skelter"**: This song became infamous as one of the songs mass murderer Charles Manson used as inspiration for his followers' killing spree, whose victims included actress Sharon Tate. Manson believed the song was about

(continued on next page)

hell and was an anthem for the race war he hoped to start in the United States. McCartney simply wrote a raucous song about a spiral playground slide.

- **"I'm So Tired"**: Lennon's song about sleeplessness, withdrawal from cigarettes, and missing Yoko Ono while he was in India.
- **"Revolution #9"**: While not specifically a song, this performance piece created by Lennon and Ono was hated by other members of the band. It represents the greatest avant-garde influence and is one of the most divisive Beatles works.

Abbey Road

In early 1969, the Beatles would begin a project that would include filming the band as it created its next album. The film and album project would end with a live concert for a few thousand selected audience members. The project, at first called *Get Back* and ultimately titled *Let It Be*, would be shelved prior to its completion, as the band members were continuing to quarrel and move in different directions. Ultimately, the *Let It Be* album and film would be released in 1970, after the Beatles had dissolved the band. In later 1969, the Beatles decided to record a new album in the spirit of their older recordings, with Martin producing it at Abbey Road Studios. This album, titled *Abbey Road*, marked the end of the band. Although the Beatles themselves never spoke of the album as being their last during the recording process, they each secretly expressed that they would go different directions in the upcoming new decade. While the album does utilize the ever-improving studio technology, the most-revered elements of the album include two tremendous songs from Harrison ("Something" and "Here Comes the Sun") and a 16-minute medley of eight separate Lennon and McCartney songs that dominates the second side.

Abbey Road Listening Examples

- **"Come Together"**: Lennon's song written for Timothy Leary's gubernatorial campaign against Ronald Reagan in California. It utilizes Lennon's lyric style of creating words that sound interesting while not always having a clear meaning.
- **"Something"**: Called one of the greatest love songs of the 20th century by Frank Sinatra, Harrison wrote this song for his wife, Patti.
- **"Here Comes the Sun"**: Another Harrison song, written in Eric Clapton's garden while skipping a Beatles business meeting. It expresses the positive outlook George believed would appear once he was away from the Beatles.

(*continued on next page*)

- **"The Medley"**: Includes "You Never Give Me Your Money," "Sun King," "Mean Mr. Mustard," "Polythene Pam," "She Came in Through the Bathroom Window," "Golden Slumbers," "Carry That Weight," and "The End."

The relevance of the Beatles continues to this day, almost 50 years after they ended their brief run as a band. Their music has influenced countless other musicians, and their legend has only grown since 1970.

Each member continued his career into the 1970s and beyond. Lennon and Ono continued their musical careers and peace activism through the 1970s while living in New York City. Lennon was shot to death by an obsessed fan in front of his New York City home on December 8, 1980. McCartney had one of the greatest solo careers in the 1970s and beyond and continues as de facto royalty of rock and roll. Harrison's career included creating the first benefit rock concert with *The Concert for Bangladesh*. His solo career continued throughout the 1970s and 1980s, including forming a supergroup called the Traveling Wilburys in the late 1980s with Bob Dylan, Roy Orbison, Jeff Lynne, and Tom Petty. Harrison died of cancer at the age of 57 in 2001. Ringo Starr continued to record and act in the 1970s and beyond. Beginning in 1989, Ringo began touring each summer with his "All Starr Band," a group made up of other famous musicians.

FIGURE 3.3 Group photograph of the Rolling Stones taken from a 1965 *Billboard* trade ad. From up to down: Mick Jagger; Charlie Watts and Keith Richards; Brian Jones and Bill Wyman.

The amount of time given to the Beatles in this text is a reflection of the author's belief that the Beatles' influence over music and pop culture will never be replicated by any other single entity within rock and roll. They were of their time, which was a rapidly changing decade, but their music transcends the 1960s in a way in which most other music from that time cannot. Although other groups such as the Rolling Stones were important and had their own fans, the Beatles stand apart in rock's history.

The Rolling Stones

In many ways, the Rolling Stones were the antithesis of the Beatles. The Stones featured two songwriters, Keith Richards (born 1943) and Mick Jagger (born 1943), who wrote songs together, whereas Lennon and McCartney rarely did so. The Stones, unlike the Beatles, would have a very long career as a band. Unlike the Beatles, who set the standard for new music in their brief career, the Rolling Stones have adapted their version of R&B to the ever-changing styles of rock music in the 50-plus years the band has continued to record. The Stones have one lead singer, although others have sung lead on rare occasions, whereas the Beatles usually had all four members sing lead at some point on every album. The Rolling Stones began when Richards and Jagger met as teenagers after having lost touch as young schoolchildren. They found they shared a common love of American blues music. In the late 1950s in England, there was a growing love amongst some teenagers of American blues music, including Muddy Waters, B. B. King, and other early American R&B performers. By 1963, drummer Charlie Watts (born 1941), bassist Bill Wyman (born 1936), and guitarist Brian Jones (1942–1969) had joined them.

While the Stones became famous in the United States in 1964, it was at first as a dangerous alternative to the Beatles. The Stones were not funny or friendly, they sneered rather than smiled, and they looked unkempt. Their interpretations of American R&B songs and bluesy originals were not as ear friendly to the American public as Beatles pop hits were at first. As Jagger and Richards began writing their own songs, their performance style as a band began to branch out, adding their British take on R&B to many styles of music. This ultimately would be what has led to their great success over their many years together. As times and musical styles have changed, the Rolling Stones have adapted yet continued to inject R&B into those new styles. In our listening examples, you will hear those changes throughout their career.

- **"(I Can't Get No) Satisfaction"** (1965): A song about sex, or the frustration with the lack thereof. The Stones were more blunt about sex, much as American blues musicians of earlier decades had been. This did result in some disapproval from the American public.
- **"Street Fighting Man"** (1968): The Stones' outwardly political response to the social and political protests of that year. While the Beatles created "Revolution," a decidedly nonthreatening political response to the violence taking place at that time, the Stones' response was supportive of the protests and even the violent uprisings that were occurring.

(continued on next page)

- **"Brown Sugar"** (1971): Mick Jagger wrote this piece with his secret African American girlfriend in mind. It deals with a group of taboo issues, including interracial couples, drug use, and slavery.
- **"Hot Stuff"** (1976): A great example of the Rolling Stones adapting to the new disco sound of the mid-1970s.
- **"Doom and Gloom"** (2013): The 70-something rockers still create relevant pop hits in the 2010s with this song.

The Who and The Kinks

Two other rock bands with success during the British Invasion would be known for their hit songs and for having a great influence on emerging styles of music in the 1970s.

The Who

The Who would become well-known for their progressive style and virtuosic playing. Formed by guitarist Pete Townshend (born 1945), singer Roger Daltrey (born 1944), bassist John Entwistle (1946–2002), and drummer Keith Moon (1947–1978), they would first hit the charts with "My Generation" in 1965. One highlight of "My Generation" includes Daltrey appearing to stutter through the entire song. What most did not know was that it was an inside joke with a group of Who fans who called themselves the Mods. The Mods were known for their amphetamine use, which would at times leave them in an altered state that included stuttering. The Mods were also known for their destructive behavior, and the Who eventually adopted this behavior in their concerts, ending the shows by destroying their instruments on stage. The Who was also known for the manic sound they were able to create as a band. Entwistle was a phenomenal bass player who could master the most complex patterns, and Moon was one of the first great rock drummers who could create drum fills where most would simply play a groove. Townshend is a great rock guitarist and composer who pushed the envelope of the simple three-minute rock composition. The Who created a sound that would be followed in the 1970s by those who called themselves **progressive** or **art** rock artists. These musicians wanted to add elements of classical and jazz music into rock music to create greater complexity. We will study more of that style of music in future chapters. In "My Generation," listen to Daltrey stutter throughout the song, and, at the end of the song, listen to the band mimic the destruction that often followed their concerts.

Listening Example

"My Generation"
— The Who

In 1969, Townshend wrote *Tommy*, an opera written with rock music about a young boy who is "blind, deaf, and dumb" yet becomes a Christ-like figure through playing pinball. Although this may seem like a strange story, it represents rock moving into the previous domain of European orchestral composers. With the innovation of the Who, rock music began to take on wider forms and concepts. In 1978, Moon died of a drug overdose, and bassist Entwistle followed in 2002. The Who has continued to tour on and off with Daltrey and Townshend.

FIGURE 3.4 The Kinks on the television program called "Fanclub."

The Kinks

The Kinks have sometimes been credited as the first punk band. While the Kinks are not a punk band, as they began a decade before punk began, certainly many of the punk bands of the mid-1970s name the Kinks as a great influence. First, the Kinks were the first band to utilize distortion in their guitar sound. While this first occurred when they used cheap amplifiers that could not hold up to their playing, they eventually cut slits into the speakers of their amps to get the distorted tone. This distortion would become a staple of rock music in the future. The Kinks also expressed a raw sound that would be embraced by punks as a reaction to the complexity of progressive rock. The Kinks, while progressive in form at times, sounded like a garage band when they played live. This sound was very different from the Beatles, the Stones, and the Who. This raw sound would become the centerpiece of punk music in the 1970s.

- **"You Really Got Me":** This version performed live gives us a glimpse into what punk would later become.

Other British Invasion Bands of Note

While the Beatles, the Rolling Stones, the Who, and the Kinks were certainly the most popular bands to come out of the British Invasion, other groups would influence the music that followed.

The Yardbirds

The Yardbirds were a blues-based band like the Rolling Stones, but unlike the Stones, the Yardbirds more strictly adhered to the blues. While the Yardbirds did not have great success in the United States, they would become famous for the guitarists they employed. Their first guitarist was 19-year-old Eric Clapton. While he did not remain in the band for long, he has become one of the most important guitarists in rock music history and a member of the Rock and Roll Hall of Fame. The Yardbirds had a hit record with "For Your Love," which was a departure from their blues sound. This turn toward pop caused Clapton to leave the band later that year. Their second guitarist, Jeff Beck, is also rock royalty. Unfortunately, his extreme talent was paired with his lack of reliability in other interactions with the group. He brought in Jimmy Page to share guitar duties and would soon leave the Yardbirds to form his own band. Jimmy Page reformed the band as the New Yardbirds with new members before changing the name of the band to Led Zeppelin. While the Yardbirds had limited success, all three of their guitarists are considered among the best in rock music history.

The Animals

The Animals were formed in 1961 in the Northeast British coal mining town of Newcastle upon Tyne. Their leader and vocalist, Eric Burdon, displayed the gritty, rough nature of the city through his growling, bluesy voice. While the Animals had 10 Top 20 hits in both the United States and the U.K., they dealt with many personnel changes throughout the 1960s. Their biggest hit, a chart topper in both England and the United States, was the often-recorded song "The House of the Rising Sun." Their blues-inspired version of this song followed recordings by Woody Guthrie in 1941 and Bob Dylan 20 years later. What makes this version different is that the folk nature of the song (it dates back to the 1800s) was altered to reflect the harder sound of the blues, while guitar riffs brought a pop flavor to the song. The song, about those living in and around a den of prostitution, was also changed to reflect the characters as male, while earlier versions dealt more with female characters.

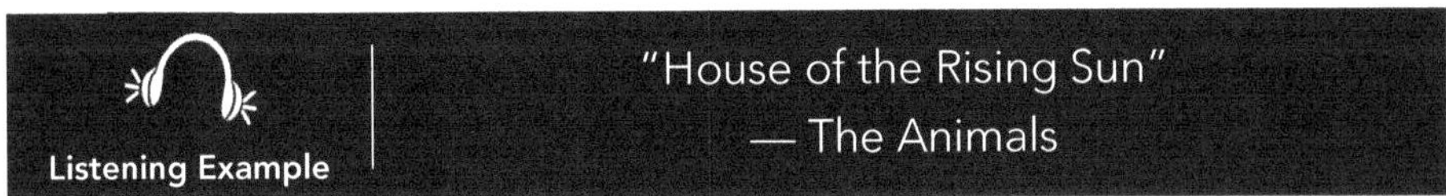

Cream

After leaving the Yardbirds in 1965, Eric Clapton (born 1945) formed his own band with drummer Ginger Baker (born 1939) and bassist/singer Jack Bruce (1943–2014). Some have called Cream the greatest rock band ever and the first heavy metal band. While Cream was an outlet for Clapton's strict adherence to the blues, it was also a power pop trio, utilizing a more strict rhythmic structure to bring the blues of Robert Johnson (1911–1938) into the rock arena. In recording Johnson's "Cross Road Blues," Cream utilized electric guitar and a steady tempo. This cranked-up blues was what Clapton had wanted to record with the Yardbirds, and he finally was able to realize his dream with Cream. Although Cream only lasted two years, it is one of the most legendary bands in rock music history. Let us compare Cream's "Crossroads" with Robert Johnson's original recording.

Although many other bands had success during the British Invasion, most were one-hit wonders or reflected a sound that did not translate well to the American *Billboard* charts. Other bands, such as the Moody Blues, would achieve fame later during the progressive/art rock era. As the British Invasion bands continued to have success in the second half of the 1960s, on the other side of the Atlantic, the new counterculture was beginning, and a new resurgence of African American music would emerge, moving young people in a new direction.

References

"500 Greatest Albums of All Time: Rolling Stone's Definitive List of the 500 Greatest Albums of All Time." *Rolling Stone*, May 31, 2012. https://www.rollingstone.com/music/lists/500-greatest-albums-of-all-time-20120531.

"Beatles' First Ed Sullivan Show, The." The Beatles Bible. Accessed July 23, 2019. https://www.beatlesbible.com/1964/02/09/the-beatles-first-ed-sullivan-show/.

"Beatles Live at Shea Stadium, New York, The." The Beatles Bible. August 15, 1965. https://www.beatlesbible.com/1965/08/15/live-shea-stadium-new-york/.

"Beatles Occupy the *Billboard* Hot 100 Top Five, The." The Beatles Bible. https://www.beatlesbible.com/1964/04/04/beatles-billboard-hot-100-top-five/. Accessed July 16, 2019.

Corliss, Richard. "A Hard Day's Night." *Time*, January 4, 2010. http://entertainment.time.com/2005/02/12/all-time-100-movies/slide/a-hard-days-night-1964-2/.

Giles, Jeff. "The Story of the Beatles' 'Sgt. Pepper' Runout Groove." Ultimate Classic Rock, April 21, 2017. http://ultimateclassicrock.com/beatles-complete-sgt-pepper-runoff-groove/.

Reising, Russell. *Every Sound There Is: The Beatles' Revolver and the Transformation of Rock and Roll*. Farnham, UK: Ashgate Publishing, 2002.

Runtaugh, Jordan. "Ten Great Beatles Moments We Owe to George Martin." *Rolling Stone*, March 9, 2016. https://www.rollingstone.com/music/music-lists/10-great-beatles-moments-we-owe-to-george-martin-14719/yesterday-1965-21934/.

Sheffield, Rob. (4 December 2015). "50 Years of *Rubber Soul*: How the Beatles Invented the Future of Pop." *Rolling Stone*, December 3, 2015. https://www.rollingstone.com/music/music-news/50-years-of-rubber-soul-how-the-beatles-invented-the-future-of-pop-59132/.

Swanson, Dave. "The Time The Beatles Met the Maharishi." Ultimate Classic Rock. February 15, 2016. http://ultimateclassicrock.com/the-beatles-india-maharishi/.

Figure Credits

IMG. 3.1: Source: https://commons.wikimedia.org/wiki/File:The_Beatles_in_America.JPG.

Fig. 3.1: Source: https://en.wikipedia.org/wiki/File:Beatles_with_Ed_Sullivan.jpg.

Fig. 3.2: Copyright © by Parlophone Music Sweden (CC BY 3.0) at https://commons.wikimedia.org/wiki/File:The_Beatles_magical_mystery_tour.jpg.

Fig. 3.3: Source: https://commons.wikimedia.org/wiki/File:Rolling_Stones_1965.jpg.

Fig. 3.4: Copyright © by W. Veenman (CC BY-SA 3.0) at https://commons.wikimedia.org/wiki/File:Fanclub_-_The_Kinks_2.png.

CHAPTER 4

The Second Half of the 1960s: Soul, Folk Rock, Psychedelic Rock, and the Blues Revival

Historical Context for the Decade

> Soul lyrics, soul music came at about the same time as the civil rights movement and it's very possible that one influenced the other.
>
> —Ahmet Ertegun

> When I was a kid, I was following black soul music.
>
> —Robert Plant (Led Zeppelin)

During the frenzy of the British Invasion and its disruption of African American success on the music charts, African American music began to rebound in new ways. This new music was a collaboration between black and white musicians and producers. It was a reaction to the popular Motown style, which had mass appeal for black and white audiences yet did not accurately reflect the traditional styles of African American music. In the South, there was a call for a "back to black," or more traditional take on African American music. That reaction became **soul** music.

While we have already established that all rock and roll is influenced by the gospel singing style, as we moved into the 1960s, African American music had begun to move away from the traditions of the Southern black gospel church. At Motown, Berry Gordy realized white Americans' ignorance of black church traditions made acceptance of black music difficult, and during the age of new advances in the civil rights movement, pushback from those resisting change made that acceptance even more difficult. Gordy chose to create music at Motown by black musicians aimed at the broadest possible audience. While soulful in nature, Motown music was not really soul music. Many of the traditions of the black gospel church were either tamed or eliminated so the larger white audience would understand and accept the music. In the second half of the 1960s, the term "soul" was used to describe the reaction to Gordy's tamed, though very successful, music.

While it is easy for 21st-century citizens to look upon white Americans' reluctance to embrace African American music as part of the U.S.'s racist past, to think in only that way is simplifying the situation. When we look at segregation in the United States, we most often think about it in terms of legal precedent. Much of organized religion in the United States would continue to be voluntarily segregated long after civil rights advances made forced segregation illegal in the public sphere, such as in schools. To this day, there are churches attended predominantly by African Americans and churches attended predominantly by white Americans. Those who choose to be religious tend to embrace the style of worship their parents and grandparents practiced. This tendency to keep a particular religious practice has led to a voluntary continuation of segregation within many houses of worship. The style of the African American gospel church scared white America because it had no reference for where the style was drawn from. The gritty, powerful attitude of gospel music had very little to do with the four-part church hymns of most predominantly white churches. When Motown eliminated much of this church-based style, white America embraced African American music. However, not all African Americans were happy with the changes occurring within black music.

Soul Music

Soul music is secularized gospel music, meaning that the music itself is completely rooted in the gospel church but with the lyric content changed to delete all religious references. This music, while referencing the vocal style of Little Richard from 1950s rock and roll, added elements from the gospel church service not seen during the beginnings of rock music.

Elements in Soul Music That Stand Out

The following are the major elements of soul music that distinguish it from other genres:

1. Using an unrestrained vocal technique, the soul singer acts as both the gospel soloist and the preacher. The soul singer is most often singing a sermon to us, much as a minister would preach in a church service. While this sermon is not religious in nature, it certainly bears the weight of the pulpit in that we are being made to look in the mirror at our faults and misgivings. This unrestrained style allows for screaming, groans, or any vocal inflection the soloist feels is needed at the time to get the message across.
2. A repeated rhythmic vamp, which is a short musical phrase played by the band, is often used throughout a soul song to provide an energetic backing music for the singer while not getting in the way of the message. Often in gospel services, the vamp was a way for the church band, which did not know the length of the preacher's sermon, to continue to stir up the congregation as the service progressed. Often this vamp would begin quietly and build in intensity and excitement over a long period. We often see this process in soul music as well. Songs may begin in a reflective, soft, and slow way but gradually build to a climax, bringing the congregation along for the ride.
3. The horn section acts as the gospel choir in soul music. While some soul musicians did use a gospel choir as backing musicians, often the horn section, comprising saxophones, trumpets, and sometimes trombones, would provide long, drawn-out notes to act as the choir singing "oohs" and "aahs."
4. Most soul music used church-based musicians, many of whom did not read music, so rarely were arrangements created. Rather, these musicians learned pieces by rote and created the arrangements themselves as they prepared in the studio.

Soul Music and the Connection to Social Change

Soul music became popular within the African American community at a time when great social changes were occurring. The civil rights advances of the 1960s, while leading our society on a path to greater equality we're treading to this day, also caused a reaction in those who opposed desegregation and equal rights for all. Art of all forms is created for and reflected by society as a whole and cannot be separated from a particular era. To provide some points of reference, here is a timeline of civil rights events of that period.

Timeline of Civil Rights Events

May 1954: The Supreme Court decision in Brown v. Board of Education ended legal segregation in schools. Many schools remained segregated through other means, and some were desegregated using forced busing for both black and white students.

December 1955: Rosa Parks refused to give up her seat to a white man on a bus in Montgomery, Alabama. She was arrested, and a yearlong bus boycott in the city began.

June 1963: President John F. Kennedy sent the National Guard to force the University of Alabama to allow two African American students to register for classes. Governor George Wallace initially blocked the move but eventually gave in.

August 1963: In front of the Lincoln Memorial, the Reverend Doctor Martin Luther King Jr. gave his iconic "I Have a Dream" speech in front of 250,000 people who marched on Washington, D.C., to protest inequality.

July 1964: President Lyndon Johnson signed the Civil Rights Act of 1964, which outlawed employment discrimination due to race, color, sex, religion, or national origin.

April 1968: Martin Luther King Jr. was assassinated in Memphis, Tennessee. Segregationist James Earl Ray was convicted of the murder. One week later, President Johnson signed the Fair Housing Act, which prevented the practice of denying real estate purchasing or renting based on race, religion, or national origin.

(History.com 2017)

Soul Singers

The struggles that occurred during this time yielded great advances for Americans who had long faced discrimination, yet with each advance came pushback and violence. Soul music became the music of this struggle, not only as a form of uniquely African American expression but also related to the church, a center of the black community. This need for a change from what some called the "whitewashed" music of Motown became a source of African American pride during very difficult times. There were many great soul singers, including James Brown, Ray Charles, Sam Cooke, and later, Aretha Franklin and Otis Redding.

James Brown

James Brown (1933–2006) was one of the most important African American musicians of the 20th century. In the 1950s, he was a rhythm and blues (R&B) artist, creating music supplemented by his own terrific dance moves. In the 1960s, he helped to lead the development of soul music and became a strong voice in the civil rights struggles of the time. He invested money in African American–owned radio stations and other businesses and provided a voice of the black pride movement, a nonviolent call to protest during the 1960s. Later, Brown was an early innovator in **funk** music, the reaction to soul music that followed in the 1970s.

FIGURE 4.1 James Brown

The following three songs represent the three styles of music Brown helped develop, from 1950s R&B to 1960s soul and finally, the music that would become funk in the 1970s. A great example of James Brown's R&B music is "Please, Please, Please" from 1956. This song shows the beginnings of the development of soul music in James's unrestrained vocals. We also hear a repeated rhythmic vamp. When Brown performed this song live, he would often collapse on stage, as if overcome by emotion, only to rebound repeatedly. This also represents some of the early stages of bringing drama onto the pop music stage.

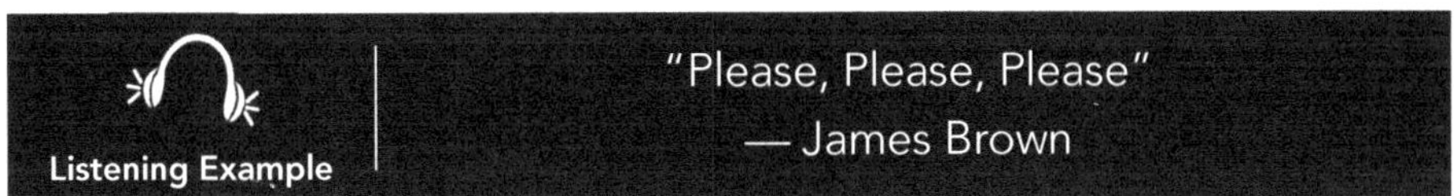

"Say It Loud (I'm Black and I'm Proud)" is a great example of soul music. In 1968, the assassination of Dr. King infuriated the African American public, and the resulting riots in many urban areas left death and destruction in their wake. Brown offered "Say It Loud" as a sermon to the African American public to help continue Dr. King's legacy. Soul music often used this technique of having the singer be the "preacher from the pulpit" to get a particular message across. In the case of "Say It Loud,"

Brown used this pulpit to encourage African American pride while continuing the peaceful protests led by Dr. King.

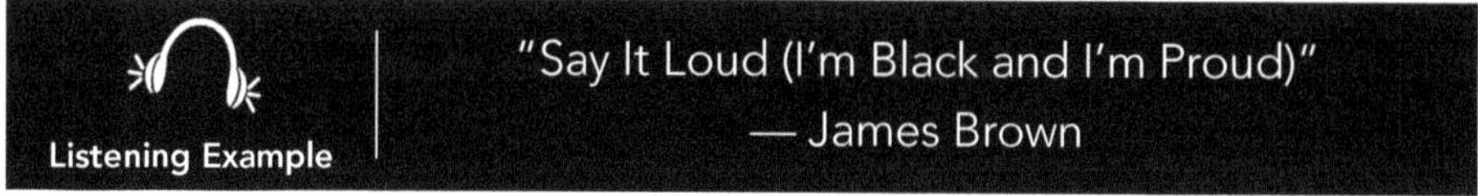

As the end of the 1960s approached, the African American public was looking for new music that would become the accompaniment to urban life in the 1970s. That music would be a reaction to the church-based music of 1960s soul—less gospel-based, stripping out much of the church-based style, including less emphasis on the singer or "preacher" singing the listener a sermon. Rather, this new music would be multi-rhythmic dance music, where almost every instrument acted as a percussion instrument, establishing a rhythmic foundation that made people move their feet. This music was called funk, and James Brown was at the forefront of its development. As you listen to "Get Up (I Feel Like Being a) Sex Machine," you will hear a greater emphasis on the bass guitar and the use of horns, not as a choir, as was common in soul music, but rather as percussion instruments used to accent offbeats for a syncopated effect.

Although Brown was an innovator, his success rarely crossed over into mainstream pop (white) music. While this may be looked upon as a detriment to his success, Brown's lack of compromise to gain crossover appeal was needed in the era of great social change, and it actually helped his career because most black music that had broader appeal was subject to the pop chart domination of the British Invasion. While Brown's music did not have broad appeal for most white Americans, it also did not suffer in the same way mainstream African American music, such as Motown and Phil Spector's groups, did.

Ray Charles

Ray Charles (1930–2004) was one of the most innovative African American musicians of the 20th century, singing both R&B and gospel music yet refusing to be defined by these styles. He also incorporated country and western, Tin Pan Alley, and other stereotypically white styles into his unique presentation. Charles's first hit, released in 1954, was "I've Got a Woman." This song is a great example of how changing music styles always tend to cause a generational backlash. For "I've Got a Woman," Charles took a gospel song called "It Must Be Jesus" and changed the words to remove the religious content, replacing it with lyrics about love and lust. This angered the older African American Christian population, who thought it blasphemous that a gospel song was transformed in this way. Charles, never short on confidence, continued to defy stereotypes with his 1962 release of *Modern Sounds in Country and Western Music, Volumes 1 and 2*. Charles's own record company did not want to release it, as they were positive that it would not only fail but also ruin Charles's career. The long-established stereotypes of white music and African American music were so established that any veering outside of those lines was considered confusing and somehow a betrayal of each particular race/culture. "I Can't Stop Loving You," written by country artist Don Gibson and recorded by Charles in 1962, broadened Charles's appeal for white listeners and earned him a Grammy Award and number one song on *Billboard*'s Hot 100 chart ("I Can't Stop Loving You" 2019). The combination of Ray Charles's gospel-influenced vocals and many different styles of music has led to his being considered a genius of 20th-century American music.

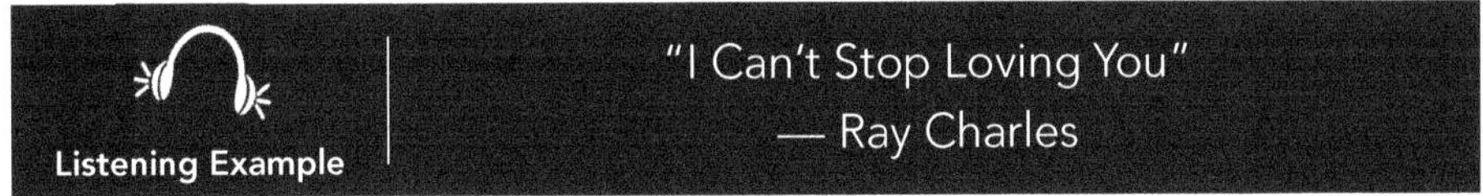

Aretha Franklin

FIGURE 4.2 Aretha Franklin

One soul artist who enjoyed the greatest crossover appeal with white audiences was Aretha Franklin (1942–2018). Franklin was raised in Detroit, the daughter of a well-known gospel preacher, and spent her early life as a gospel singer. Her first several years as a professional musician were with Columbia Records, where she was groomed to sing jazz. Her career did not take off, however, until she signed with Atlantic Records and traveled to Fame Studios in Muscle Shoals, Alabama, to record with soul musicians. Franklin's unrestrained gospel technique was now in the forefront, and her career exploded. In songs like "Respect" and "Think," she is delivering the sermon with all the power and emotion of the gospel church. Her career continued into the 1970s and beyond, breaking the barriers of style and race by recording pop and even opera. Listen to the song "Think" and focus on the singer as preacher, the repeated rhythmic vamp played at the very beginning by the piano, and the horns as gospel choir, mentioned earlier as great examples of soul music. Franklin became popular as a soul crossover artist just as soul music was beginning to transition to funk for much of the African American community. Her desire to branch out into other forms of music has established her as one of the greatest vocalists of the 20th century.

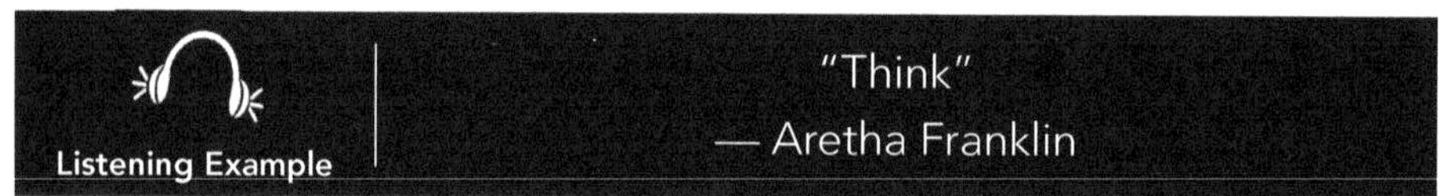

Memphis and Stax Records

Memphis, Tennessee, became one of the centers of soul music in the 1960s. Stax Records, formed by Jim Stewart and his sister Estelle Axton in 1961, would become known as the most successful soul-based record company of the 1960s. Much of this success was due to the house band, Booker T. and the MGs. This unique collaboration among African American members Booker T. Jones (organ), Al Jackson Jr. (drums), and white musicians Steve Cropper (guitar) and Donald "Duck" Dunn (bass) became the sound of soul in the 1960s. Unlike the musicians from Motown, these musicians didn't read charts but rather learned by rote and were so experienced playing with one another that they used nonverbal cues while recording to complete instrumental arrangements. Both Dunn and Cropper would later go on to be part of the Blues Brothers, both on tour and in the movie of the same name. Stax Records recorded legendary artists such as Isaac Hayes, Mavis Staples, Otis Redding, Sam and Dave, and Johnnie Taylor. One great example of Memphis soul is "Who's Making Love" by Johnnie Taylor (1934–2000). This soul sermon, with Taylor as the "preacher," first warns men of the dangers of "cheatin' on your woman," then gives a verse with the same warning for women, and follows with Taylor's own experiences. The song builds in intensity throughout, with a repeated bass guitar riff and the horns providing the "choir" response. "Who's Making Love" sold more than one million copies in 1968, making it one of Stax Records' biggest-selling singles (Whitburn 2004).

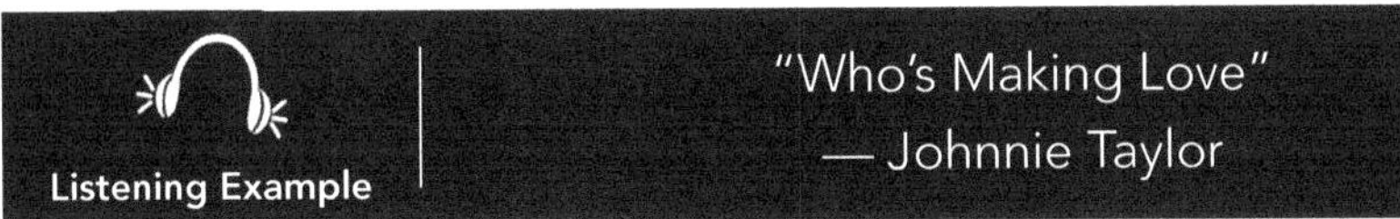

The biggest success story from Stax Records was that of Otis Redding (1941–1967). Redding grew up as a gospel singer and would go on to be considered one of the greatest singers in the history of American music. He worked as a backing musician for Little Richard and later as a driver and backup singer for Johnny Jenkins and the Pinetoppers. One day when he was at Stax Records working on a record with the Pinetoppers, Redding was overheard singing by himself, which impressed the staff. He was signed to Stax in 1962. Redding was a huge hit at the Monterey Pop Festival in 1967, which was a surprise, as almost all of the fans and other acts were white and part of the emerging counterculture. Unfortunately, Redding's biggest crossover success would come posthumously. Redding was killed in a plane crash on December 10, 1967, three days after completing recording on "(Sittin' On) the Dock of the Bay," a song that would become the first number one posthumous hit. Redding's broader appeal came from his ability to sing with a raw emotion rarely equaled in popular music.

The Beatles + Bob Dylan = Folk Rock

The folk rock style of music that was popular in the second half of the 1960s was a combination of the intelligent, socially conscious lyrics of Bob Dylan (born 1941) and the popularity of the "Beatle Beat." This hybrid style had broad appeal, as it leaned on the urban folk revival that had occurred with Dylan's success in the early 1960s along with the mainstream popularity of the British Invasion. The meeting between the Beatles and Bob Dylan in 1964 became more than just a conversation between an urban folk icon and a group of long-haired British rockers. The meeting caused both to change what they did musically. The Beatles began writing music that was more personal, adult oriented, and serious. Dylan, whose devotees rejected the use of electric instruments and drums as teen fodder, began to experiment with electric guitars, eventually hiring a band of Canadian R&B musicians to back him up. While this caused many of Dylan's fans to reject his new musical ideas, it helped lead the Beatles to unparalleled success and complexity never before achieved in rock music.

One band that best represents folk rock borrowed heavily from both Dylan and the Beatles. The Byrds were a folk group before viewing the Beatles film *A Hard Day's Night* in 1964, an event they considered life-changing. After seeing the movie, they sold their acoustic guitars and mandolins and bought electric instruments. Their first hit, "Mr. Tambourine Man," was an interesting conglomeration of musical styles. The song, written by Dylan, was greatly altered by the Byrds, who added a four-beat rock meter, a syncopated rhythm heard in a Beach Boys song, and an introduction based on Johann Sebastian Bach. They also altered much of the lyric content from Dylan's original, making the song half the length of the original and focusing more on the chorus. These changes turned Dylan's folk song (which did not have any chart success) to a *Billboard* chart-topping single and elevated the Byrds to become one of the first American groups to challenge the dominance of the British Invasion groups of the mid-1960s. As you listen to both the Dylan original and the Byrds cover version, focus on the following differences:

FIGURE 4.3 Bob Dylan

1. Dylan's meter is two beats per measure, while the Byrds use 4/4 time.
2. Dylan's original is based on music fitting around his lyric content, which was a basic construct of the urban folk tradition. The Byrds altered the lyrics to fit into the 4/4 meter of their version of the song. This is a predominant technique used in more mainstream popular music.
3. Listen to the instrumentation. Dylan's version is primarily acoustic guitar and harmonica, with a sparse electric guitar countermelody very much in the background. The Byrds use a more full rock instrumentation, including electric and acoustic guitars, bass guitar, drums, and three-part vocal harmonies. (It should be stated that Dylan was impressed with the Byrd's version of his song, stating, "Wow, you can dance to it."

Following the Byrds' instant success, many would capitalize on this new style. Groups such as Peter, Paul and Mary, Sonny and Cher, Simon and Garfunkel, and Buffalo Springfield would have folk rock hits. Even the Beatles, at the height of their Beatlemania success, recorded *Rubber Soul* in 1965, which is considered a folk rock album.

The Counterculture and Psychedelic Rock

Earlier we discussed the rapid changes in civil rights that occurred during the 1960s. Change was not confined to issues concerning just race but also included the greatest generational disconnect in U.S. history. The baby boomers, born in the years just after the end of World War II, had very different ideas about many aspects of life than their parents did. For those parents, often now called the "Greatest Generation," the idyllic life after World War II was to get married, buy a suburban single-family home, and have children. These ideals led to the emergence of suburban subdivisions with cookie-cutter homes. This "normalcy" included a great need to conform to the prevailing American culture. While rock and roll was at times disturbing to these parents in the 1950s, the rebellion that occurred in the second half of the 1960s was unprecedented.

Some teenagers in the 1960s began to rebel against their parents in a way that defied the traditional parent/child norms of previous generations. This new way of thinking was embraced by the teenagers of the second half of the 1960s through the counterculture that developed. The members of this counterculture, often called "hippies," fundamentally disagreed with most of the cultural norms in which their parents believed. They had a great distrust of the centers of power, including schools, the police, government, and established religion. They believed no one over 25 years of age could be trusted. They also believed certain hallucinogenic drugs, such as LSD and marijuana, would help them achieve new levels of consciousness, which would in turn help them create a new, better society. Although some humans have always searched for ways to alter their consciousness through drug use, the main difference between past eras and 1960s counterculture was that at no time prior (or since, for that matter) had a subgroup of a population not only accepted this type of recreational drug use but actually seen it as a preferred way of life. This use of drugs, along with a desire for communal living, were the foundation of this new philosophy of life.

Much of this great change was directed toward the role of the United States in the Vietnam War. In the past, there had been very few protests against the U.S. government when it came to military intervention. The hippies saw this war, which escalated during the 1960s, as unjust, and high school and college students protested loudly against the war's continuation. While the height of the counterculture lasted, at best, for five years, it did have a profound effect on how that generation and future generations would question authority. Those who were part of the counterculture have claimed they were responsible for several enormous changes in American culture. While some of these changes did occur, others did not. The hippies have claimed their protests stopped an unjust war. While the protests did help to change how Americans questioned the legitimacy of the government involving the country in armed combat, the Vietnam War did not end until 1975, long after the counterculture had peaked. The hippies have also claimed they helped remove a corrupt president from office. Although the hippies were very much against the presidency of Richard Nixon, he won reelection and resigned from office in 1974 due to the Watergate scandal. The counterculture also makes great claims about helping advance civil rights for African Americans and women. Although the hippies were inclusive of minorities and women, neither were ever in positions of power within the counterculture base.

San Francisco and Acid Rock

One of the new developments of the counterculture was a music based around the new drug culture. This music, called psychedelic or acid rock, was created by those consuming hallucinogens, was meant to be listened to by those consuming hallucinogens, or, at the very least, was representative of this new culture. This counterculture found its home in San Francisco, California. Up until this time, San Francisco had never been a musical center in the United States. San Francisco has a concentration of many cultures due to its role as a port city and has always been accepting of different cultures and the norms associated with a very diverse population. This willingness to "live and let live" made San Francisco the perfect location in which the counterculture could grow. In January 1967, the "Human Be-In" was held in Golden Gate Park. It was a gathering of 20,000 young people that included poetry readings and music. This gathering made national headlines, and as San Francisco began to be associated with this new counterculture, tens of thousands of teenagers ran away from home to join this new movement. Hundreds of rock bands ended up in San Francisco, and the music began to have a profound impact on young people across the world who considered themselves a part of this movement. A few of the bands involved had great success.

The Grateful Dead

One of the greatest and longest-lasting musical acts to emerge from the San Francisco scene was the Grateful Dead. The band was formed as the Warlocks in 1965. The name the Grateful Dead was created as founder Jerry Garcia (1942–1995) was looking in a dictionary and found the two words separately. The Grateful Dead combined musical elements of the blues, country, bluegrass, jazz, and long improvisational breaks with what Garcia called "a lot of weirdness" (Conefrey 1995). Though the Grateful Dead have sold more than 35 million records worldwide, they are most well-known for their live performances and their extremely dedicated fan base, the Deadheads. These fans would travel from concert to concert, setting up small villages in the parking lots and living by trading communally.

The band's early success was due in part to their becoming one of the house bands for the "acid tests," which were organized by writer Ken Kesey to experiment with LSD. The improvisational style the Grateful Dead practiced was the perfect soundtrack for these experiments. Twenty- to 40-minute jams, which would normally not be accepted by an audience, worked well as an accompaniment for the actual show, which was the audience experimenting with LSD.

The song **"Dark Star"** exemplifies this improvisational experimentation. It is 23 minutes in length and considered required listening for those who want to learn more about the Grateful Dead. Although this song is mostly instrumental (it does contain some lyric content), it was often the basis for many of the extended jams the band performed live over their 30-year career.

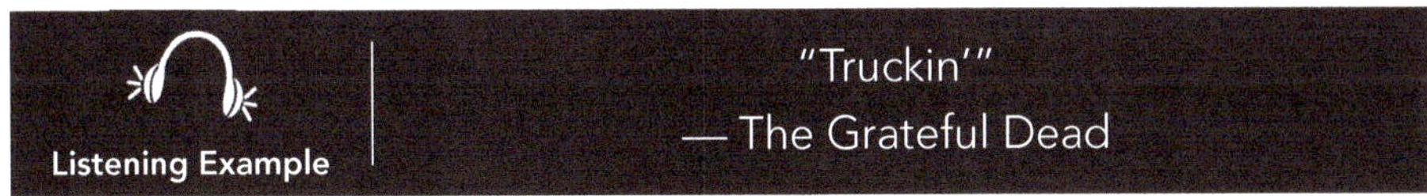

This song, from the *American Beauty* album of 1970, did get radio airplay, though the first and only top ten record by the Grateful Dead would not occur until the song "Touch of Grey" hit number nine in 1987.

Although the Grateful Dead officially ended in 1995 with the death of Garcia, members would continue to tour in various groups, and in 2015, the surviving members reunited for what they termed their final performances together. The greatest legacy left by the Grateful Dead is their blending of musical styles and their history of live performances, which overshadowed their studio recordings and pop radio hits.

Jefferson Airplane

Jefferson Airplane was one of the first bands out of the San Francisco counterculture scene to achieve mainstream popularity and radio success. Formed by Paul Kantner (1941–2016) in 1965, Jefferson Airplane combined mainstream pop with folk and psychedelic rock. They featured two female lead singers, Signe Anderson (1965–1966) and Grace Slick (1966–1973). Slick brought the psychedelic "White Rabbit" to Jefferson Airplane, who would go on to record the song as an anthem to the "Summer of Love" in 1967. The song, from the 1967 album *Surrealistic Pillow,* peaked at number eight on the *Billboard* Hot 100 ("Hot 100" 2018). "White Rabbit" was written in response to the perceived hypocrisy of parents who dismissed the counterculture and its acceptance of hallucinogens yet accepted the consciousness-altering effects of alcohol and prescribed drugs. In "White Rabbit," Slick uses *Alice's Adventures in Wonderland*, a 19th-century story by British author Lewis Carroll, to show how a traditional children's story can be compared with the new drug culture in the mid-1960s. "White Rabbit" is also unusual in that it rejects the normal verse-chorus form of most popular music of the time. Listen to the lyrics, which glorify the adventures you can have when altering your consciousness through chemicals.

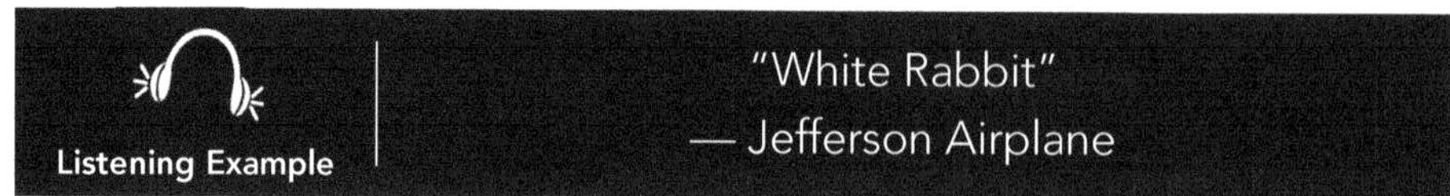

Jefferson Airplane, which would breakup in 1974, would go on in various forms, including Jefferson Starship (1974–1984) and Starship from 1985 to the present.

Janis Joplin: The First Female "Rocker"

Janis Joplin (1943–1970) was one of the most celebrated blues and soul singers of the late 1960s and the first truly independent female rock and roll star. She grew up in Port Arthur, Texas, was an outcast as a teen, and preferred to listen to the great blues performers of the past, such as Ma Rainey and Bessie Smith. She traveled back and forth between Texas and San Francisco several times before being recruited to sing for the San Francisco acid rock band Big Brother and the Holding Company. She officially joined Big Brother in 1966 and recorded two albums with them prior to beginning a solo career in 1968. From 1968 until her death on October 4, 1970, a heroin overdose, Joplin formed two other bands and recorded two additional albums, the last of which was released after her death. Joplin was not only one of the greatest female rock vocalists but also the first to be treated as an equal in what was previously a male-dominated business. Previous female singers, such as those who became famous through Motown or Phil Spector, had been packaged or promoted as sex objects. They had been made to look and sound a certain way to achieve the vision of the older male producer. Joplin was treated not as a female singer but as a blues singer on equal footing with the men with whom she worked. She was the first female singer given true respect and control of her own career path. Listen to the raw blues sound of Joplin in these two recordings.

Jimi Hendrix and the Rebirth of the Rock Guitar

Jimi Hendrix (1942–1970) is arguably the greatest single instrumentalist in the history of rock and roll. Though his career was only four years long, his guitar playing redefined what was considered possible on the instrument. During his posthumous induction into the Rock and Roll Hall of Fame, the following was written about Hendrix: "Hendrix expanded the range and vocabulary of the electric guitar into areas no musician had ever ventured before. His boundless drive, technical ability, and creative application of effects such as wah-wah and distortion forever transformed the sound of rock and roll" ("Jimi Hendrix" n.d.). Hendrix utilized amplifier feedback (previously thought of as a mistake on the instrument) and could fret with his thumb, creating combinations of lead and rhythm parts not previously created by any other musician. Following a brief time in the Army, Hendrix worked as a rhythm guitarist for Little Richard and the Isley Brothers. He moved to England in 1966 and hired Chas Chandler, a former bassist with the British rock group the Animals, to be his manager. He achieved almost instant success in England, where members of the Beatles, the

Who, the Rolling Stones, and others attended his live performances. His performance prompted Pete Townshend of the Who to declare, "With Jimi, I didn't have any envy. I never had any sense that I could come close" (Fricke 2010). Hendrix became famous in the United States after his performance at the Monterey Pop Festival in 1967 and continued with a legendary performance at the Woodstock Festival in 1969. He died on September 18, 1970, from an accidental overdose of barbiturates. Listen to the recordings of "Purple Haze" and the live performance of "The Star-Spangled Banner" from the Woodstock festival.

Eric Clapton

Considered one of the greatest guitarists in rock music history, Eric Clapton (born 1945) is the only person elected to the Rock and Roll Hall of Fame three times (as a member of the Yardbirds and Cream and as a solo artist). Clapton was influenced by the blues from an early age and, at sixteen, was already being noticed for his playing. His performances in the Yardbirds, Cream, and Blind Faith as well as his solo work under both his own name and Derek and the Dominos are some of the most iconic examples of blues-based guitar playing. While not as groundbreaking as Hendrix, Clapton has been equally influential and was named the fourth-greatest guitarist in rock music history by *Rolling Stone* magazine (Fricke 2010). He is credited with helping to revive the careers of several American blues musicians, including B.B. King and Buddy Guy. Clapton's career has spanned more than 50 years interpreting traditional African American blues. His interpretation of Bob Marley's reggae recording of "I Shot the Sheriff" brought reggae to a larger audience in the United States. His 1991 recording of "Tears in Heaven," a song written after his four-year-old son accidentally fell to his death, and the *Unplugged* album won six Grammy Awards in 1992.

FIGURE 4.4 Eric Clapton

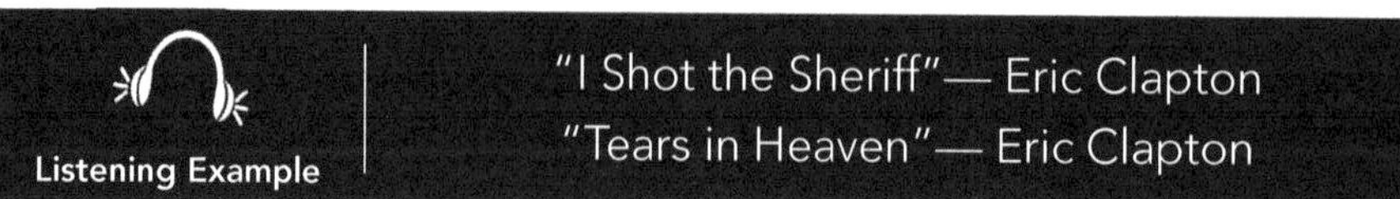

The Doors

The Doors were unlike any other popular band from the second half of the 1960s. Raymond Manzarek (1939–2013) and Jim Morrison (1943–1971), who met as film students at UCLA, formed the band in 1965 in Los Angeles. Their backgrounds in the visual arts were highly influential on their music. The music they would create was not of the counterculture that was prevalent at the time but instead drew from emotions such as jealousy, rage, and antagonism, which would later become staples of heavy metal music. Morrison's poetry, along with Manzarek's organ playing, Robby Krieger's guitar, and John Densmore's drumming, would appeal to an audience that was not part of the hippie subculture. Morrison's stage personae, sometimes referred to as "The Lizard King," would evolve to include his ability to manipulate his audience, sometimes through anger or antagonism, to riot. This behavior caused Morrison to be arrested on stage once and have several other legal charges filed. His behavior became more erratic, and he left the United States for Paris in 1970. In July 1971, he was found dead in his hotel room and was buried in Pere Lachaise Cemetery in Paris. The Doors would become one of the first rock bands to achieve great success on FM radio, as up to that point AM radio played mainstream pop music. The Doors were also influential in the beginning of 1970s-era theatrics in rock and roll, paving the way for more developed acts such as David Bowie, Alice Cooper, and Kiss.

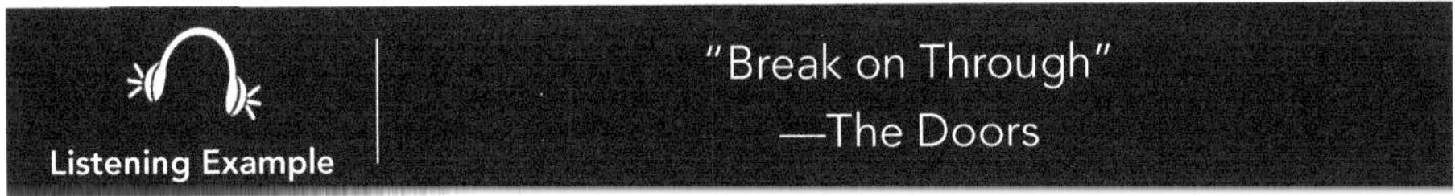

The Monkees

One other band that formed during this time was created specifically to be visual in nature, as its existence was created for television. The Monkees were formed in 1965 through an ad in the *Hollywood Reporter* announcing a casting call for actors to join a TV show about a rock group. The show was created as an American reaction to the Beatles and their fun antics in *A Hard Day's Night.* While the Beatles had moved on to greater complexity in their music, the Monkees would fill a void for younger teenagers who may not have been ready for the more complicated music coming from the Fab Four. The Monkees, who sang but were not allowed to play on early records, were truly the original boy band. Conflict soon occurred as Michael Nesmith (born 1942), Peter Tork (1942–2019), Davy Jones (1945–2012), and Micky Dolenz (born 1945) fought with producers over being allowed to write and perform their own material. Brill Building composers Tommy Boyce and Bobby Hart, with contributions from Gerry Goffin and Carole King and Neil Diamond, wrote the Monkees' first hits. Though the television show only lasted from 1966–1968, the Monkees continued to record albums through 1971 and have reunited on several occasions since for new releases and tours. The success of the Monkees marked the end of the Brill Building/assembly-line style of pop songwriting that was so successful in the 1960s.

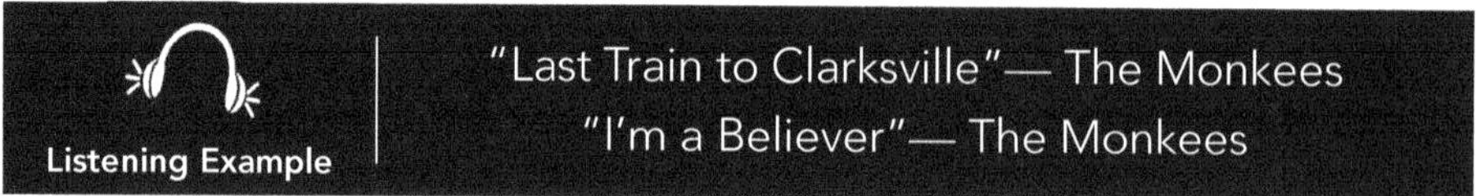

The Woodstock Music and Arts Festival

As the 1960s ended, the final meeting of the counterculture occurred in Bethel, New York, on August 15–18, 1969. The "Three Days of Peace and Music" was held on Max Yasgur's 600-acre farm and was attended by nearly 500,000 hippies. The 32 acts that performed included Ravi Shankar, Country Joe MacDonald and the Fish, Arlo Guthrie, Joan Baez, Santana, the Grateful Dead, Crosby, Stills, and Nash, Janis Joplin, Creedence Clearwater Revival, Jefferson Airplane, and Jimi Hendrix. This concert became the final symbol of the late 1960s counterculture and is still considered one of the greatest events in rock music history. It showed the world that half a million young people could gather peacefully. Unfortunately, the Woodstock Music and Art Fair was an anomaly. A similar festival was set up in California in December of 1969. The Altamont Festival was billed as the "West Coast Woodstock" but ended up as an example of poor planning and excessive drug and alcohol use, which caused violence and the deaths of three attendees.

FIGURE 4.5 Woodstock

As the turbulent 1960s ended, another void would soon form as music moved into the new decade. The Beatles broke up in early 1970. Janis Joplin and Jimi Hendrix would join the "27 club" of musicians who did not live past that age in 1970.

Jim Morrison would join the next year. As times changed and the counterculture fell apart, music would change as well. Rather than mimicking the producer-driven styles that dominated the early 1960s, the music of the 1970s would branch out in many directions, diversifying for new audiences based on age, race, and musical styles. No longer would one style dominate, but artists as diverse as James Taylor and Alice Cooper would have their place in the rock landscape of the 1970s.

References

"Ahmet Ertegun Quotes." Brainy Quote. Accessed February 2, 2018.

Conefrey, Mick, prod. *Rock and Roll: Crossroads/Blues in Technicolor.* WGBH, Boston and British Broadcasting Corporation, 1995. VHS.

Fricke, David. "100 Greatest Guitarists: David Fricke's Picks." *Rolling Stone,* December 3, 2010. https://www.rollingstone.com/music/music-lists/100-greatest-guitarists-david-frickes-picks-146383

Fricke, David. "Eric Clapton." *Rolling Stone,* December 2, 2010. https://www.rollingstone.com/music/music-lists/100-greatest-guitarists-david-frickes-picks-146383/eric-clapton-9-164848/. History. "Civil Rights Movement Timeline." Accessed Retrieved February 3, 2018. www.history.com/topics/civil-rights-movement-timeline.

"Hot 100 the Week of July 29, 1967, The." *Billboard.* Accessed February 6, 2019. https://www.billboard.com/charts/hot-100/1967-07-29.

"I Can't Stop Loving You." Songfacts. Accessed February 3, 2018. https://www.songfacts.com/facts/ray-charles/i-cant-stop-loving-you.

"Jimi Hendrix." http://www.perryscope.us/jimi-hendrix. Perryscope. Accessed January 18, 2018. https://www.brainyquote.com/quotes/ahmet_ertegun_539129

"Robert Plant Quotes." Brainy Quote. Accessed February 2, 2018. https://www.brainyquote.com/quotes/robert_plant_472854.

Whitburn, Joel. *Top R&B/Hip-Hop Singles: 1942–2004.* Record Research, 2004.

Figure Credits

IMG. 4.1: Source: https://commons.wikimedia.org/wiki/File:Martin_Luther_King,_Jr..jpg.

Fig. 4.1: Copyright © by Heinrich Klaffs (CC BY-SA 2.0) at https://commons.wikimedia.org/wiki/File:James_Brown_Live_Hamburg_1973_1702730029.jpg.

Fig. 4.2: Source: https://commons.wikimedia.org/wiki/File:Aretha_Franklin_1968.jpg.

Fig. 4.3: Copyright © by Chris Hakkens (CC BY-SA 2.0) at https://commons.wikimedia.org/wiki/File:Bob_Dylan_1978.jpg.

Fig. 4.4: Copyright © by Matt Gibbons (CC BY 2.0) at https://commons.wikimedia.org/wiki/File:Eric-Clapton_1975.jpg.

Fig. 4.5: Copyright © by Derek Redmond and Paul Campbell (CC BY-SA 3.0) at https://commons.wikimedia.org/wiki/File:Woodstock_redmond_stage.JPG.

1970s

CHAPTER 5

The First Half of the 1970s

Historical Context for the Decade

The beginning of the 1970s marked a major shift in the music industry that would be reflected in the music that was available to listeners across the world. The Beatles would break up in April 1970, finishing their dominance at the top of the charts. Before the end of the year, Janis Joplin and Jimi Hendrix would both become victims of accidental drug overdoses. By the time the Woodstock Festival occurred in August of 1969, it was clear that major changes were taking place. The counterculture's plans to begin a new society and end the Vietnam War would prove futile. It was clear in the 1967 "Summer of Love" and through the remainder of the 1960s that the drug-fueled hippy rebellion would ultimately fail. Those who had turned on to LSD and marijuana had begun to grow up and move on. The "innocence" of those recreational drugs had proved not so innocent. As musicians from that time moved on, new styles emerged as Americans moved into the new decade.

Although some musicologists love to hate the music of the 1970s, that opinion is often based on confusion over the lack of one dominant musical style. The 1970s ushered in an explosion of new arenas in rock, providing a wider variety of sounds that each listener could make their own. Singer-songwriters appealed to 20-something adults who had graduated from the counterculture. Heavy metal was consumed by teenagers who were either too young to be hippies or rejected the counterculture and needed an outlet for their pubescent frustration. Progressive or art rock appealed to those who enjoyed the complexity of classical music and jazz and loved the virtuosity and advanced songwriting of bands like the Who and the Beatles. Southern rock would combine a stronger shot of the blues with elements of country music. Funk music would become the new African American urban sound. These new subgenres, along with many others, would cause an explosion in the music industry in the 1970s, with unprecedented numbers of albums and singles being sold. Music was no longer dominated by one band (the Beatles) or one style (psychedelic rock) but now offered more diverse sounds that could fit a listener of any age, gender, or race. Music would diversify, no longer marketed based on age alone. New musical styles grew out of either a negative reaction to a previously established style or as a combination of two or more previously established styles. In the 1970s, this new diversity was unparalleled. This chapter will focus on the first half of the 1970s and the new styles. The most dominant new music style was characterized by the singer-songwriter.

Singer-Songwriters

The tradition of the singer-songwriter in American popular music can be traced to Bob Dylan and the folk musicians who influenced him (e.g., Woody Guthrie). Singer-songwriters are musicians who write their own lyrics and compose and perform their own music, often accompanying themselves. While this was true of Dylan and many other urban folk musicians who used musical accompaniment only as background or incidental music to support their poetry, the 1970s singer-songwriter usually employed a full band while attempting to focus on lyric content. This style was dominated by musicians who were part of the counterculture of the 1960s but had moved on, grown up, moved into their mid-20s, and started creating music that was introspective (examining one's own mind or thoughts). This music was much more personal than the music of the counterculture, relying on the musician's personal experiences rather than the more common themes of love and conflict often used as the basis for psychedelic rock. The singer-songwriters used personal reflection as a basis for much of their music, sometimes as a way of dealing with their own issues as they emerged from the turbulence of the 1960s. We will discuss several of these singer-songwriters, all of whom brought different personal and musical elements to this subgenre, which was the most dominant form of pop in the early 1970s.

James Taylor

James Taylor (born 1948), a five-time Grammy Award winner and Rock and Roll Hall of Fame inductee, is the quintessential American singer-songwriter, having sold more than 100 million records in his career of more than 50 years. In 1967, following a failed career attempt in the United States, a stay in a mental hospital, and recovery from heroin addiction, Taylor moved to London. With the help of Peter Asher, a former British Invasion singer who had become head talent scout for the Beatles' Apple Records, Taylor auditioned for Paul McCartney and George Harrison and became the first American musician signed to Apple Records (Reed 2015). Taylor's mellow baritone voice, great vocal phrasing, and complicated life gave him the authority of someone much older than his 20 years. His song "Fire and Rain" is autobiographical, dealing with his heroin addiction and the suicide of a close friend. The song is personal to Taylor yet deals with the cliché "If you love someone, tell them, because you never know when they might be gone."

FIGURE 5.1 James Taylor

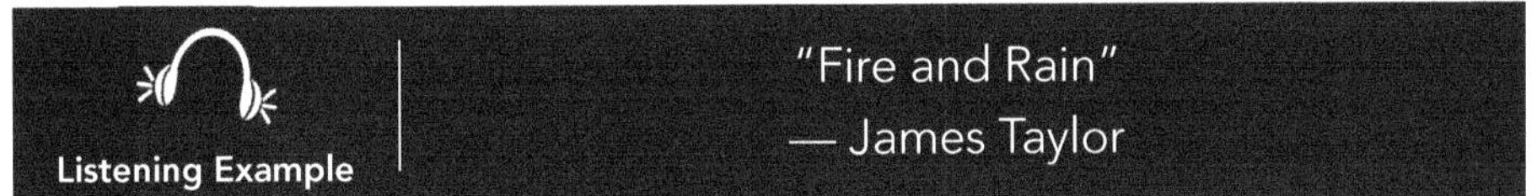

Taylor's career has continued throughout the past 50 years. His newer releases, while not played on the radio or having single chart success, have been critically praised. His 2001 album *New Moon Shine* gave us "The Frozen Man," a song about the possibility of bringing someone back to life.

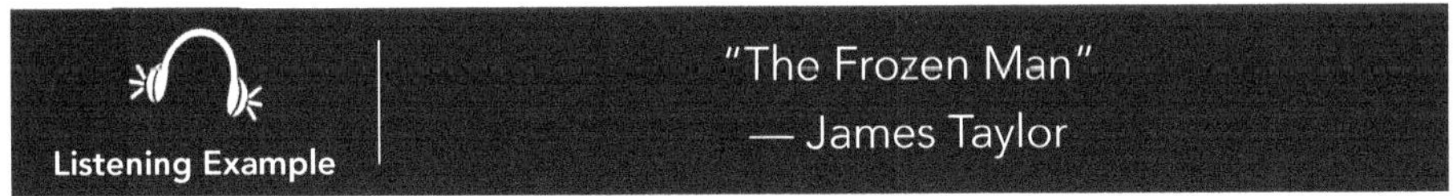

Taylor has been linked to former Brill Building composer Carole King through shared concert tours and his popular recording of her song "You've Got a Friend."

Carole King

Carole King (born 1942) is the most successful female songwriter of the second half of the 20th century. King's career as a singer-songwriter was delayed over a decade due to her success as a songwriter creating the Brill Building pop sounds of the early

1960s with her then-husband Gerry Goffin. Her album *Tapestry,* released in 1971, topped the charts for 15 weeks in 1971 and won four Grammy Awards. She has sold 75 million albums worldwide (Kasper n.d.). The album contained the hit songs "You've Got a Friend" (made famous by James Taylor) and "It's Too Late."

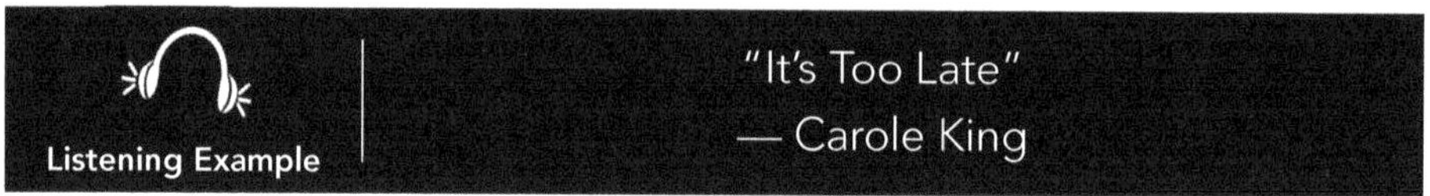

Joni Mitchell

Other female artists would achieve success as singer-songwriters in the 1970s. Joni Mitchell (born 1943) is a Canadian singer-songwriter whose songs often included social themes, environmental activism, and themes of love and loss. The song "Big Yellow Taxi" is a great example of a song dealing with loss on multiple levels. Mitchell refers not only to environmental concerns but also to a loss of love, echoing the James Taylor sentiment of "Fire and Rain."

> "Oh, it always seems to go, that you don't know what you've got till it's gone."
>
> ("Big Yellow Taxi" 2010).

This line refers to concerns about how we treat our environment and then segues into the loss of "my old man." Mitchell's quirky voice has never achieved mainstream popularity, yet her albums and songs have been praised by critics and covered by many artists. After listening to "Big Yellow Taxi," we will see how an unusual tone quality can be a positive in getting creative lyrics across to an audience.

Another 1970s singer-songwriter who was a great storyteller was Harry Chapin.

Harry Chapin

Harry Chapin (1942–1981) was a singer-songwriter, environmental activist, and humanitarian who served on the first Presidential Commission on World Hunger. Although he was best known for his number one hit song "Cat's in the Cradle" (1974), many of Chapin's songs were **ballads** (complete short stories told in songs), which made them too long for radio. One such song is a love song about a down-and-out night watchman and the waitress he tells his story to after his shift one morning. Listen to this great example of a **ballad** called "A Better Place to Be." Chapin's life would end following a traffic accident at the age of 38.

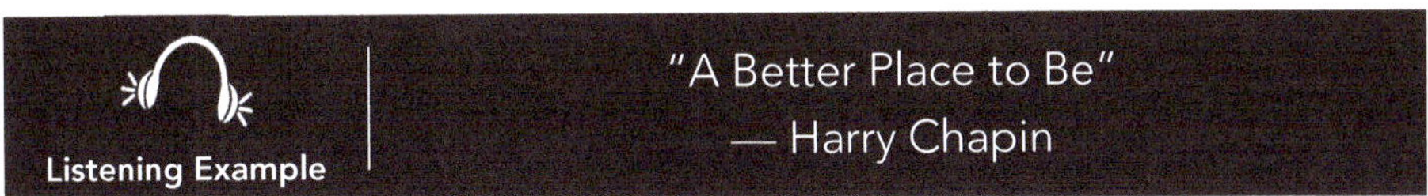

Warren Zevon

The quirky music of Warren Zevon (1947–2003) did not yield large numbers of pop hits, but his music is respected by singer-songwriters and many other musicians. His biggest hit, "Werewolves of London," is a staple on classic rock radio. His music had recurring themes of the macabre, dealing with death at times in a comic, flippant manner. His 1978 album *Excitable Boy* included the hits "Werewolves of London," "Excitable Boy," and "Lawyers, Guns, and Money." In "Excitable Boy," Zevon uses his interest in the macabre to tell a story about a boy, moving through periods of the boy's life and increasingly psychotic behavior, always with the excuse "Oh, he's just an excitable boy," a phrase used to describe hyperactivity in the past. What makes this song so unique is that while documenting these horrific chapters in the subject's life, we hear a fun, bouncy song with doo-wop background singers. It is Zevon's use of this musical style that gives the song a comic element.

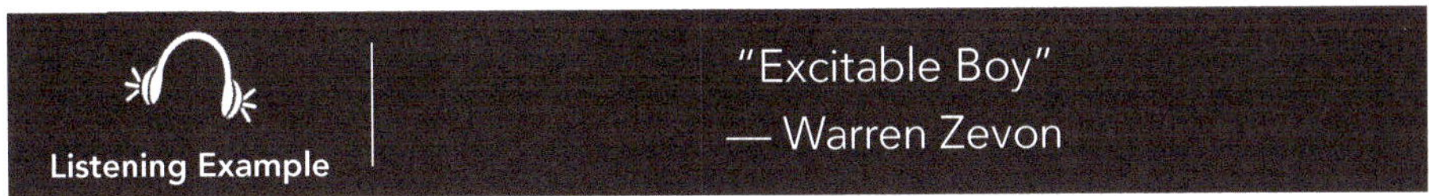

A Musical Battle, an Unusual Mashup, and a Unique Goodbye

In 1970, Canadian singer Neil Young wrote and released "Southern Man," a song documenting the treatment of slaves by slave owners and relating that bigotry to the current times. In 1974, the Southern rock group Lynyrd Skynyrd responded to Young with the song "Sweet Home Alabama." In the song, they called out Neil Young with the line "Well I hope Neil Young will remember, Southern man don't need him around anyhow"(Greene 2015). While the members of Lynryd Skynyrd were fans of Neil Young's music and later became friends with Young, the response song provided a musical battle of the North versus the South. In 1980, Zevon decided to become involved by writing a third song to respond to "Sweet Home Alabama." In "Play It All Night Long," Zevon stereotypes Southern white men as drunken, racist, incestuous, and insane. Although Zevon did not have a part in the original "Southern Man"/"Sweet Home Alabama" battle, he decided to become involved, even commenting on the plane crash that killed three members of Lynyrd Skynyrd in 1977. "Sweet home Alabama, play that dead band's song, turn those speakers up full blast, play it all night long" (Cochran 2009).

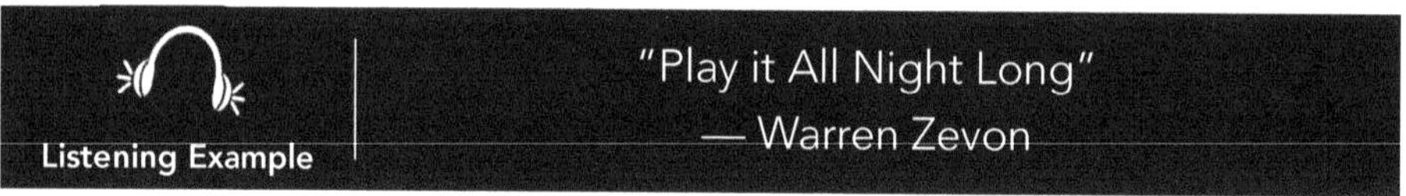

One interesting addition to this musical saga: in 2008, Kid Rock had his most successful single with "All Summer Long," which was a mashup of Skynyrd's "Sweet Home Alabama" and Zevon's "Werewolves of London." The author has never been able to discover whether Kid Rock wrote this song knowing about the Neil Young/Skynyrd/Zevon battle.

In 2002, Zevon announced he was terminally ill with lung cancer. He spent the last few months of his life recording *The Wind*, an album composed to say goodbye to family, friends, and fans. The album, full of guest appearances by many famous musicians, was nominated for five Grammy Awards and won two (Grammy, n.d.). His final recording became his final goodbye in "Keep Me in Your Heart."

Billy Joel

One of the most successful artists in rock music history is Billy Joel. His hit songs spanned the 1970s through the 1990s, and his string of once-a-month concerts at Madison Square Garden have sold out since 2014. Known as "The Piano Man," he is the third most successful solo act in U.S. history. Only Elvis Presley and Garth Brooks have sold more records (Lewis 2015). Joel (born 1949) grew up in Long Island, New York. His career began in the 1970s, and after three moderately successful albums, Joel became famous with his commercially successful and critically praised album *The Stranger.* The next release, *52nd Street,* was an homage to the culturally diverse music of New York City. In 1980, he released *Glass Houses*, a harder rock sound, which featured his first number one hit, "It's Still Rock and Roll to Me." He won the Grammy Award for best male rock vocal performance for the album, and it was nominated for Album of the Year. In 1982, he released *The Nylon Curtain,* an album in which he wanted to pay tribute to the brilliance of the Beatles. It was also nominated for Album of the Year. In 1983, he released *An Innocent Man,* which paid tribute to doo-wop and Motown, the music of his youth. The album had six Top 40 singles and three Top 10 singles, including the hit "Uptown Girl," accompanied by the video starring his then-girlfriend, supermodel Christie Brinkley. After releasing *The Bridge* in 1986 and *Storm Front* in 1989, Joel released his final album, *River of Dreams*, in 1993. Since that album, Joel has largely avoided writing pop music. From *The Stranger,* "Scenes from an Italian Restaurant" is a song that was written as two separate songs and then combined. It is the story of a meeting between two old friends at an Italian restaurant that flashes back to their years in high school. In between the two song sections is a piano solo.

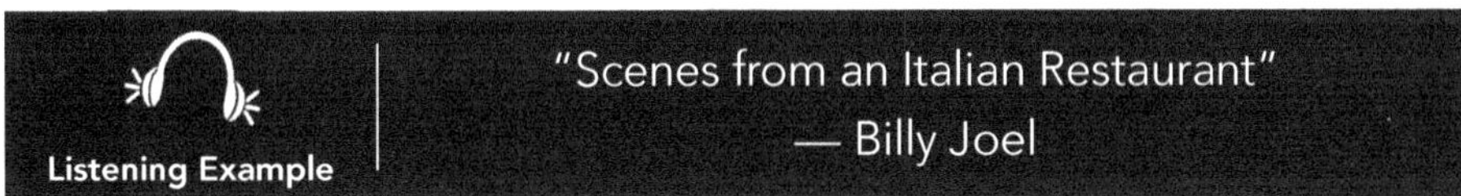

Elton John (born 1947)

Another artist often compared to Billy Joel is Elton John. John is one of the most successful artists of all time, having at least one song in the *Billboard* Top 100 every year for 31 consecutive years (1970–2000; Weiser n.d.) He is not technically a singer-songwriter, as he does not write the lyrics to his music. His partnership with poet/lyricist Bernie Taupin has continued since 1967. Elton's song "Candle in the Wind 1997," a remake of his 1970s song with new lyrics in tribute to the late Diana, Princess of Wales, is the highest-selling single in the history of the US and UK pop music charts (Guinness n.d.).

Heavy Metal

Unlike the work of the singer-songwriters, some musical styles continued to be aimed at the teenager. Heavy metal music developed in the late 1960s and early 1970s out of the blues-dominated rock music of British bands, including the Rolling Stones, Cream, and the Who, as well as American Jimi Hendrix. The term is attributed to the Canadian rock band Steppenwolf, whose lyrics to "Born to Be Wild" included the term "heavy metal thunder." Although meant to describe the sound of motorcycles in the song, it also reflected the chemical composition of some metals, which were toxic, and the term "heavy metal" was often used in military circles to describe large tanks or guns (Walser 2014). The music was typified by a massive sound with highly distorted electric guitars and strong drumbeats, creating a very powerful sound with extremely high decibel levels. The music stressed aggression and the attitudes of young teenagers (primarily teenage boys) who were dealing with the angst and sexual frustration of the postpuberty, pre-adult time in their lives. This rebellion and anger was served well by heavy metal in that it provided a musical style that seemed to reflect the anger, confusion, and stress many teens feel. As critic Robert Cristgau stated, "Heavy metal is an expressive mode [that] seems to be with us for as long as ordinary white boys fear girls, pity themselves, and are permitted to rage against a world they'll never beat" (Christgau 1998).

The subject matter of heavy metal has taken much criticism based on not only sex but also its darker themes and depressing subject matter. This criticism is also directed toward the audience for heavy metal. The music consumed by teen populations has traditionally been viewed as shallow, silly, and overemotional. Older populations have always dismissed these strong emotions felt by teenagers, and any art form associated with such a group will usually be similarly dismissed.

Heavy metal gained inspiration from a number of sources. Heavy metal artists such as Alice Cooper and Black Sabbath relied on the pop culture staples of comic books and horror movies to express their frustration. While that frustration was aimed at established authority such as government or overall societal norms, it translated to teenagers as a general frustration about finding one's place, sex, and the male battle for dominance in a common social group.

Motor City Five (MC5)

MC5, or the Motor City Five, was formed outside Detroit, Michigan, in 1964, but became better known following an article in *Rolling Stone* magazine in 1969. Their dense, heavy sound was ahead of its time, sounding more like the established heavy metal of three or four years later. While their original lineup only lasted until 1972, and they had very little chart success, MC5 is considered one of the most important early American heavy metal groups. They would influence many metal and punk acts that would follow, and some critics refer to MC5 as "proto punk." (The author of this text does not consider "proto" to be an adequate prefix for any style, as it forces us to form a comparison with something that did not yet, technically, exist.) MC5 was criticized for its raw sound, radical political affiliations, and foul language. The song "Kick Out the Jams" is a great example of early heavy metal. In reviewing the release of the album *Kick Out the Jams, Rolling Stone* critic Lester Bangs referred to the album as "A ridiculous, overbearing, pretentious album" (Bangs 1969). In retrospect, this is exactly what heavy metal would become—raw emotions contained in a blues-based package kicked up on steroids.

Black Sabbath

Black Sabbath was formed in Birmingham, England, in 1968 by guitarist Tommi Iommi, bassist Geezer Butler, singer Ozzy Osbourne, and drummer Bill Ward. Their initial album, *Black Sabbath*, was released on Friday the 13th in February 1970. Although it did not receive good reviews, it was very successful on the British charts, reaching eighth place. Black Sabbath's music was a reaction to the vibe of the psychedelic hippie movement and the British society's class system, which made it very difficult for someone to raise his or her social status. Black Sabbath's response was what Osbourne once referred to as "doom" music. They wanted to rebel against the authorities through a horror vibe in music. The song "Iron Man" best reflects this attitude, as it describes the story of a Frankenstein-type creature who is betrayed by those in power and now seeks his revenge.

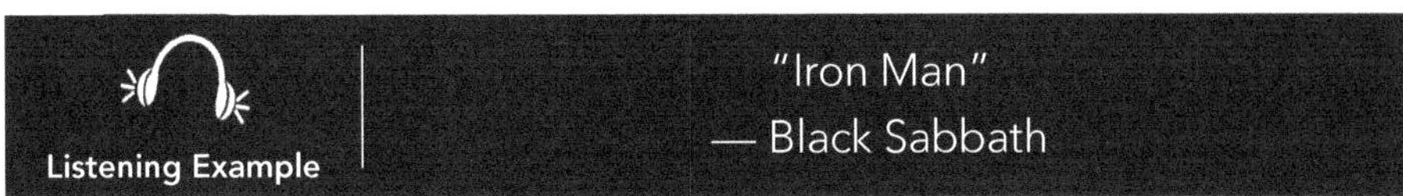

Alice Cooper

Vincent Furnier (born 1948), the lead singer and leader of the band Alice Cooper, has in the nearly 50-year history of the band adopted that name as his own. The group formed in Detroit, and its purpose was to "drive a stake through the heart of the love generation" (Alice Cooper.com 2012). They wanted to take all the taboos of what Cooper called the "class-less" pop culture and throw them in front of a live audience. At first, the band cross-dressed, which was meant to shock the norms of the time. America was not ready for the androgynous look, and the band shifted to a campy, fun horror vibe. Alice became a Frankenstein's monster–type character on stage, incorporating the cartoon-ish look of horror movies with props and costumes, special effects (including Alice guillotining himself on stage), and all the drama of a live Broadway show. This new look became incredibly important for rock in the 1970s as the economics of touring increasingly required that artists create huge shows that could fill arenas and stadiums. The show was now much more than a concert; rather, it was a multisensory experience.

FIGURE 5.2 Alice Cooper

One such manifestation of this new stage presentation involved the story of Alice and the chicken. Supposedly, during a concert in Toronto in 1969, a fan threw a live chicken onstage. Alice thought it would be great art to throw the chicken out over the audience to watch it fly away. Instead, the fans tore it into pieces and threw the newly deceased chicken's parts back up onto the stage. The next day, the press wrote stories portraying Cooper biting the head off the live chicken and drinking its blood. Before Cooper could deny the story, Frank Zappa called him and asked if it was true. Alice's reply was "Of course not! That's disgusting!" Zappa's response was "Whatever you did, keep doing it!" (Superseventies, n.d.). This myth helped Alice Cooper sell out concerts for the next 20 years, and to this day, fans want to go to Alice Cooper concerts to see what might happen onstage. The 1975 album *Welcome to My Nightmare* and the following tour were two huge events in the heavy metal landscape of the 1970s.

Deep Purple

Deep Purple, a British band formed in 1968, is one of the pioneering bands of heavy metal music. The lineup of Ian Gillan (vocals), Ritchie Blackmore (guitar), Jon Lord (keyboards), Roger Glover (bass), and Ian Paice (drums) was their best-known grouping, and their 1973 hit "Smoke on the Water" is their best-known song. "Smoke on the Water" was inspired by the fire that burned down the Montreux, Switzerland, casino Deep Purple had planned to use to record their next album. The night before they were to begin recording, a fan attending the Frank Zappa concert shot a flare gun into the ceiling, which caused the destruction of the entire casino as the members of Deep Purple watched from their hotel nearby (Zappa 1990). The song tells the story of the casino fire and the smoke that flowed across the lake.

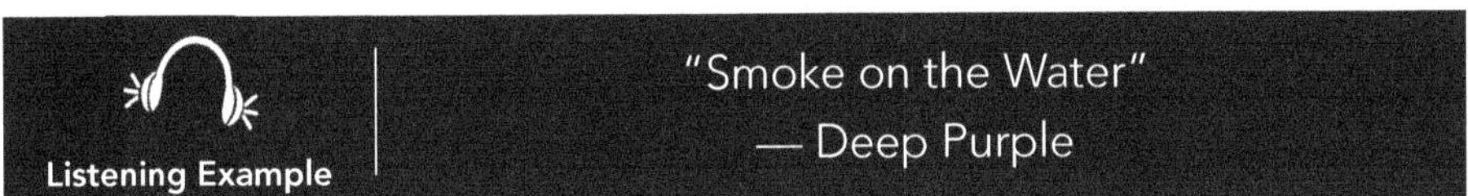

Led Zeppelin

Led Zeppelin is one of the most successful, innovative, and influential rock bands in pop music history. While many consider Led Zeppelin the greatest heavy metal band of all time, their style drew from many areas, and their music was reflective of that diversity. The members of the band do not like the use of the term "heavy metal" to describe their music, considering the term too narrow in scope. Guitarist Jimmy Page (born 1944) formed the band in 1968 out of the remnants of the New Yardbirds to fulfill the Yardbirds' previously scheduled events. Page then hired Robert Plant (born 1948), who recommended John Bonham (1948–1980). John Paul Jones (born 1946), who had previously played with Page, was then hired as bassist and keyboardist. The name Led Zeppelin came from a quote by the Who's drummer, Keith Moon, who believed the new group would fail, or "sink like a lead balloon" (Greene 2018). The term "lead zeppelin," later changed to "led" to avoid mispronunciation, became the band's name.

FIGURE 5.3 Led Zeppelin

Although the band wanted to perform the blues, they also added elements of psychedelic rock, folk music, and reggae. Their success in heavy metal in the 1970s was unprecedented. Their album releases have sold in excess of 300 million units worldwide (Beech 2018). Many heavy metal acts that followed would be greatly influenced by Led Zeppelin's heavy, thunderous sound. Their fourth album, *Led Zeppelin IV*, would also produce "Stairway to Heaven," considered to be the most-played single of the 1970s. The group became associated with the heavy metal lifestyle, with a reputation for excess related to drugs, women, and destroying hotel rooms. The group ended their run in 1980 when drummer Bonham died from an overdose of alcohol. The song "Whole Lotta Love," which is ranked 75th on *Rolling Stone*'s list of the top 500 songs of all time, became their first hit single in the United States. From their second album, *Led Zeppelin II*, this 1969 song crushes the counterculture vibe of peace and love while adding an element of psychedelia in the middle section. This song provides an early look into the heavy metal scene of the 1970s.

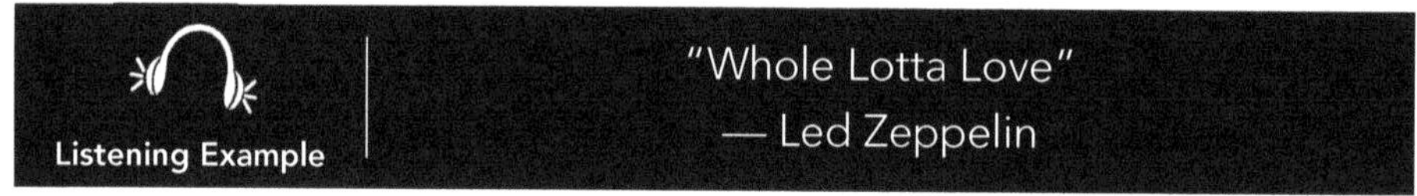

The surviving members of Led Zeppelin continued to work on solo projects through the 1980s and beyond and reunited on occasion, sometimes with Bonham's son Jason on drums. There have been rumors of an upcoming reunion.

Aerosmith

Aerosmith was formed in the Boston, Massachusetts, area in 1970. Their well-known lineup of Steven Tyler (lead vocals), Joe Perry (lead guitar), Tom Hamilton (bass), Brad Whitford (guitar), and Joey Kramer (drums) started in 1971. Their sound was based on British blues–oriented bands such as the Rolling Stones and Cream, but they would get much of their influence from Led Zeppelin. Their string of hit records, including "Dream On," continued through the 1970s until drug abuse caused Perry and Whitford to quit the band in the late 1970s. The band experienced an unusual comeback in 1986 when their song "Walk This Way" was covered by rap group Run-D.M.C. Perry and Tyler appeared in the music video with Run-D.M.C., and the collaboration was fruitful for both groups. Run-D.M.C., with the help of the single, had the first million-selling rap album, and Aerosmith's career was resurrected (Price 2016).

Aerosmith's career continued through the 1990s and 2000s. In 2018, they planned a long farewell tour that was scheduled to include a residency in Las Vegas in 2019.

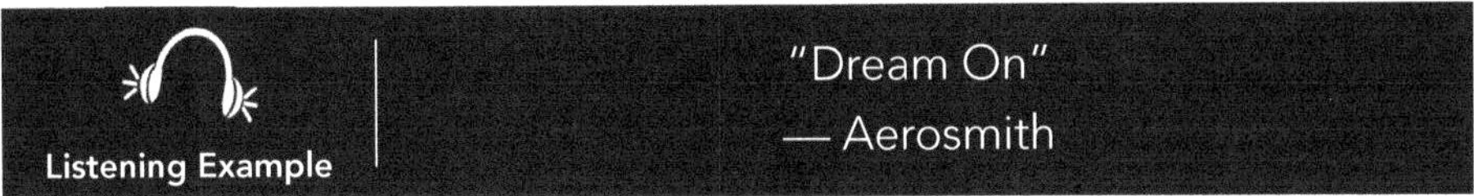

Van Halen

Van Halen was formed in 1974 in California by brothers Eddie and Alex Van Halen (on guitar and drums, respectively), David Lee Roth on vocals, and Michael Anthony on bass. The band was discovered by Kiss bassist Gene Simmons and had their first hit in 1978 with "You Really Got Me" a cover of the Kinks song cited in Chapter 3. From 1984 to the present, the band has continued, alternating David Lee Roth and Sammy Hagar on lead vocals and replacing Michael Anthony with Wolfgang Van Halen, Eddie's son, on bass. The most important aspect of Van Halen's music is Eddie Van Halen's guitar playing. Eddie Van Halen is one of the best guitar players in rock music history and certainly of the greatest and most influential since the death of Jimi Hendrix. His ability to play incredibly fast patterns and passages provided a blueprint for what heavy metal guitar playing would become in the 1980s and beyond. Van Halen also provided a transition from the darker elements of heavy metal in the 1970s to the more mainstream pop sounds of the hair bands of the 1980s. Eddie's use of synthesizer, coupled with the band's sense of showmanship onstage and in videos, would provide the perfect pop heavy metal act for MTV and the 1980s.

Heart

Heart, fronted by sisters Ann and Nancy Wilson, formed in 1974 in Seattle, Washington. Ann Wilson is considered one of the greatest female singers in rock history. Although Heart's sound in the 1970s also incorporated folk and mainstream pop, Wilson's voice is the greatest example of the female heavy metal sound of the 1970s. They were inducted into the Rock and Roll Hall of Fame in 2013.

Southern Rock

Southern rock is a subgenre of rock developed from the blues, country music, and mainstream rock and roll. The majority of the bands that played this music were from the Southern states and felt contributions from the South had been minimized in rock's history. Southern rock's signature sound has long electric guitar solos and a greater emphasis on the blues. Southern rock was a reaction to the complex, complicated music of the psychedelic movement, adding folk elements to give the music greater legitimacy. Two great examples of the Southern rock sound are the Allman Brothers and Lynyrd Skynyrd.

The Allman Brothers

One of the best-known Southern rock bands, the Allman Brothers Band was formed in 1969 in Florida by brothers Duane Allman (1946–1971) and Gregg Allman (1947–2017). Their third album, *At Fillmore East,* recorded live in 1971, has been called "one of the best live recordings ever committed to vinyl" (Kemp 2002). As teenagers, the Allman brothers were introduced to rhythm and blues (R&B) and soul music through an African American friend. Prior to forming the Allman Brothers Band, Duane Allman worked as a session guitarist at Fame Studios in Muscle Shoals, Alabama, where he played with great soul musicians, including Aretha Franklin and Wilson Pickett. Once the band formed, Allman was instructed to move the band to either New York or Los Angeles so they could become more popular. He refused, wanting the band to stay in the South. The band's members also realized they couldn't reproduce their live performances with a studio record and decided to record a live performance. *At Fillmore East* not only quickly climbed the charts; it also stood the test of time. In 2004, it was selected to be preserved in the Library of Congress by the National Recording Registry as "culturally, historically, and aesthetically important" (Library of Congress 2004). Though Duane Allman was killed in a motorcycle accident in 1971 and fellow bandmate Berry Oakley (1948–1972) died the next year in a motorcycle accident just miles from where Allman died, the band continued through 2014. The band's song "Whipping Post," from their live album, became their signature song.

Lynyrd Skynyrd

Lynyrd Skynyrd was formed in Jacksonville, Florida, in 1969 and became the most famous example of a Southern rock band. Their hit songs "Sweet Home Alabama" and "Freebird" are staples of classic rock radio to this day. The name for the group was created by founding member Ronnie Van Zant, who at first called the band Leonard Skinnerd, a mocking callout to their former high school gym teacher, Leonard Skinner, who was against any male high school student having long hair. By 1970, the better-known spelling was used, and the band later invited Skinner to introduce them onstage (*New York Times* 2010). The band had many hits through 1977, when tragedy struck. Ronnie Van Zant, guitarist Steve Gaines, and backup singer Cassie Gaines, along with three other people, were killed when the plane the band had chartered crashed in Mississippi. The group disbanded immediately after the accident and did not reform until 10 years later with Ronnie Van Zant's younger brother Johnnie as the singer and songwriter. The band continues to tour and record, announcing their "Farewell Tour" in 2018.

As we discussed earlier in the chapter, "Sweet Home Alabama" was a song written as a response to Neil Young's "Southern Man." While the feud between the band and Young seems to be overblown and each has shown respect for the other's music, it is interesting to hear Ronnie Van Zant call out Neil Young in the song. "Sweet Home Alabama" is often used as an anthem for Southern pride and is sometimes associated with the racist policies of Southern states in the historically segregationist South. While the members of Lynyrd Skynyrd have discredited those associations, Skynyrd's use of the Confederate flag as a backdrop for its concerts has provoked outrage, since the use of that flag has been associated with white supremacy and bigotry. In the past few years, Lynyrd Skynyrd has stopped using the Confederate flag at most of their concerts, preferring to perform in front of an American flag. They claim to this day, however, that their use of the Confederate flag was never about race but simply a show of Southern pride.

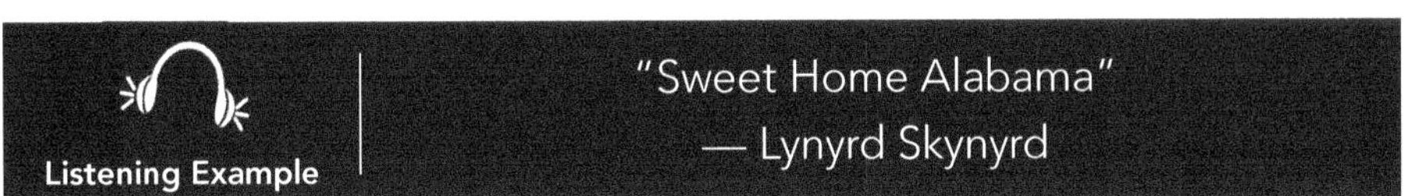

Progressive (Art) Rock

The terms "progressive" and "art" rock are used to describe musicians who were influenced by jazz and classical music, respectively. Although some musicologists differentiate between the two, most progressive and/or art rock musicians utilized influences from both styles, so for the purposes of this text, the terms progressive and art rock will be considered synonyms. Progressive rock developed in the late 1960s and early 1970s, utilizing the sounds, compositional techniques, and virtuosity previously attributed to jazz and classical musicians. While the genre was created in both the United States and Britain, the British had a greater tendency toward progressive rock for two reasons. First, British kids grew up hearing more classical and jazz music than American teenagers did, as British radio was less commercial and tended toward older forms of music prior to accepting American rock and roll. Second, there was a void at the end of the 1960s as many of the most successful British artists left England due to the taxes they were forced to pay.

Progressive rock began as an outgrowth of the music the Beatles and the Who began composing in the mid-1960s. This music included the introduction of unusual instrumentation, virtuosic (great technical ability) playing, and changes in meter. Some will trace progressive rock back to *Sgt. Pepper's Lonely Hearts Club Band,* recorded by the Beatles in 1967. The use of string instruments, the trace of a concept within the album, and the fact that the album was recorded without any assumption of live performance led to the Beatles garnering respect that in the past had only gone to musicians such as Ludwig Van Beethoven or modern American composers such as George Gershwin. The term "composer" was applied to those who created a greater art, excluding rock musicians as writers of trivial, banal songs to which "little kids could dance." Once the Beatles began to garner respect with songs that no longer fit that stereotype, music critics could no longer dismiss rock music completely. The Who, known for having superbly talented players, created songs that showed that talent and created music that no longer fit into the pre-established forms of rock. *Tommy,* an opera composed by Pete Townshend, showed rock music could work as a long-form theatrical work. Many other musicians followed what the Beatles and the Who began in the mid-1960s and expanded on that complexity in the 1970s. Progressive rock developed in many different ways, depending on the groups that performed it. We will look at several different progressive rock bands, each of which brought something new to listeners in the early 1970s.

Emerson, Lake, and Palmer

Keith Emerson, Greg Lake, and Carl Palmer each played in other bands before coming together in England in 1970. They brought with them a love for both classical music and jazz, relying on Emerson's use of the Hammond organ, Moog synthesizer, and other keyboard instruments to create rock-based symphonic compositions. Although their music included acoustic vocal and mainstream rock songs, they became better known for their rock adaptations (arrangements) of previously written material, including an album of rock music based on arrangements of Russian composer Modest Mussorgsky's *Pictures at an Exhibition*, a suite of 10 short pieces meant to be played at one time. Originally composed in 1874, it is known as both a piano masterpiece and a popular arrangement for full orchestra. This style of composition was prevalent during the Classical (1750–1820) and Romantic (1820–1900) periods of the European tradition of music. During those time periods, composers created longer works based around shorter sections, often called movements. While the shorter works or movements can stand alone, each are related to the other and are intended to be played as one work.

As an example, a symphony from Beethoven might be 35 minutes in length, with four movements, each individual yet related to one another and ultimately meant to be performed and/or listened to as one work. The Emerson, Lake, and Palmer (ELP) arrangement of Mussorgsky's work includes some of the pieces originally written and others added by the band. ELP also interpreted American orchestral music. One composer whose music they adapted was Aaron Copland (1900–1990), who is considered one of the great masters of American orchestra music. ELP arranged a piece called "Fanfare for the Common Man," a brass and percussion piece originally composed by Copland in 1942. ELP transformed the piece into a rock shuffle.

Yes

The group Yes formed in England in 1968. Though it had a core of musicians, including Chris Squire and Jon Anderson, there have been more than 20 full-time members in the group in its 50-year history. One of the most successful and influential progressive rock bands, Yes has sold more than 13 million albums (RIAA 2019) in the United

States. They were inducted into the Rock and Roll Hall of Fame in 2017. Yes created rhythmically complex music with the addition of tight vocal harmonies. They employed only the most talented players and singers, creating rock music using Classical and Romantic-based forms.

In "I've Seen All Good People," a song written by Anderson and Squire, Yes uses the game of chess as a metaphor for life. In dividing the song into two parts: A ("Your Move") and B ("All Good People"), the song takes on the quality of a suite. In this song, we hear varied meter changes. Meter is the regularly defined grouping of beats that provide a pattern for the listener. When meters change regularly in a piece of music, it provides a musical suspense, keeping the listener surprised. Regular meter changes in a song will tend to make the song undanceable. While Classical and Romantic composers tended to utilize changing meters in music, pop music and rock usually avoid this, as dancing was a big part of the appeal of mainstream rock and roll. The lyric content also requires interpretation. This deeper lyric content is often avoided by mainstream rock, as teen audiences wanted a succinct, clear message. Listen to "I've Seen All Good People." As you listen to the B section, "All Good People," listen to the repetition of the phrase "I've seen all good people turn their heads each day so satisfied I'm on my way." While this repetition might seem tedious, Yes uses the repetition to make subtle changes to each line, either through changes in instrumentation or pitch. This process tends to mimic what many orchestral composers practiced during the 18th and 19th centuries —taking a simple musical idea and spending at least several minutes to create many possible sound combinations from that simple melody.

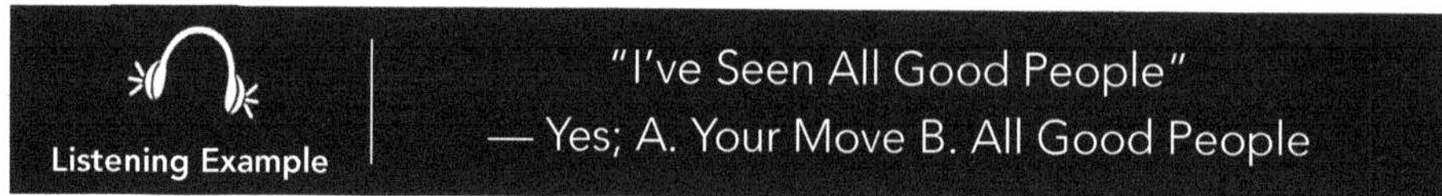

Jethro Tull

In Jethro Tull, we see a different approach to progressive rock. Formed in England in 1967, they have continued to perform intermittently through 2018. Described by *Rolling Stone* magazine as "One of the most commercially successful and eccentric progressive rock bands" (Macaluso 2016), much of Jethro Tull's sound relies on charismatic singer/flautist/composer Ian Anderson, who has been the lone constant member of the band. Jethro Tull combines elements of British folk music, heavy metal, and the blues, often taking inspiration from the madrigal songs of the Renaissance period in music (1450–1600). Anderson's flute playing brings a different element to their music, and the band's biggest hit, "Aqualung," still receives regular airplay on classic rock radio. A great example of the combination of sounds utilized by Jethro Tull can be heard in the 1977 song "Songs from the Wood." In the song, we hear elements from the older British folk music of the 1600s, followed by a hard rock sound. Within the piece are constantly changing meters, providing an almost disjointed sound. The music shows off the technical virtuosity of the band's members. The often thick sound is meant to sound complex but changes often enough to avoid becoming repetitive.

FIGURE 5.4 Ian Anderson with flute from Jethro Tull

The Moody Blues

The Moody Blues were initially an R&B band formed in Birmingham, England, in 1964. Although they had a Top 10 hit in the United States with "Go Now" in 1965, it would be their 1967 album *Days of Future Passed* that would establish the band as pioneers in the development of progressive rock. The Moody Blues' approach on *Days of Future Passed* was to create a concept album about the passing of the day as compared to the journey through life. In this album, the Moody Blues employ the London Festival Orchestra to provide a bold orchestral sound in music interludes throughout the album. The orchestra joins the band on the final chart, "Nights in White Satin (Late Lament)." This huge orchestral sound was a first in rock music. While many (from Motown to the Beatles) had added orchestral instruments, no band had utilized the enormous sound of a full orchestra. The album is a great combination of an early concept album, a dose of psychedelia appropriate for 1967, and early progressive rock. It is interesting to know that although the album was released in 1967 and made the British charts, its impact was not felt in the United States until 1972, when "Nights in White Satin" became a Top 5 hit. Listen to both "Nights in White Satin," the conclusion of the album, and its attached poem, "Late Lament." The combination of the song and poem is meant to end our listening experience, similar to the way the day ends.

Pink Floyd

Pink Floyd (named after American blues musicians Pink Anderson and Floyd Council) began as a blues and psychedelic rock group in 1965 with Syd Barrett as its lead singer, guitarist, songwriter, and leader. He was joined by fellow college students Nick Mason (drums), Roger Waters (bass and vocals), and Richard Wright (keyboards). The psychedelic influence Barrett brought to Pink Floyd yielded two 1967 hits in England: "Arnold Layne" at number 20 and "See Emily Play" at number six. By this time, it was already apparent to the other members of the band that Barrett was suffering from a mental illness, believed to have been caused by excessive LSD use. His behavior became erratic, and he could no longer be counted on to attend live gigs. If he did attend, he might not sing any of his parts. In December 1967, Pink Floyd added David Gilmour as a fifth member of the band, hoping his addition would take some of the pressure off Barrett and also allow the band to continue if Barrett was not available. While they wanted to keep Barrett involved, if only as a composer, his behavior grew increasingly strange and they decided in early 1968 that he would no longer be a part of the band.

The four members continued, eventually releasing *Dark Side of the Moon* in 1973. The album is one of the most successful albums in rock music history. It has sold in excess of 45 million albums worldwide and remained on the US charts for an astonishing 14 years (Gallucci n.d.). Recorded at Abbey Road Studios, it utilized the latest technology, using tape loops and analogue synthesizers. It is a concept album, containing 10 tracks that each represent different points in someone's life and the conflicts that arise. These conflicts include greed, death, anger, insanity, and our race against time. The songs "Brain Damage" and "Eclipse" are the final tracks on the album. Though it is believed that in "Brain Damage," the lunatic is a reference to Barrett, it is also reflective of the *Dark Side of the Moon* being a mental state or condition, and the term "lunatic" referred to someone who was insane, which was at one time thought to be caused by the moon. "Eclipse" ends the album with a summary of all the emotions and trials of life. Waters would leave the group in 1985, and the three remaining members would record through the mid-1990s. The band was inducted into the Rock and Roll Hall of Fame in 1996 and has sold more than 250 million albums worldwide.

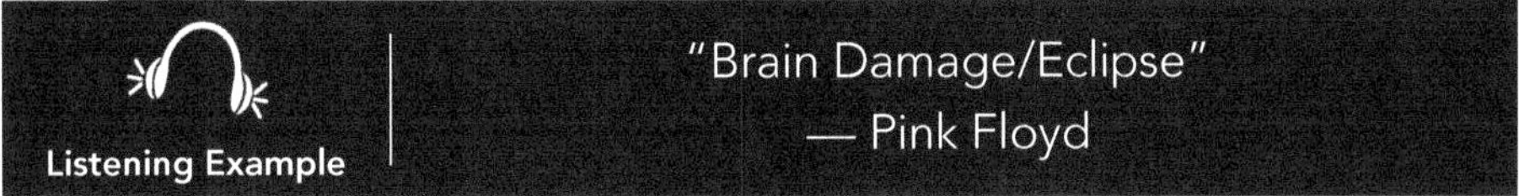

Frank Zappa

FIGURE 5.5 Frank Zappa

American Frank Zappa (1940–1993) became one of the most experimental musicians of the progressive rock movement. In fact, some believe Zappa should not be included as a progressive rock artist, instead deserving his own subgenre. While he grew up on rock and roll, his musical tastes included avant-garde composer Edgard Varese, jazz, R&B, and doo-wop. He was a staunch advocate for freedom of expression by artists, even testifying in front of the U.S. Senate's Commerce, Technology, and Transportation Committee to protest the censorship of musicians and artists in general. Zappa also believed American culture was dominated by conformists. His music either made fun of that conformity or made a conscious effort to reject it. Zappa realized his music would not become popular, and he reveled in that fact. His group, the Mothers of Invention, utilized extremely complex rhythmic patterns and unusual instrumentation. The musicians employed by Zappa became famous because they were able to play his incredibly difficult music. Later in his life, Zappa would compose music for orchestras. Though Zappa died in 1993, he recorded more than 60 albums, and his music lives on, performed by his son, Dweezil. One of the most unusual things about Zappa's music is the group of musicians who have listed him as an influence. The group includes musicians as diverse as Paul McCartney, John Frusciante (of Red Hot Chili Peppers), Kraftwerk, Devo, Trey Anastasio (Phish), Jimi Hendrix, and funk musician George Clinton. The song "Truck Driver Divorce" is a great example of the diverse sounds heard in Zappa's music. It begins as a tale of a truck driver on the road and what might be happening at home when he is away and changes to a long free-form jazz exploration.

Glam and Glitter Rock

The influence from the Velvet Underground became important in glam and glitter rock in the 1970s. Singers David Bowie and Iggy Pop and bands such as Kiss began to create stage personas that involved makeup, cartoonish outfits, and a flare for androgyny. The Velvet Underground were a band formed in the 1960s by artist Andy Warhol to provide accompaniment to the theatrical presentations of his group, the Exploding Plastic Inevitable. While creating interesting, if not commercially successful, music, the Velvet Underground would become influential on the often escapist glam rock of the next decade.

David Bowie

Bowie (1947–2016) began as a British folk singer in 1969 with the song "Space Oddity." While considered a novelty hit, "Space Oddity," based on Bowie's love for the Stanley Kubrick movie *2001: A Space Odyssey*, would provide a look into what Bowie's music would become in the next few years. In 1973, Bowie created the character Ziggy Stardust, which would lead to the release of *Ziggy Stardust and the Spiders from Mars*. This character, an alien being who was not quite male or female, appealed greatly to a new group of music fans who wanted an alternate reality. Bowie grew up in the suburbs of London, saw the city as a wasteland and himself as an outcast, and wanted to get away from that area to be able to find his identity. His fans in the 1970s saw him as the famous musician they could see themselves in, as someone who does not fit in his or her current environment. Bowie became a hero to those who were living in the closeted 1970s, becoming the first entertainer to publically declare his bisexuality.

Much like glam and glitter rock in general, Bowie's music was not of a single style but varied based on his musical preferences throughout his career. Rather, it was about the theatrics of a performance. Bowie, trained in acting and mime, used his talents to create an alternate universe while performing a rock concert. Bowie continued to perform throughout the 1970s and through to 2016, when he passed away after a battle with cancer. His final album, *Blackstar*, released just two days before his death, was met with great critical acclaim and was intended by Bowie to be his parting gift to his fans. The legacy of Bowie is one of giving many of the uncool kids a hero of their own and creating for them an escape from the expectations of society.

FIGURE 5.6 David Bowie as Ziggy Stardust

Kiss

Much like Alice Cooper, the members of Kiss were fans of pop culture, including comic books, science fiction, and horror movies. In 1973, Kiss formed in New York, creating a look not previously seen in rock music. Their full cartoon makeup and crazy outfits cast them as alien superheroes. Part of the mystique of Kiss was that the band never appeared without their full makeup and costumes during the height of their career. In the 1980s, they had some personnel changes and dropped the makeup, returning to it in later years. Band cofounder Gene Simmons wanted to create a group as a reaction to what he saw in the 1960s as ambivalence to live audiences by the groups onstage. Kiss would be a reaction to the jam bands of the psychedelic era that sometimes turned their backs to the audience. He wanted to make sure every eye would be on the band, so the act included

FIGURE 5.7 Kiss

Simmons breathing fire and appearing to spit blood (through a well-disguised theatrical blood packet hidden in his mouth).

The scenery used by Kiss during rock shows rivaled that of a full stage set usually reserved for Broadway theater productions. These developments in the visual aspect of live performances by artists in the 1970s would directly lead to the popularity of music videos and MTV in the 1980s.

Queen

The last group we will cover in this section is Queen. Queen, formed in England in 1970, became one of the biggest-selling bands in British history and has sold in excess of 200 million records worldwide. While the name was meant to imply androgyny or homosexuality, it was singer Freddy Mercury's (1946–1991) flamboyant stage persona, four-octave vocal range, and musical diversity that almost immediately made the band famous in England. Along with guitarist Brian May, bassist John Deacon, and drummer Roger Taylor, Mercury created music that crossed many subgenres, including progressive and heavy metal, and included tight vocal harmonies. While all four members of the band composed, it was Mercury's "Bohemian Rhapsody" from the 1975 album *A Night at the Opera* that became one of the most praised songs in rock music history. It also became an early example of music video several years before MTV would make the video a popular form. Queen performed at the Live Aid concert in 1985, a performance that is considered one of the greatest live performances in rock history. Mercury, unfortunately, became one of the first well-known musicians to die during the AIDS epidemic, passing away in 1991. The band continued throughout the 1990s and beyond, using singers Paul

FIGURE 5.8 Queen

Rodgers (formerly of Bad Company) and Adam Lambert (from the *American Idol* TV reality show).

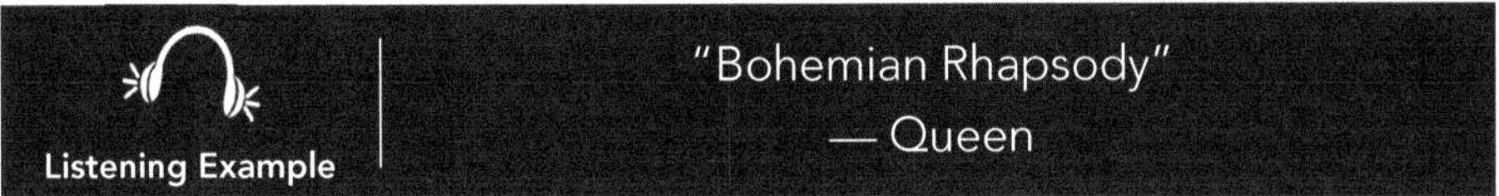

California Rock and The Eagles

The California rock sound is not so much a subgenre but rather a well-produced, tight sound played by professional musicians and a laid-back sound indicative of the California lifestyle. While country music certainly was a part of this style, it also included mainstream pop, rock and roll, folk music, and vocal harmonies descended from the Beach Boys and Crosby, Stills, and Nash. The genre included the Eagles, singer-songwriters Jackson Browne and Warren Zevon, vocalist Linda Ronstadt, and blues-influenced Fleetwood Mac.

The Eagles

Linda Ronstadt recorded an album in 1971 with a backing band of session musicians, including Detroit guitarist Glenn Frey, guitarist Bernie Leadon, bassist Randy Meisner, and drummer Don Henley. Once they finished the album for Ronstadt, she helped them form their own band. The Eagles would become one of the biggest bands of all time and as of 2018 have the top-selling album of all time in the United States (*The Eagles Greatest Hits 1971–1975*), moving ahead of Michael Jackson's *Thriller* (USA Today 2018). With the exception of Frey and Henley, the personnel changed in the 1970s, and the band broke up in 1980. They reformed in 1995 with the group that finished in 1980, including Frey and Henley, bassist Timothy Schmit, and guitarists Don Felder and Joe Walsh, and released *Hell Freezes Over* (the term used by the members of the band in the past when asked when they would get back together). They have continued to perform since that time, adding country singer Vince Gill and Deacon Frey following Glenn Frey's death in 2016. Their most iconic song is "Hotel California" from the 1976 album of the same name. The song is about drug addiction or their "interpretation of the high life in Los Angeles." The song ends with long alternating guitar solos from Felder and Walsh that were named among the greatest guitar solos of all time by *Guitarist* magazine in 1998 (Barber 1997).

The first half of the 1970s yielded many new forms of music, from the laid-back sounds of the singer-songwriters to cranked-up heavy metal to the complexity of progressive pock. Rock would now appeal to a wider audience than ever before. However, as the 1970s progressed, a new dance style would begin to dominate the airwaves, charts, and popular culture.

References

"Alice Cooper—In His Own Words." Superseventies.com. Accessed July 26, 2019. https://www.superseventies.com/ssalicecooper.html.

Associated Press. "Leonard Skinner, Rock Band Muse, Dies at 77." *New York Times*, September 21, 2010. https://www.nytimes.com/2010/09/21/arts/music/21skinner.html.

Bangs, Lester. "Kick Out The Jams." *Rolling Stone*, April 5, 1969. https://www.rollingstone.com/music/music-album-reviews/kick-out-the-jams-252641/.

Barber, Brandon. "Hotel California Voted Best Guitar Solo." *Rolling Stone*, December 17, 1997. https://www.rollingstone.com/music/music-news/hotel-california-voted-best-guitar-solo-255269/.

Beech, Mark. "Led Zeppelin Adds to 300 Million Sales With Live Album, 50th-Anniversary Surprises." *Forbes*, January 27, 2018. https://www.forbes.com/sites/markbeech/2018/01/27/led-zeppelin-adds-to-300-million-sales-with-live-album-50th-anniversary-surprises/#78253cd8ca59.

"Big Yellow Taxi." Genius. Accessed December 16, 2018. https://genius.com/Joni-mitchell-big-yellow-taxi-lyrics.com.

Christgau, Robert. "Nothing's Shocking." *The Village Voice*, October 13, 1998. https://www.villagevoice.com/1998/10/13/nothings-shocking/.

Cochran, Jeff. "Warren Zevon: Play it All Night Long." LikeTheDew.com, August 16, 2009. https://likethedew.com/2009/08/16/warren-zevon-play-it-all-night-long/#.XTsCkOSG_IU.

"Eagles Fly Past Michael Jackson, Now Have the Best-Selling Album of All-Time, The." *USA Today*, August 20, 2018. https://www.usatoday.com/story/life/music/2018/08/20/eagles-michael-jackson-best-selling-album-thriller/1040092002.

Gallucci, Michael. "The Day *The Dark Side of the Moon* Ended Its Record Chart Run." Ultimate Classic Rock. https://ultimateclassicrock.com/dark-side-of-the-moon-ends-chart-run/.

Greene, Andy. "The 10 Wildest Led Zeppelin Legends, Fact-Checked." *Rolling Stone*, July 26, 2019. https://www.rollingstone.com/music/music-lists/the-10-wildest-led-zeppelin-legends-fact-checked-153103/keith-moon-of-the-who-gave-led-zeppelin-their-name-154053/.

Greene, Mike. "Flashback: Neil Young Covers 'Sweet Home, Alabama' in 1977." *Rolling Stone*, January 20, 2015. https://www.rollingstone.com/music/music-news/flashback-neil-young-covers-sweet-home-alabama-in-1977-186638/.

Guinness World Records. https://www.guinnessworldrecords.com/world-records/59721-best-selling-single?fb_comment_id=729040983851955_1622492151173496.

Kasper, Mike. "Grammy Winner Carole King's Idaho Home For Sale." Mix106radio. Accessed June 18, 2019. https://mix106radio.com/grammy-winner-=carole-kings-former-idaho-home-for-sale-pics-video/.

Kemp, Mark. "At Fillmore East." *Rolling Stone*, July 16, 2002. https://www.rollingstone.com/music/music-album-reviews/at-fillmore-east-2-192971/.

Lewis, Randy. "Garth Brooks Again Surpasses Elvis as US Solo Sales Champ." *Los Angeles Times*, January 12, 2015. https://www.latimes.com/entertainment/music/posts/la-et-ms-garth-brooks-elvis-presley-album-sales-20150112-story.html.

Library of Congress. "About This Program." Accessed July 26, 2019. https://www.loc.gov/programs/national-recording-preservation-board/about-this-program/?dates=2002-2099.

Macaluso, Scott. "Snubbed: 3 Artists that Should Be in the Rock and Roll Hall of Fame." JBonamassa.com. Accessed July 26, 2019. https://jbonamassa.com/snubbed-3-artists-rock-and-roll-hall-of-fame/.

"Old School Box—Special Edition." Alice Cooper.com, November 13, 2012. https://alicecooper.com/980-2/.

Price, Simon. "Walk This Way: How Run-D.M.C. and Aerosmith Changed Pop." *The Guardian*, July 4, 2016. https://www.theguardian.com/music/musicblog/2016/jul/04/walk-this-way-run-dmc-aerosmith.

Recording Academy. "Winners: Best Rock Performance by a Duo or Group with Vocal." Accessed December 17, 2018. https://www.grammy.com/grammys/artists/warren-zevon.

Recording Industry Association of America. "Gold and Platinum." Accessed July 26, 2019. https://www.riaa.com/gold-platinum/?tab_active=top_tallies&ttt=TAA#search_section.

Reed, Ryan. "Watch James Taylor Recall 'Nervous' Beatles Audition for Apple Records." *Rolling Stone*, June 19, 2015. https://www.rollingstone.com/tv/tv-news/watch-james-taylor-recall-nervous-beatles-audition-for-apple-records-57543/.

Walser, Robert. *Running With the Devil: Power, Gender, and Madness in Heavy Metal Music*. Wesleyan University Press, 2014.

Weiser, Carl. "Elton John's 31-Year Hit Streak." Songfacts. Accessed January 12, 2015. https://www.songfacts.com/blog/writing/elton-john-31-year-hit-streak.

Zappa, Frank, and Peter Occhiogrosso. *The Real Frank Zappa Book*. Touchtone Publishers, 1990.

Figure Credits

IMG. 5.1: Copyright © by Mind2mind (CC BY-SA 4.0) at https://commons.wikimedia.org/wiki/File:1970s.png.

Fig. 5.1: Source: https://commons.wikimedia.org/wiki/File:James_Taylor_-_Columbia.jpg.

Fig. 5.2: Copyright © by Sven Mandel (CC BY-SA 4.0) at https://commons.wikimedia.org/wiki/File:Alice_Cooper_-_2017217165130_2017-08-05_Wacken_-_Sven_-_1D_X_MK_II_-_0928_-_B70I1993.jpg.

Fig. 5.3: Copyright © by Jim Summaria (CC BY-SA 3.0) at https://commons.wikimedia.org/wiki/File:Jimmy_Page_with_Robert_Plant_2_-_Led_Zeppelin_-_1977.jpg.

Fig. 5.4: Copyright © by Jean-Luc (CC BY-SA 2.0) at https://commons.wikimedia.org/wiki/File:Jethro_Tull_Ian.jpg.

Fig. 5.5: Copyright © by Helge Øverås (CC BY-SA 3.0) at https://commons.wikimedia.org/wiki/File:Zappa_16011977_01_300.jpg.

Fig. 5.6: Copyright © by Rik Walton (CC BY-SA 2.0) at https://commons.wikimedia.org/wiki/File:David-Bowie_Early.jpg.

Fig. 5.7: Source: https://commons.wikimedia.org/wiki/File:Kiss_at_backstage_(1975).jpg.

Fig. 5.8: Copyright © by Carl Lender (CC BY-SA 3.0) at https://commons.wikimedia.org/wiki/File:QueenPerforming1977.jpg.

CHAPTER

6 The Second Half of the 1970s

Historical Context for the Decade

The second half of the 1970s was dominated by political upheaval in the United States. Jimmy Carter was elected President in 1976 after Gerald Ford pardoned Richard Nixon, who resigned from office in 1974 following the Watergate scandal. The country was beset by a recession that included high unemployment, gasoline shortages, and a greater distrust of government following the Nixon scandal. The music of this era was a reflection of those times. While some styles became the soundtrack to escapism and excess (disco), other subgenres were a reaction to the slick, adult medium rock had become.

Though the period was dominated by **disco**, there were several other subgenres of rock that catered to each individual, whether younger or older, dancer or listener. Some of the styles did not gain fame during the 1970s but greatly influenced the music moving forward into the 1980s and beyond. While certainly not competing with disco for radio airplay, one style that would become important later was **punk**.

Punk Rock

The musical style called punk rock developed as a reaction to the complexity of the musical styles of the early 1970s. The complicated, technically advanced sounds of progressive rock were leading listeners, radio programmers, and the industry in general to believe that rock and roll was now an adult medium to be played by great musicians, produced to emphasize technical brilliance for an audience ready to consume the complex sounds. The original idea that you could play three chords, form a band, and get up on a stage in weeks (rather than practicing for years) was seemingly lost. Although the progression to more complex sounds is natural and will gradually occur over a given period, the reaction against this buildup will usually be sudden. A younger generation, often the siblings of those consuming the complexity, will decide that they need their own sound, something that appeals to their less sophisticated, more emotional minds. Punk became this reaction to more complex music in the 1970s. Punk was a loud, aggressive style with a fast tempo that at first used simple chords and instrumentation. The musical style got its name from the term "punk," which had been used for a long time as a negative term for a person.

Punk developed in the United States in East Coast cities such as Boston and New York City and spread down the coast to Philadelphia, Baltimore, and Washington, D.C.. While punk claimed to be averse to any influence, it is impossible not to be influenced by the music and musicians of the past. Punk did draw from the garage band sounds that had some success in the 1960s as well as the avant-garde sounds of the Velvet Underground.

Early Influences on Punk

Lou Reed (1943–2013), along with Sterling Morrison (1942–1995), Maureen (Moe) Tucker (born 1944), and John Cale (born 1942), formed the Velvet Underground in 1965 upon meeting artist Andy Warhol (1928–1987). The combination of Reed's pop songwriting ability and Cale's classical training and interest in avant-garde music created a new sound relying on repetitious, drone-like chords and simple melodies. The group provided background music for Warhol's theatrical presentations while being supported in their musical endeavors by Warhol's fame and influence. A friend of Warhol's, Nico (1938–1988) was added as a singer, and in 1967, they released the album titled *The Velvet Underground and Nico*. The album contained songs about the street hustlers, prostitutes, and drug addicts of New York City life in direct contrast to the new counterculture and the Summer of Love. Critics did not appreciate the music, and almost no one bought the album, but it did provide an alternative to the West Coast peace, love, and flowers vibe that was becoming very prominent at that time.

Over the next few years, the counterculture would fail, and many teenagers in the 1970s would reject the procession from psychedelic rock through to the singer-songwriters and progressive rock. The Velvet Underground would be a great example of a band that did not achieve any commercial success while creating music yet would go on to influence many who would create music later. The song "I'm Waiting for the Man" details a man waiting to get heroin from a dealer. The repeated rhythmic pattern played by every member of the band provides a sonic representation of the desperation of someone suffering from withdrawal symptoms while waiting for a fix.

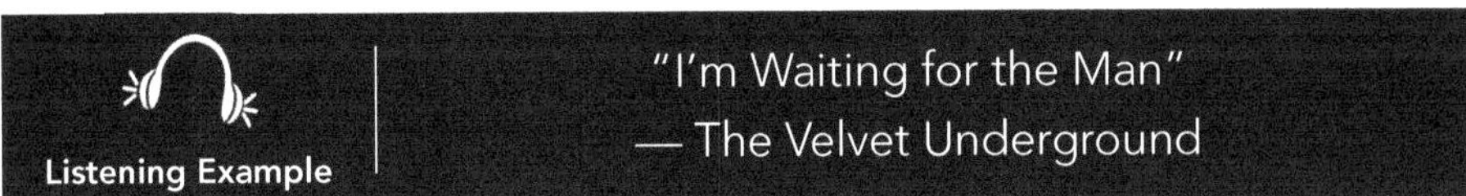

Another band that had a great influence over what would become punk rock in the 1970s was the Kinks. As discussed in Chapter 3, the Kinks had a sound that was closer to garage rock than the other British Invasion bands popular at the time. Ray Davies, the primary songwriter and lead singer of the Kinks, also was more likely to create lyrics that were controversial and spoke about taboo subjects, including the cross-dressing that was the subject of "Lola." The first song to become popular about a transvestite, "Lola," though not punk-like in its presentation, was nonetheless one of many Kinks songs to greatly influence the punk scene.

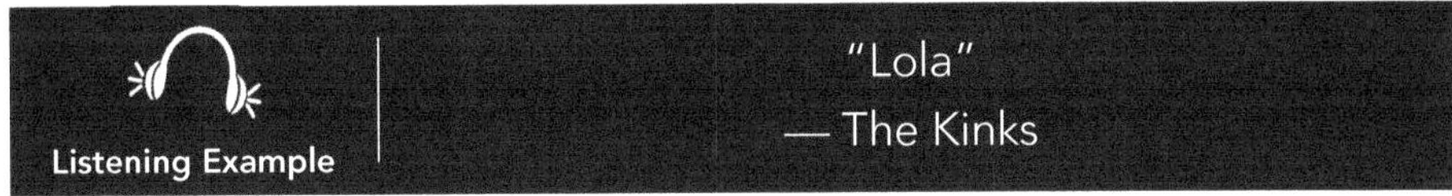

Punk in the 1970s

One of the earliest examples of punk came from a Boston-area band led by Jonathan Richman (born 1951). As a teenager, Richman became a huge fan of the Velvet Underground, even moving to New York for a few months to hang out with the group. When he returned to Boston, he formed the Modern Lovers. The Modern Lovers, influenced by the Velvet Underground, would become popular in the Boston area. The band would include Richman, keyboardist Jerry Harrison (later of Talking Heads), and drummer David Robinson (later of the Cars). The band failed to find an audience outside of Boston, and it disbanded in 1974. In 1976, while Richman was moving in a new musical direction, their previous record company released an album of their original demo sessions. That album, *The Modern Lovers*, was released in 1976. The album contained songs about the awkwardness of teen life, driving around in cars, and living in Massachusetts. The song "Roadrunner," recorded in 1972, is a great track of early punk that would influence the Ramones and Television.

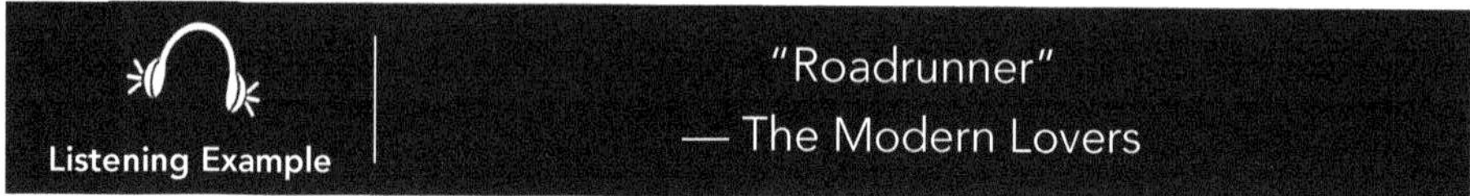

The New York Punk Scene

The New York City punk scene developed in several locations. The Mercer Arts Center in Greenwich Village housed a space for the visual arts that eventually included musicians. Many of the musicians who frequented Mercer ended up becoming regulars at CBGB's, a club on the Lower East Side of Manhattan. The letters in the club's name, which stood for **c**ountry, **b**lue**g**rass, and **b**lues, were not representative of the music performed there. Hilly Kristal opened the club in 1973, planning to have country, bluegrass, and blues groups perform, but its location soon drew musicians and fans who wanted the do-it-yourself music of punk. Patti Smith, Talking Heads, Television, the Ramones, and Blondie all became regulars in the venue. The club continued primarily as a hardcore punk venue until 2006, when it lost its lease.

The Ramones

The Ramones were formed in the Queens borough of New York City in 1974. The members of the band all adopted the Ramone surname, even though none of the members were related. Their simple garage band sound, with no more than three chords (at first), became a model for the punk rock sound. Their lyric content rejected the normal subject matter of love, cars, and sex, instead reflecting their feelings of boredom and their predisposition to sniffing glue. Though they did not have commercial success, they were listed as one of the all-time greatest bands by *Rolling Stone* magazine and were inducted into the Rock and Roll Hall of Fame in 2002 (Kaye 2010). The band continued to record and tour nonstop until 1996. As of 2014, all

FIGURE 6.1 The Ramones

four original members had passed away. The Ramones' debut single, "Blitzkrieg Bop," released in 1976, is considered the national anthem of punk. Also listen to "I Wanna Be Sedated," the most commercially successful of the band's singles.

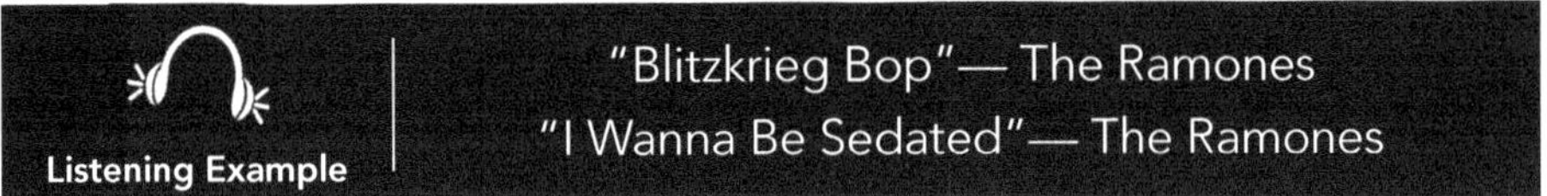

Patti Smith

Poet Patti Smith (born 1946) became a punk music icon by accident. Working at a bookstore and writing poetry, she began performing her poetry live with a band that included friend Lenny Kaye. She began attending shows at CBGB's and soon began performing there. Her first album, *Horses,* was released in 1975 to great critical praise. Although not a mainstream album and with no commercially successful singles, the album did cross into the Top 50 on the *Billboard* album charts. The album is known for its mix of songs and poetry. It includes a cover of the Van Morrison–composed "Gloria." Former Velvet Underground member Cale produced the album.

Talking Heads

Talking Heads was formed in New York in 1975 by vocalist and guitarist David Byrne, bassist Tina Weymouth, and drummer Chris Frantz. Keyboardist Jerry Harrison, formerly of the Modern Lovers, later joined them. Their first gig was as an opening act for the Ramones at CBGB's in 1975. Talking Heads was an interesting example of a punk band. College educated, the band's members became known for their unusual songs, led by Byrne, and their regular look. Rather than constructing three-chord songs at a fast tempo, Talking Heads rejected that style, instead best representing the do-it-yourself ideals around which punk flourished. They rejected the punk clothing styles of leather jackets and slicked-back hair, instead wearing the clothes "that they were sent for Christmas" onstage. Though Talking Heads had some limited success with songs such as "Psycho Killer," from their 1977 album *Talking Heads: 77*, they would become better known in the 1980s for their more mainstream pop, infusing elements of the avant-garde and world music sounds. Their 1983 breakout album, *Speaking in Tongues*, contained the Top 10 hit "Burning Down the House." Though often not realized as a legitimate punk band, Talking Heads was a regular at CBGB's. Unlike many punk bands, their music escaped the reins of the 1970s. They continued to grow musically, moving on to eclectic mainstream rock in the 1980s. They disbanded in 1991.

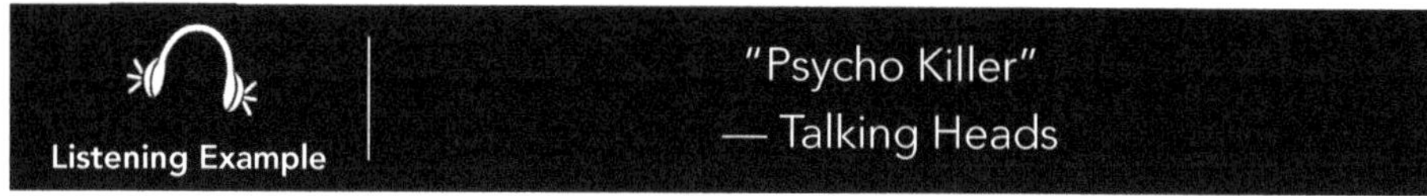

Punk music, though important and influential on several styles of music that would emerge in the 1980s, was not commercially successful in the United States. Punk was not played on mainstream radio, and punk songs did not make the charts. Most of America really did not know what punk was. If you lived in Boston, New York City, Philadelphia, or other East Coast cities, you could find punk, but you had to know where to go. The rest of the United States never knew what punk was in the 1970s. For the most part, the original groups either died away, became commercially irrelevant, or moved on to more commercially viable styles. This lack of acceptance of punk is not surprising, given the environment of the country and the music industry at the time. The United States is an enormously large country. Any style of music would naturally need more time to become big. However, the most important reason for punk's lack of acceptance in the United States was American's collective skepticism toward new cultural developments. The United States has been known throughout its history as a socially conservative country. Settled by those seeking religious freedom, it remains socially conservative, even though great advances have occurred over the years. New things will take time, and the first response is often to reject new ideas (political, social, or musical). Although the new ideas will usually be accepted eventually, smaller, more socially progressive countries may have a quicker response time. This was the case with punk, which began in the United States but exploded in the U.K.

Punk in the United Kingdom

While needing to change to conquer American radio, punk blew up like a rocket in the U.K., reaching the main streets of every midsized or larger city. The fan base in Britain included many young kids who were rejecting the new progressive rock style, looking at the establishment of pop music with the same contempt with which they viewed the British government. In London, Malcolm McLaren, a British businessperson and sometime musical manager, returned to the U.K. from the United States after a several-month stay and opened up a clothing store called Sex. The name, meant to shock the public, sold rubber bondage and S&M gear but also sold T-shirts with lists of what McLaren thought were cool and awful. The kids who came into the shop to buy T-shirts would become the first punks in the U.K. Some of those early shoppers would audition for a band that McLaren would form, the Sex Pistols.

The Sex Pistols

The Sex Pistols became the face of British punk and are considered one of the most important punk bands of the era. McLaren was managing a band called the Strand, based out of his clothing store, which included Steve Jones on vocals and Paul Cook on drums. McLaren made several attempts to hire a singer from the US punk scene, including Sylvain from the New York Dolls and Richard Hell, formerly of Television. When both refused, McLaren held an audition, and Johnny Rotten (John Lydon, born 1956), who hung out around the store, auditioned holding a shower attachment, lip-syncing to Alice Cooper's "I'm Eighteen." Rotten's attitude and look, rather than his ability to sing, got him the job. McLaren's goal was to create a vibe, a fashion trend, and a following rather than a great musical group. Rotten later described the social and economic situation in Britain that led to the development of the Sex Pistols and British punk in general:

> Early seventies Britain was a very depressing place. It was completely run-down, there was trash on the streets, total unemployment—just about everybody was on strike. Everybody was brought up with an education system that told you point blank that if you came from the wrong side of the tracks … then you had no hope in hell and no career prospects at all. Out of that came pretentious *moi* and the Sex Pistols and then a whole bunch of copycat wankers after that (Langley 2010).

The copycats Rotten spoke of in this quote would include dozens of the band's fans who would go on to form their own groups. These included Joe Strummer of the Clash, Siouxsie Sioux, and Billy Idol. Some of the early concerts began to involve a greater degree of violence, both from the band members and the audience. The Pistols would begin trashing their instruments and gear (often borrowed from another band), throwing chairs into the audience, and repeatedly insulting their fans. This animosity was the spark that ignited British punk. The fans, fueled by their hatred of the British establishment, fed off the apparent hatred of the band toward their fans.

In 1976, the Sex Pistols were signed to EMI Records, and their first single "Anarchy in the U.K." was released. Though some critics praised the song, punk was immediately looked upon as a lifestyle choice, ushering in a new political era for disaffected British youth. This eventually moved the band away from music as its primary interest, rather using chaos to promote the punk lifestyle. Their first publicity stunt occurred when they were asked to replace Queen on a live television show called *Today*. The show's host, Bill Grundy, gave the band alcohol prior to having them on the show and then proceeded to antagonize and instigate the members of the group to use foul language on the live show. Between dropping "f-bombs" and using the word "s**t," the band's appearance had the tabloid newspapers spending several days reporting on the band's performance, including the now-famous *Daily Mirror* headline "The Filth and the Fury!" (Peacock 2017). The show made the Sex Pistols famous in every corner of Britain, and punk immediately became mainstream. The mainstream media and political establishment constantly commenting on how horrible this group and music were continued to fuel the punk fire.

In 1977, Sid Vicious (John Ritchie, 1957–1979) joined the Sex Pistols as a bass player. Although he could not play the instrument at first, he was hired because the band liked the look and attitude he brought to the band. His heroin use became an increasingly big problem and helped to lead to the destruction of the band in early 1978. In March 1977, the Sex Pistols signed with A&M records, only to be dropped six days later after the band trashed the record company's offices. In May 1977, they signed with Virgin Records and released "God Save the Queen." The single, off *Never Mind the Bollocks,* became a huge hit, which was surprising, as every radio station in England banned the track. The song was released to coincide with the 25th anniversary of the coronation of Queen Elizabeth II. It sold massively in the weeks leading up to the anniversary and became number one but was shown only as a black mark where "God Save the Queen" and the Sex Pistols should have been on the chart ("Sex Pistols Cover Tops Charts" 2017). On the evening of the anniversary, the band chartered a boat and played "God Save the Queen" as the boat flowed down the Thames River. This act of defiance is looked upon as one of the great events in punk music history.

In January 1978, the Sex Pistols embarked on a tour of the United States. McLaren booked the band in small, deep-South country bars where he knew there would be conflict with the fans. Vicious was out of control, picking fights with everyone, including the other band members, and hitting one concert attendee over the head with his bass guitar. When the tour got to San Francisco, the band members were not talking to each other, and Rotten decided, after one song, to leave the stage and end the Sex Pistols' turbulent brief career. Vicious would move to New York with his girlfriend, Nancy Spungen. He would later be accused of her murder and die from a heroin overdose while awaiting trial for the crime. The other members would reunite for tours from 1996 through to 2008. In 2006, they were inducted into the Rock and Roll Hall of Fame. They refused to attend, and Rotten sent a fax to the Hall of Fame, calling them a "piss stain" ("Johnny Rotten's Cordial Letter" 2013). While the Sex Pistols often turned out to be a publicity stunt group, their influence over British youth and the rock music that would follow was monumental in scope.

FIGURE 6.2 The Sex Pistols

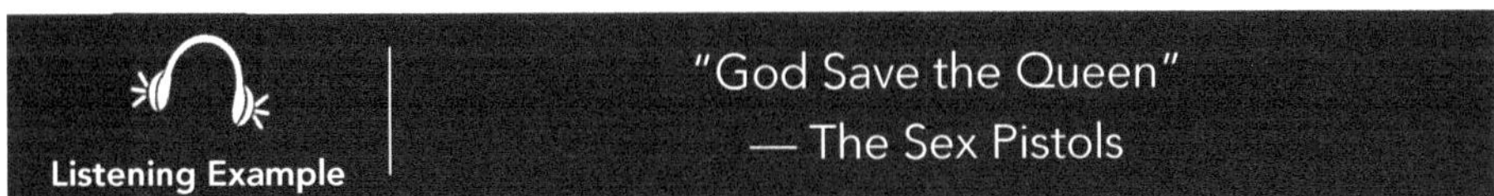

The Clash

While the Clash formed at nearly the same time as the Sex Pistols, their music would include wider elements such as reggae, ska, funk, and rockabilly. The Clash achieved greater success and praise than most of their punk counterparts. The band, with guitarist Joe Strummer (1952–2002), vocalist and guitarist Mick Jones, bassist Paul Simonon, and drummer "Topper" Headon, earned immediate commercial success in England with their 1977 release *The Clash*. They achieved international success with their third album, *London Calling*, released in the United States in 1980 and considered one of the best albums of the 1980s. It is ranked eighth on *Rolling Stone*'s list of the 500 greatest albums of all time (*Rolling Stone* 2012). The band disbanded in 1986 and was inducted into the Rock and Roll Hall of Fame in 2003.

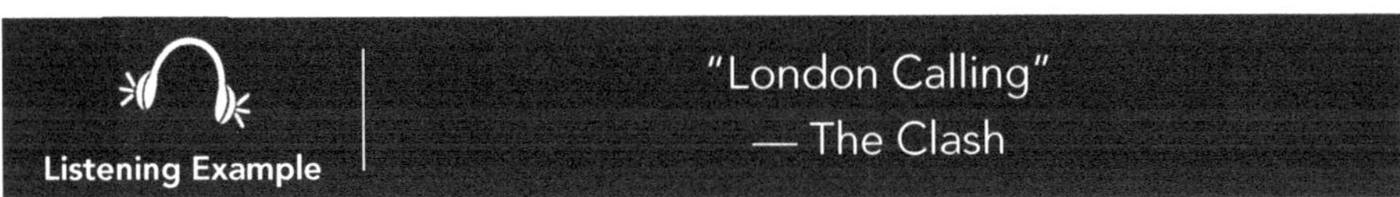

The Influence of Reggae on British Punk Rock

The Clash was greatly affected by reggae, as it was the only music being played in London at the beginning of the punk scene that was truly "revolutionary." The British punks and the Jamaican reggae musicians felt a common connection. They felt oppressed and abandoned by their government. Reggae was played in London's punk clubs before there were any punk records to play. Though reggae was developed on the island of Jamaica, it would have a close bond with British punk and greatly influence the music that would follow into the 1980s.

Reggae

Reggae originated in Jamaica in the late 1960s and had several influences. Mento (Jamaican rural dance music), in combination with the sounds of Fats Domino and other New Orleans artists of the 1950s, led to the earlier forms called ska and rock steady. One theory suggests that Jamaican teens listening to radio broadcasts out of New Orleans in the 1950s misinterpreted rhythms from Fats Domino songs and, in recreating the sounds from memory, created the new rhythmic idea that would be the basis for reggae. This rhythm involves staccato guitar chords played on the offbeats (halfway between each beat).

Reggae was also influenced by the Rastafari religion, developed in Jamaica in the 1930s. The religion is Afrocentric, meaning its followers believe in Africa as the Promised Land. It also practiced the ritualistic smoking of herb (marijuana). The religion was developed as both a religious and political movement by Afro-Jamaicans who were under the oppression of British colonial rule. For economic reasons, the British government awarded Jamaica independence in 1962. Although technically independent, there were many years when Afro-Jamaicans fought for fundamental rights, and the Rastafari religion strengthened. As it did, reggae followed. As residents of a former colony, Jamaicans were able to travel to and from England very easily, and as Jamaica continued to be a Caribbean resort for the British, England became a landing spot for many Afro-Jamaicans looking for work or escaping the difficult economic situation at home. Although reggae was well-known to British kids and in Jamaica, it would only achieve world success through the music of Bob Marley.

Bob Marley

Bob Marley (1945–1981) grew up in Nine Mile, a rural farming community in Jamaica. When he was 12, he moved to the capital of Kingston and joined forces with Neville Livingston (later known as Bunny Wailer). They formed the Wailers in 1963 and had a number one hit in Jamaica in 1964. By the late 1960s, reggae had become successful throughout Jamaica, and by 1973, Marley was becoming better known in England. Guitarist Eric Clapton, who was given the Wailers' first album as a gift, liked it so much that he recorded a version of the Marley song "I Shot the Sheriff," which became a number one *Billboard* hit in 1974 (Breihan 2019). It is the only Top 10 single penned or performed by Marley in the United States. Marley's fame continued to rise, and in 1976, he was getting ready to play a concert organized by the Jamaican prime minister. The concert was meant as a show of solidarity between two opposing political parties, but some looked at Marley's upcoming performance as a show of support for one party. Two days before the concert, gunmen broke into his home and shot Marley, his wife, and his manager. All three survived, and Marley gave his performance two days later. Fearing for his life, Marley left Jamaica and moved to England. He immediately became famous there with the release of *Exodus*, which stayed on the British charts for 56 weeks with four hit singles (O'Neil 2009).

In 1977, Marley was found to have a melanoma on his toe, which he refused to have amputated. By 1980, the melanoma had spread, and Marley died in a Miami, Florida, hospital on May 11, 1981. Marley's legacy is much greater than that of most musicians. His outspoken opposition to apartheid in South Africa and his political statements, both in music and in verse, resonated (and still resonate) with many oppressed peoples around the world. He is looked upon by many as a prophet, leading a desire for the unification of peoples of African descent from all parts of the world. His music did not have an immediate impact in the United States, but it would greatly influence musicians from many other parts of the world. We will listen to two Marley songs. "Get Up, Stand Up" is a song of standing up for one's rights against your oppressor. "One Love/People Get Ready" is a song with religious content about redemption and people coming together.

FIGURE 6.3 Bob Marley

Not only did reggae greatly influence British punks, it also led to a revival of ska in England. Ska, a form that predated reggae, was embraced by British punks for its faster tempo. The British bands Madness and the Specials became known during this ska revival.

As punk and reggae were related in England and had common themes, it should be noted that in the years that followed, some skinhead and neo-Nazi groups adopted forms of punk that included ska rhythms. It is interesting to see how time can change any art form to serve the needs of its users, even if that change involves completely altering its original intent.

The British music scene would contain many examples of the influence of reggae in the 1980s, including the music of the Police, Elvis Costello, and UB40. The great combination of reggae, punk, disco, and R&B would continue into the 1980s in the form of dance pop and new wave. As we will discuss further in Chapter 7, reggae and the music of Jamaica would be the direct ancestor of rap and hip hop music, developing in the 1970s in the Bronx borough of New York City and becoming mainstream by the middle of the 1980s.

Funk

As previous chapters have discussed the integration of the European and African musical traditions, the difficulty with which the two styles have integrated is obvious. After many years of this integration, American music still has subgenres that have been created by and appeal to (at least at first) only one race. Motown was brilliant at integrating African American music styles into mainstream pop, but the reaction of soul moved African American music back from the center. This would continue as the 1960s moved into the 1970s. The church-based, gospel-dominated sound of soul music was replaced by the more outrageous rhythmic dance music known as funk. Funk was the African American urban dance music of the 1970s, incorporating new musical ideas, a less serious attitude, and the escapism of science fiction and comic books.

In Chapter 4, the elements of soul music were discussed. An important musician in the development of soul and the transition to funk was James Brown. In the mid-1960s,

Brown developed a new dance form with an emphasis placed on the first beat of every measure, a sound he called "the One." It also involved the bass guitar in a way not commonly used prior. The bass guitar in funk music would play a syncopated melodic line, and that syncopated rhythm would play against rhythms from all of the other instruments in the band. The vocals become far less important in funk music, and the idea that the singer in soul music was preaching us a sermon was gone. Below is a chart that compares the differences between soul and funk music.

Outlining the Differences Between Soul and Funk

	Soul		**Funk**
1	The singer as preacher or gospel soloist	1	The singer is less important
2	A repeated instrumental rhythmic vamp allowing improvised instruments	2	Intense syncopation from singer to all
3	Horn section acting as gospel choir	3	Horns acting as additional percussion instruments
4	Bass guitar in traditional form, providing rhythmic pulse	4	The bass guitar takes center stage, providing melody and percussion with slap bass technique
5	Matching tailored suits	5	Costumes that emphasized cartoonish supernatural characters

The greatest musical development in funk music was the new use of the bass guitar. By bringing the bass guitar and drums to the foreground, rhythm was emphasized over traditional chord progressions and the melody of vocals. This new style, with its greater rhythmic contrast, was perfect for dancing. The new style bypassed the straight grooves of modern African American music, instead taking greater influence from the more intense polyrhythmic patterns of sub-Saharan Africa through the musical melting pot of New Orleans. These African and indigenous sounds bypassed the development of African American music in the 19th and 20th centuries. Although cousins of African American music, the funk cousins grew up in a different world.

James Brown

In the 1960s, James Brown (1933–2006) was already established as a hero and spokesperson for African Americans and African American music. In the 1950s, he was part of the early R&B explosion that became rock and roll. In early 1960, he was a forerunner in the establishment of soul music as a reaction to the middle-of-the-road treatment of black music by Motown. He anticipated the next change in African American music with his 1965 recording of "I Got You (I Feel Good)." In this piece, listen to the bass guitar and its syncopated rhythms and the use of the horns to play percussive, staccato, short bursts of sound. Although Brown's gospel roots are still evident in his vocals, the rest of the song is clearly different than soul.

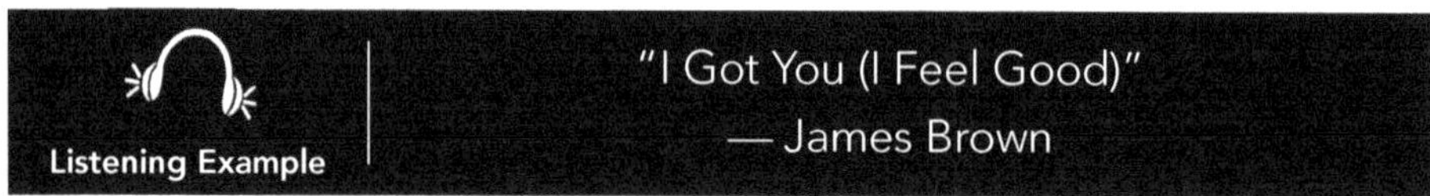

Sly and the Family Stone

Another important band in the development and popularity of funk music was Sly and the Family Stone. Based out of San Francisco, Sylvester Stewart (born 1943) came from a musical family and began as a gospel singer. He became proficient at keyboards at an early age but decided to focus on the guitar as a teenager. He formed Sly and the Family Stone in 1966. The band was unusual for the time in that it contained both black and white musicians as well as male and female musicians. The musicians included Sly's brother Freddie on guitar, sister Rose on keyboards, Cynthia Robinson on trumpet, Jerry Martini on saxophone, Greg Errico on drums, and Larry Graham on bass guitar. The band's music was a great combination of funk styles combined with the psychedelic rock that was dominating the airwaves in the 1960s, particularly in San Francisco. The band's music contained a great amount of social commentary, including songs about bigotry. "Everyday People" is a song that deals with social and racial divides while not taking any particular side in the debate. In "Thank You (Falletinme Be Mice Elf Agin)," we hear the trademark slap bass technique from Graham that would make him famous and one of the great innovators in bass guitar playing.

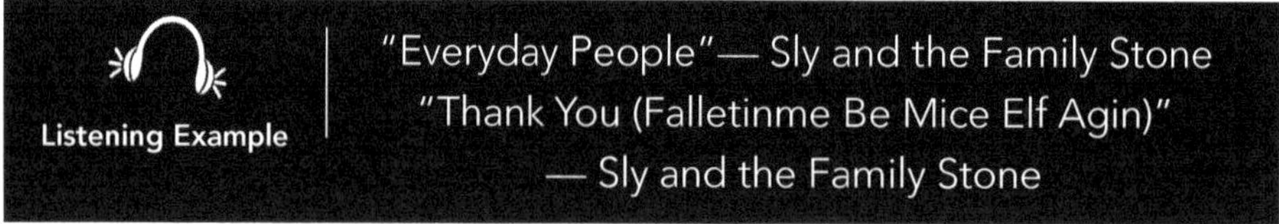

Parliament/Funkadelic

Singer-songwriter George Clinton (born 1941) formed Parliament and later Funkadelic, two bands that would exchange members and eventually record together but remain two separate entities. The name Parliament-Funkadelic would eventually be used to describe any incarnation of either group, with a large number of rotating musicians. Parliament-Funkadelic created a stage show that used crazy costumes and a science fiction/alien vibe; members of the group created stage personas and adopted alien names. The humor Clinton added to the stage shows created a fantasy world for African Americans in a way that Bowie and Kiss did for more mainstream white audiences. Two prominent members of Funkadelic were William (Bootsy) Collins (born 1951) and George (Bernie) Worrell (1944–2016). Collins is recognized as one of the greatest bass guitar players of the 20th century, often called the Jimi Hendrix of the bass guitar. Prior to joining Funkadelic, Collins spent a year in James Brown's band, helping Brown create a great funk sound with his long, complicated solos and slap bass sound. Worrell was a classically trained pianist, having studied at the Julliard School and the New England Conservatory of Music. His early work using keyboards to double the bass guitar created a new sound for funk that was perfect for the science fiction vibe of Funkadelic.

FIGURE 6.4 Parliament/Funkadelic

Funkadelic could have as many as 30 musicians on stage, an elaborate stage setup that at times included a spaceship landing onstage, and "Dr. Funkenstein" emerging from the spaceship to "deliver the funk." It was a silly, purposely over-the-top presentation directed at African Americans who were looking for a new identity following the violence of the late 1960s and the assassination of Dr. Martin Luther King Jr. The song "Flash Light," recorded by Parliament in 1977, became the first hit for Parliament/Funkadelic to have success on the mainstream U.S. pop charts. This was significant because although funk had become important to the African American community and scored successes on the R&B charts, similar success had not occurred on the pop charts since the late-1960s success of Sly and the Family Stone. "Flash Light" combines the funk bass sound with the new addition of Worrell's Moog synthesizer as an added bass texture.

Philadelphia Soul

While the music was called Philly soul, it was really a combination of soulful vocals, funk-laced instrumentals, and lush arrangements involving strings and horns. It is a great example of a peripheral style (funk) being brought into the mainstream for a wider base of popularity. Fred Wesley, a veteran of both James Brown's band and Funkadelic, said it best when he stated that the smoother Philly sound was about "putting a bow tie on funk" (Winistorfer 2019). Producers Kenny Gamble and Leon Huff of Philadelphia International Records recorded a string of musicians in the 1970s and had 175 gold and platinum records. This music would lead effortlessly to disco, and there is no clear delineation between where Philly soul ends and disco begins.

"If You Don't Know Me by Now," recorded in 1972 by Harold Melvin and the Blue Notes with Teddy Pendergrass as lead singer, is a great example of the combination of soul vocals and a lush disco-friendly treatment. The song later won a Grammy for Gamble and Huff after it was covered by British group Simply Red in 1989.

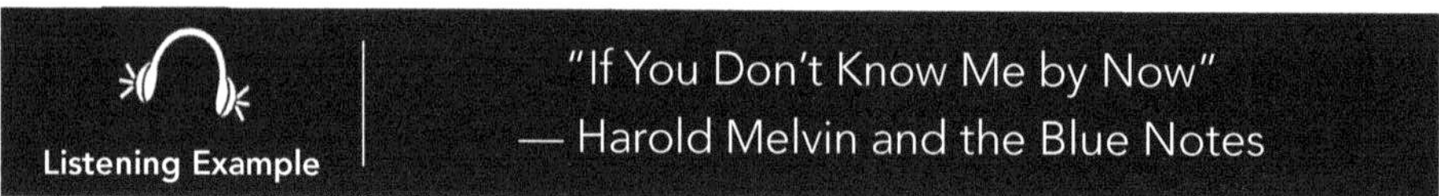

One of the most successful songs by Gamble and Huff is "Me and Mrs. Jones," recorded by Billy Paul. The song, one of the biggest-selling singles of 1972, would help to popularize the Gamble and Huff sound (Theroux 2016). It tells the story of the singer's infidelity and knowing that it is wrong but being unable to break off the relationship. Listen for the lush string arrangement included in the song.

The sounds we heard above set the tone for the dance-friendly music that would dominate the radio and record charts during the second half of the 1970s.

Disco

Disco, a much-maligned dance music, dominated the record charts and radio airplay from 1976 through 1980. In the 1940s, going out to dance at swing clubs became the dominant form of entertainment for young people. Disco had similar success in the 1970s. Disco was first developed in European dance clubs and became popular in the United States in New York City and Philadelphia. Disco borrowed heavily from many styles, including the danceable tracks of Motown, the soul music of the late 1960s, and the dance grooves of the psychedelic movement. The smooth Philadelphia sound, discussed earlier, provided an easy transition for a mass audience to accept disco. The very loud sounds of the dance clubs allowed for a communal feeling, an escape from everyday life, and an excuse to overindulge.

One of the earliest disco clubs in the United States was The Loft, a private club in New York City that became an early escape for the gay community, whose members were not welcomed and were often discriminated against in mainstream society. In the 1970s, expressing any alternative lifestyle out in the open was, at best, uncomfortable and, at worst, dangerous. The police regularly harassed gays in bars and dance clubs. The Loft allowed same-sex dancing, which was rare in the early years of the 1970s.

The music relied on a very steady beat with smooth production, often including strings and horn sounds. While Latin rhythms and percussion instruments were often used, they remained in the background to allow the steady beat to dominate the song. As with funk, the vocals were less important than in past rock music and were often considered just "another instrument."

Disco once again brought the producer into the forefront, as dance records relied less on the star power of established rock stars. In the clubs, any danceable groove was accepted, and most who danced to the songs never knew who many of the performers of those songs were.

There are several reasons why disco is often derided by newer generations of musicians and listeners. It was producer driven, so the personality-driven rock stars were less important than in the past. Some rock stars looked down on the music as being shallow, as its lyric content became less important. Almost all rock and rollers are poets first, and disco downplayed that poetry. The best disco was repetitive, hoping to keep people on the dance floor for a long time, so some of the songs included long instrumental passages. One of the innovations of the era was the 12-inch single, a rearrangement of a three-minute single to a 20-minute song, taking up an entire side of an LP. These 12-inch singles were not played on the radio but were loved in clubs. Much of what gave disco a bad reputation was how it was perceived as a lifestyle. The disco lifestyle was extravagant, including a dress code that included three-piece suits for men, long flowing gowns for women, platform shoes and high heels, long necklaces and gold medallions, and glitter. While fashion is also cyclical, the last 40-plus years have not brought back the fashion of the disco era into prominence.

The disco club became a location where attendees could overindulge in alcohol, illicit drugs, including cocaine and amphetamines, and rampant casual and (at times) public sexual activity. This was reflective of the disco being the place where you could live out your fantasies under cover of darkness. It became a matter of "what happens in a disco stays in a disco." Much of this illicit sex was unprotected, as the HIV/AIDS epidemic was not yet occurring. Clubs such as Studio 54 in New York City became places for the rich and famous to "see and be seen." The movie *Saturday Night Fever* (1977), starring John Travolta, brought disco out of the cities and into main street America. Suddenly, there were discos in almost every midsized town, and although most of those clubs were not as hedonistic as the clubs in New York and Miami, what we now know as risky behavior was still common. Though disco usually sold better in singles than in album form, the soundtrack to *Saturday Night Fever* became the highest-selling soundtrack of all time and remained so until the release of *The Bodyguard* (Whitney Houston) 15 years later. The music of *Saturday Night Fever* was dominated by the most successful disco group, the Bee Gees.

FIGURE 6.5 The Bee Gees

The Bee Gees

The Bee Gees were formed in 1958 by the Gibb brothers: Barry (born 1946) and twin brothers Robin (1949–2012) and Maurice (1949–2003). The group had two periods of success, first as a pop/folk group in the late 1960s and early 1970s and then, after relocating to Miami, Florida, and hearing the Latin-infused music, as a disco act in the mid-1970s through the early 1980s. Barry's falsetto vocals became the most recognizable sound of the disco era. The tight harmonies and brilliant songwriting made the Bee Gees one of the top-selling acts in rock history. They have sold more than 220 million records worldwide (Petridis 2013). Unlike many of the one-hit wonder disco acts, dominated by producers and having no real star power to put with the music, the Bee Gees toured, created early music videos, and became recognized around the world. The song "You Should Be Dancing" was one of their first disco hits. During a nine-month period beginning in December 1977, songs recorded by or written by the Bee Gees held the number one spot on the *Billboard* pop charts for 27 of 37 consecutive weeks (Bee Gees.com, n.d.). They had three chart-topping hits from *Saturday Night Fever*, including "Stayin' Alive," "How Deep Is Your Love," and "Night Fever." Their career would continue with great success until disco fell from grace in 1980.

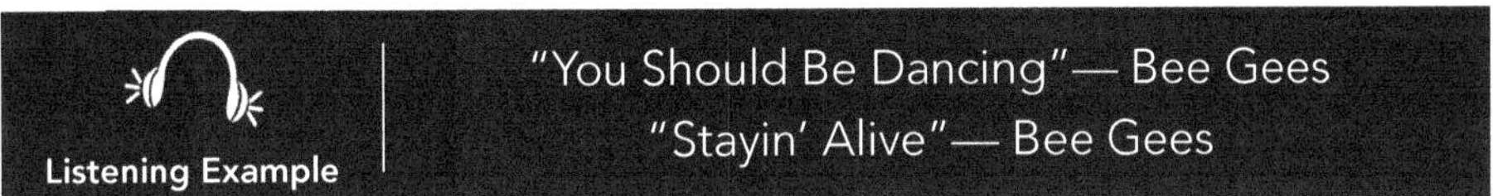

Donna Summer

Donna Summer (1948–2012) became one of the few artists associated with disco to have a successful career after the disco era and became the most successful female disco artist. She was later dubbed "The Queen of Disco." Her gospel-influenced voice, paired with Italian record producer Giorgio Moroder's great ability to create dance grooves, was hugely successful. Songs such as "Love to Love You Baby," were huge disco hits, and dance versions were created that were more than 20 minutes in length. Her most successful hit, "Hot Stuff," was number one for four consecutive weeks in the United States in 1979 (*Billboard* n.d.)

The Village People

The influence of the gay community on disco and its early club scene in New York City was made evident by the success of the Village People, a vocal group dressed in costumes, including those of a policeman, a biker, a cowboy, a Native American, and a construction worker. Songs such as "YMCA," "In the Navy," and "Macho Man"

FIGURE 6.6 The Village People

became huge hits, but most who heard the songs never realized the existence of the group and many of its songs included inside jokes aimed at the gay community. At a time when alternative lifestyles were not accepted by society as a whole, people loved their catchy songs, not realizing the inferred meaning behind the lyric content.

Earth, Wind & Fire

While Earth, Wind & Fire, formed in 1970, are considered a funk, Afro-Cuban, and soul band, their greatest success was with disco. As we have studied, bands that were a part of the funk, reggae, and punk scenes in the early 1970s rarely had mainstream success with those styles but could go on to have hits if they crossed over into the disco mainstream. The song "September" from 1978, with its great horn blasts and upbeat tempo, give it an energy that makes it a great dance song.

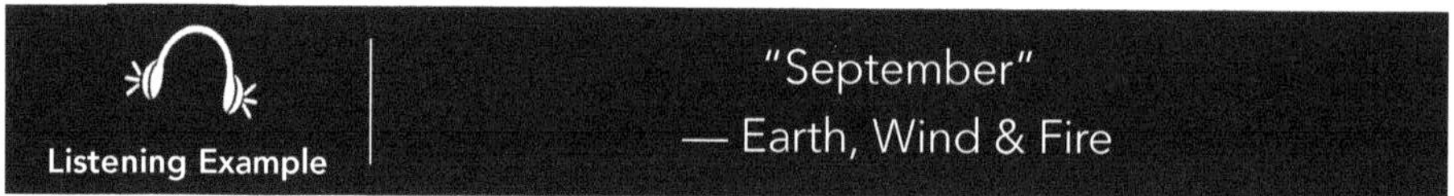

Blondie

Blondie was a punk band that performed at CBGB's early in their career yet went on to much greater success and fame once they moved away from the punk sound. Formed in 1974 by vocalist Debbie Harry and guitarist Chris Stein, they had commercial success in England and Australia but achieved success in the United States when they began to combine elements of disco, reggae, pop, and rap music. In 1978, the band released their third album, *Parallel Lines.* The album, produced by Mike Chapman, contained the reworked reggae song "Heart of Glass." Chapman told the band the

FIGURE 6.7 Blondie

song was great but would not work as a reggae song. The song was changed to be a perfect disco hit, and on the strength of the song, the album sold 20 million copies worldwide. In 1980, Blondie had the biggest-selling single of the year on *Billboard*'s chart with "Call Me" and late that year released the song "Rapture," the first song to feature rapping to reach number one in the United States (Trust 2014). The greatness of Blondie was their need to try anything new. While some accused them of "selling out" by creating disco hits, pandering to British punks by performing reggae, and attempting to defy racial norms by rapping, Blondie's embrace of new ideas has enabled the band to continue to exist to this day and be considered one of the greatest bands to emerge from New York City.

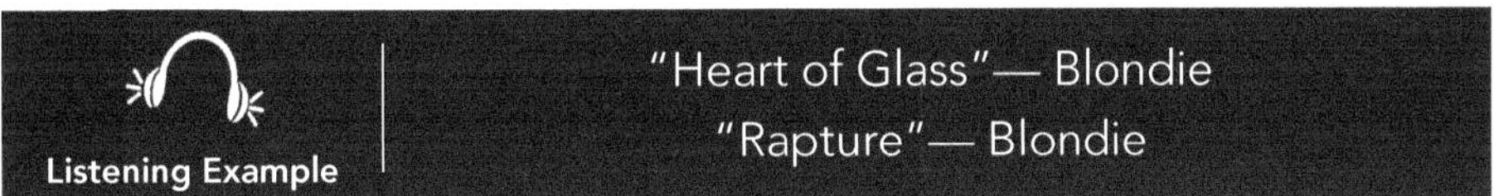

The Downfall of Disco

As discussed above, there were many reasons disco thrived in the late 1970s, but it appeared that by 1979, disco was in decline. Many popular DJs and rock artists began expressing their dislike for disco, and mainstream rock and roll, which had taken a backseat to disco for the previous few years, was on the rise. Just as the rise of disco was quick and monumental, so was its death. No single event would represent this change in music more than Disco Demolition Night. On July 12, 1979, disgruntled DJ Steve Dahl, who had lost his job a few months earlier when his station changed to an all-disco format, staged an anti-disco promotion between two double-header games by the Chicago White Sox. The promotion, sponsored by Dahl's new radio station and the White Sox themselves, offered to allow fans into the game for 98 cents if they brought a disco record, which would be collected and then destroyed in a controlled explosion between the two games. The White Sox, which was not a good team, saw the promotion as a way to get a few extra fans into the ballpark.

What occurred was that 35,000 extra fans attended, many of the records were not collected, and a riot broke out between the two games that included throwing seats onto the field, hurling records as Frisbees, and general damage to the field and stands. The explosion occurred, tearing a huge hole in the outfield grass, and fans stormed the field, ripping up the bases, stealing materials, and getting into fistfights. Many arrests were made, and the White Sox had to forfeit the second game, as conditions were ruled unsafe on the field (Costello 2009).

While this incident did not cause the end of disco, it did represent the change that was happening throughout the United States. Although some disliked disco from the beginning of its success, even those who embraced it seemed to be reacting to its excesses. Some have claimed the newfound dislike for disco was a homophobic and racist reaction by those who did not like the advances made by the gay community and the success of African American disco artists. As discussed in past chapters, when new social change occurs, there will be loud protest, as social change, though destined to occur, is scary and painful for those who do not understand it. Although this does describe some of the backlash to disco, it cannot account for the entirety of its fall from grace. The entire country was changing. The political scene was switching from the perceived failure of the Jimmy Carter presidency to the socially conservative era of Ronald Reagan. The ebb and flow of culture was ready for a change, powering the wheel of the short attention spans of the listening public. It seemed as if the pop fan was now looking again for a poet/rock and roller. In reality, as we move into the 1980s, dance music will still dominate, even though the term "disco" became a taboo word. The biggest-selling studio album in history will soon follow, and even though it would essentially be a disco album, it will be categorized as "dance pop," two words that perfectly described disco.

References

"500 Greatest Albums of All Time, The." *Rolling Stone*, May 31, 2012. https://www.rollingstone.com/music/music-lists/500-greatest-albums-of-all-time-156826/the-clash-london-calling-2-52521/.

Breihan, Tom. "The Number Ones: Eric Clapton's 'I Shot the Sheriff'." Stereogum. June 3, 2019. https://www.stereogum.com/2046093/the-number-ones-eric-claptons-i-shot-the-sheriff/franchises/the-number-ones/.

Costello, Brian. "Postcards from Disco Demolition Night." *Chicago Reader*, July 9, 2009. https://www.chicagoreader.com/chicago/postcards-from-disco-demolition-night/Content?oid=1148642.

"Hot 100: 1979 Archive." *Billboard.* Accessed October 19, 2018. https://www.billboard.com/archive/charts/1979/hot-100.

"Johnny Rotten's Cordial Letter to the Rock and Roll Hall of Fame: Next to the Sex Pistols, You're 'a Piss Stain'." OpenCulture. July 10, 2013. http://www.openculture.com/2013/07/john-rottens-cordial-letter-to-the-rock-and-roll-hall-of-fame.html.

Kaye, Lenny. "100 Greatest Artists." *Rolling Stone*, December 3, 2010. https://www.rollingstone.com/music/music-lists/100-greatest-artists-147446/the-ramones-91915/.

Langley, William. "Malcolm McClaren: What a Magnificent Failure." *The Telegraph*, April 11, 2010. https://www.telegraph.co.uk/culture/7575721/Malcolm-McClaren-What-a-magnificent-failure.html.

"Making History: Consecutive Chart-Topping Singles." BeeGees.com. Accessed October 21, 2018. https://www.beegees.com/making-history-consecutive-chart-topping-singles/.

O'Neil, Dennis. "The Exodus is Here." *Leo Weekly*, July 22, 2009. https://www.leoweekly.com/2009/07/the-exodus-is-here/.

Peacock, Tim. "The Filth and the Fury! How the Sex Pistols Sparked a Media Outrage." Udiscovermusic, October 25, 2017. https://www.udiscovermusic.com/stories/sex-pistols-media-outrage/.

Petridis, Alexis. "Barry Gibb of the Bee Gees: 'I Want to Keep the Music Alive.'" *The Guardian*, July 18, 2013. https://www.theguardian.com/music/2013/jul/18/barry-gibb-bee-gees-music-alive.

"Sex Pistols Cover Tops Charts." BBC, October 25, 2017. http://news.bbc.co.uk/2/hi/entertainment/1219770.stm.

Theroux, Gary. "The History Behind 'Me and Mrs. Jones' by Billy Paul." *Goldmine*, November 23, 2016. https://www.goldminemag.com/articles/history-mrs-jones-billy-paul.

Trust, Gary. "Rewinding the Charts: Blondie's 'Rapture' Rules *Billboard* Hot 100." *Billboard*, March 28, 2014. https://www.billboard.com/articles/columns/chart-beat/6022002/rewinding-the-charts-blondies-rapture-rules-billboard-hot-100.

Winistorfer, Andrew. "A Philadelphia Soul Primer." Vinyl Me, Please, March 28, 2019. http://www.vinylmeplease.com/magazine/best-philly-soul-albums/.

Figure Credits

IMG. 6.1: Source: https://commons.wikimedia.org/wiki/File:Nixon_edited_transcripts.jpg.

Fig. 6.1: Copyright © by Plismo (CC BY-SA 3.0) at https://commons.wikimedia.org/wiki/File:Ramones_Toronto_1976.jpg.

Fig. 6.2: Copyright © by Koen Suyk (CC BY-SA 3.0) at https://commons.wikimedia.org/wiki/File:Sex_Pistols_in_Paradiso.jpg.

Fig. 6.3: Copyright © by Eddie Mallin (CC BY 2.0) at https://commons.wikimedia.org/wiki/File:Bob-Marley.jpg.

Fig. 6.4: Copyright © by Joe Loong (CC BY-SA 2.0) at https://commons.wikimedia.org/wiki/File:Parliament-Funkadelic_Capitol_City_Carnival_07_(1431862160).jpg.

Fig. 6.5: Source: https://commons.wikimedia.org/wiki/File:Bee_Gees_Midnight_Special_1973.jpg.

Fig. 6.6: Copyright © by Mario Casciano (CC BY-SA 3.0) at https://commons.wikimedia.org/wiki/File:Village-People1978.jpg.

Fig. 6.7: Copyright © by Rdikeman (CC BY-SA 3.0) at https://commons.wikimedia.org/wiki/File:Blondie1977.jpg.

WARNING
Tone of this
record unsuitable
for minors

CHAPTER 7

The 1980s

Historical Context for the Decade

The move into the 1980s brought significant change to rock and roll, reflecting changes to society as a whole. The United States elected former actor and governor of California Ronald Reagan as president. His more conservative views reflected society's backlash to the liberal politics and moral practices of the 1970s. By the end of the 1980s, the Cold War would end with the dissolution of the Soviet Union. The Berlin Wall, separating Germany into two post-World War II halves, would be torn down. The backlash to liberalism was also reflected in society's reaction to music. The wives of prominent Washington, D.C., insiders, including Tipper Gore, the wife of future vice president Al Gore, formed the Parents Music Research Center (PMRC). They created the group to increase parental control over the access children had to music deemed inappropriate because of its sexual, violent, or drug-related themes. They proposed a warning sticker be placed on all LPs, cassettes, and compact discs the group deemed inappropriate for children. During the hearings, Frank Zappa, Twisted Sister's Dee Snider, and folk musician John Denver testified against the proposal. After the hearings, and with pressure put on the recording industry, the Recording Industry Association of America (RIAA) compromised and agreed to add the sticker. The generic parental advisory sticker was introduced in 1985. While some stores, such as Wal-Mart, refused to sell any album with the sticker and other stores restricted access by age, many stores ignored the sticker and found the sticker increased the sales of some of the albums (United States Senate 1985).

New technologies also became more available to musicians. Synthesizers became cheaper and more portable, allowing musicians to utilize the technology in their music like never before. Before the end of the 1980s, compact discs would outsell both vinyl albums and cassette tapes. Digital recording became very popular in the 1980s, with the first digitally recorded album having success in the United States in 1979. MTV and basic cable television would begin to dominate our entertainment. Disco was pronounced dead, but dance music would still be very popular with different terminology.

On December 8, 1980, rock fans the world over mourned the assassination of John Lennon, who was shot in front of his home in New York City by an obsessed fan. His career had been restarting after he had taken the previous five years off to help raise his son. This was the first stalking murder of a world-famous musician, and his murder is one of the reasons why most famous people now have security guards, as Lennon felt comfortable without one.

The Introduction of Music Television (MTV) and the New Music Revolution

FIGURE 7.1 MTV

The greatest musical innovation of the 1980s, and one of the most influential changes in the history of popular music in the United States, was MTV. MTV, or Music Television, began broadcasting on August 1, 1981, and quickly changed the way music was marketed and consumed. The channel began as a 24-hour pay cable channel that played music videos introduced by video disc jockeys, or VJs. Music videos were not new in 1981, but the rapid explosion of MTV's viewership made the concept of these short promotional films wildly popular.

The concept of the music video was a process many years in the making. Some trace it back to Walt Disney's *Fantasia*, the 1940 full-length cartoon film accompanied by orchestral masterpieces. While it did not fit the mold of the modern music video, it does entertain in a similar way. The next advancement in music videos involved musical numbers from movies cut to act as music videos within the films. Elvis Presley's movies were often edited in this way. The Beatles became very important to the development of music videos in the 1960s. In *A Hard Day's Night,* several Beatles songs show them performing or just goofing around while we hear one of their songs in the background. The first examples of music videos produced as independent entities can be attributed to the Beatles as well. In 1967, as they were working on *Sgt. Pepper's Lonely Hearts Club Band*, the group's record company was becoming impatient with the amount of time it was taking the Beatles to finish the album. To appease their record company, the Beatles decided to release two songs as singles. For each song, they also created a short promotional film to be run while the song played. The two songs, "Strawberry Fields Forever" and "Penny Lane," become the first two modern music videos created as single entities. While most others did not create music videos until much later, the Doors and Queen did create some short videos later.

The creation of MTV was considered counterintuitive by some advertisers. Why would someone want to watch a commercial (a music video is a commercial trying to sell a song, after all) and then more commercials, and why would they want to do that 24 hours a day? The marketing research conducted by MTV showed the channel would attract an audience consisting of teenagers and early 20-somethings, a prize market in music publishing. The beginnings of MTV also coincided with the rise of basic cable television. At first marketed to those who lived in rural and suburban areas due to a lack of reception of city television channels, MTV determined its market share would be white teenage boys. There was no perceived urban market for cable television, as those who lived in cities could already get all the necessary stations with rooftop or TV-mounted antennas.

The eventual effect of music videos on the music industry would be profound. Immediately upon MTV taking the airwaves, record stores in MTV's broadcast areas were getting requests for records local radio stations were not playing. This marks the first time since the popularity of radio in the 1930s when radio did not completely determine which records sold. Before the end of the 1980s, MTV would change the way people dressed, how television shows were made, and how popular music was perceived. It almost immediately changed what music we would buy at the record store.

British groups, who had a longer history of creating music videos, would become instantly popular on MTV, and a new British Invasion would begin that would rival the success of the Beatles-led 1964 revolution. While MTV would cater to these British groups and American acts such as the Cars, Pat Benatar, REO Speedwagon, and Styx, they refused to play music by African American artists. While MTV has been accused of race bias for these early decisions, they later admitted that while whey had their own preferences in music, they were also concerned their white market would be opposed to black music. They would soon realize their mistake.

American Mainstream Pop

Michael Jackson

FIGURE 7.2 Michael Jackson

The pop stardom of Michael Jackson (1958–2009) in the 1980s and the rise of MTV went hand in hand. Jackson, later known as "The King of Pop," was an incredibly gifted singer, songwriter, and dancer who became, by the mid-1980s, the most famous musician and entertainer on Earth. Jackson grew up in Gary, Indiana, the eighth of 10 children in the Jackson family. From the time Jackson was six years old, he was a member of the Jackson 5 with his brothers. By the time he was nine, they had signed with Motown Records after having won a talent contest at the Apollo Theater. The group's first four singles—"I Want You Back," "ABC," "The Love You Save," and "I'll Be There"—all reached number one on the *Billboard* Hot 100 charts (Huey 2018). Jackson released several solo albums in the 1970s and established his solo career with the release of *Off the Wall* in 1979. The album was produced by Jackson and Quincy Jones and included songs written by Stevie Wonder, Paul McCartney, Jackson, and others. The album was a huge success, with four Top 10 singles and more than 20 million records sold. Jackson's next album, released in late 1982, would change the world. Teaming up again with Quincy Jones, Jackson made *Thriller,* which would win eight Grammy Awards and include seven Top 10 singles (Grein 2017). It remained the best-selling album in U.S. history until 2018, when it was passed by *The Eagles Greatest Hits.* It remains the best-selling studio album throughout the world.

When a video for the song "Billie Jean" was sent to MTV, however, the station refused to show it, as MTV believed it should only play "rock" music. MTV executives believed African American music, such as rhythm and blues (R&B), and country music were different and would not appeal to MTV viewers. Walter Yetnikoff, the president of CBS Records, threatened to pull MTV's rights to play all other CBS artists unless MTV played "Billie Jean." MTV ran the video, and it was an immediate hit. The video became so popular so quickly that some people subscribed to cable television just so they could get MTV and watch Jackson in "Billie Jean." Jackson's dance moves and onscreen personality helped make MTV more popular and would help to change the music industry. Music was now becoming a multimedia experience, and MTV was the way to get that experience. Jackson took full advantage of the new medium, creating videos for other songs from *Thriller*, including "Beat It" and a 14-minute mini-movie for the song "Thriller" directed by John Landis. The special effects, lighting, and storyline made the "Thriller" video a worldwide phenomenon. More than 35 years later, the dance moves are still being imitated today in dance clubs and at wedding receptions.

Jackson's next album, *Bad*, was released in 1987. This album produced seven singles in the United States, including a record five number one singles The album sold 45 million copies worldwide and was the best-selling album of 1987 and 1988 (Unterberger and Christman 2017). His 1991 album *Dangerous* sold nearly 30 million copies worldwide ("Michael Jackson's Best-Selling" 2009). From 1993 until his death in 2008, Jackson's career was marred by controversy. His increasingly erratic and bizarre behavior, paired with allegations of inappropriate contact with minors (though he was acquitted on all charges), served to slow his career and change his public image. In 2009, Jackson announced he would be performing a series of concerts that would amount to a farewell tour and lead to his retirement. While in the process of rehearsing for those concerts, Jackson died in his sleep from an accidental overdose of sleeping medications.

Jackson's death on June 25, 2009, triggered an outpouring of grief from fans not seen since John Lennon's murder 29 years earlier. Following his death, Jackson again became the most popular artist of 2009. His records sold more than 35 million copies worldwide, and he became the first artist to have more than one million of his songs downloaded in a week. Three of his older albums sold more than any new album, and four of his albums reentered the Top 20. Since his death, Jackson's estate has earned in excess of $500 million per year, making his estate the highest grossing of any late celebrity (Kaufman 2016).

Jackson was more than just a great musician. He is the most successful entertainer of all time and had a greater effect on music, dancing, film, and fashion than any other musician. To best appreciate his talent, it is important to view the videos of his songs. Here is a short list of those videos that best represent his career as the "King of Pop."

- "Billie Jean"
- "Beat It"
- "Thriller"

- "Bad"
- "Man in the Mirror"
- "Smooth Criminal"

Madonna

Madonna (born 1958) was born and raised in the Detroit area and moved to New York City in 1978. She is another artist whose career was greatly influenced by MTV, leading her to become the most recognized female musician in the world by the late 1980s. Her success with MTV videos, movies, and albums led her to be referred to as "The Queen of Pop." She was signed to Sire Records and released her eponymous debut album in 1983. She is recognized as the best-selling female artist of all time (Hamill 2018).

Madonna was the perfect artist to become an MTV star in the 1980s. For an audience of teenage boys, she became the perfect sex symbol, pushing the boundaries of what was considered appropriate for the times. Her live performance on the *MTV Video Music Awards* show in 1984 was very controversial. She wore a white wedding dress while rolling around on the floor in a provocative manner. Although this would not garner much attention today, conservative groups considered it indecent and sought to have the video banned. As her career progressed, videos for the songs "Open Your Heart" and "Like a Prayer" received criticism for their sexual content. In 1990, a video for "Justify My Love" was banned by MTV for its strong sexual content and brief nudity. Her tour in 1993 included topless dancers, and her television appearances all sought to push the boundaries of the perceived decency of the time. It began to affect her career, as even her fans began to question her behavior. By the mid-1990s, she had begun to tone down that element of her career. Madonna has always been an artistic chameleon, changing her looks and sound with almost every new album and tour. This was perfect for the ever-changing era of MTV in the 1980s. Her music continued to change as well, adding greater elements of electronic dance music (EDM) to her pop songwriting. Her career as an actress was often panned, but her performance as the title character in the film *Evita* was praised.

Madonna's fashion sense dictated female trends throughout the 1980s. For teenage girls, she became the first "girl power" artist, not shying away from her independence and bold sexuality. This attitude would help to usher in the era of record charts being dominated by female artists in the 1990s. Although Madonna's public persona has both enhanced and, at times, negatively affected her career, she continues to release albums that are critically praised. She is also involved in many charitable projects, including funding the building of schools and hospitals in Africa.

FIGURE 7.3 Madonna

Prince

Prince Rogers Nelson (1958–2016) was another artist who dominated the 1980s, using MTV as a way to promote his music, fashion, and dance moves. He is considered one of the greatest guitarists of the 20th century, but this instrumental talent was often overlooked, as Prince was better known for his great vocal range, terrific dance moves, and often provocatively sexual lyrics. His musical style reflected a wide variety of influences, including funk, R&B, rock, psychedelia, and soul. He won eight Grammy Awards and an Academy Award for his 1984 film *Purple Rain* (Princevault n.d.).

Prince, like Michael Jackson, was someone whose onstage personality demanded that everyone watch his every move, but his offstage personality was quiet and reserved. His personality on MTV represented the sex-obsessed teen male. As a musician, he was a perfectionist, leading to his now-famous battle with Warner Brothers Records, with whom Prince had signed a multi-album contract. In a move to get out of the contract, he began changing his name—at first to "The Artist Formerly Known as Prince," then "The Artist," and finally, an unpronounceable symbol. During this period, he released many albums quickly to fulfill his record contract and appeared live with the word "Slave" written on his face to represent his contract. In 2000, he went back to using the name Prince. Two of his great performances include a guitar solo played on "While My Guitar Gently Weeps" during a tribute to George Harrison at the Rock and Roll Hall of Fame induction ceremony in 2004 and his Super Bowl XLI halftime show in 2007. He continued to perform and create new albums until his accidental overdose death in 2016.

FIGURE 7.4 Prince

Prince was a phenomenally talented musician of the 1980s and beyond. His ability to merge rock and soul and black and white music styles helped to further integrate music. His song "When Doves Cry" from the *Purple Rain* soundtrack album is a great example of this integration. His extreme vocal range, use of electric guitar, and replacing a bass guitar with an 808 drum machine utilized the new technology while still providing mainstream rock appeal.

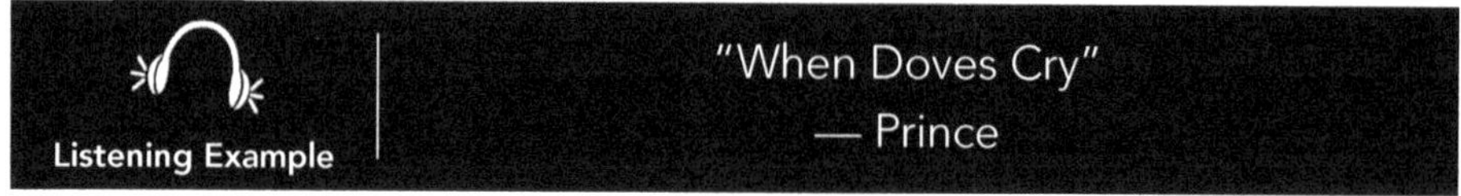

The New British Invasion or New Wave

New wave in the 1980s was a combination of many of the styles that were popular and influential from the second half of the 1970s, including punk, disco, reggae, and mainstream pop. The rise of MTV and its early refusal to play African American music did create a void that provided British musicians a new entrance into American mainstream rock. The British were always ahead of the Americans when it came to the visual aspect of rock and roll. Pete Townshend of the Who pointed out that many of the British rockers of the original British Invasion were art school students. These art schools were places where students who were not necessarily considered "university material" could distinguish themselves and graduate to entry-level jobs in design and fine arts. They were schools where an interesting mix of students from different classes could learn on an equal footing, which was very rare in Britain. These were not universities; rather, they were closer to technical colleges in the United States. Many of these students, including early British Invasion alum John Lennon, received a greater sense of the visual arts and, in turn, added that element to their careers when they became successful musicians.

This trend seemed to continue through to the 1980s and was a perfect match for MTV. During the early years of MTV, a new British Invasion occurred, and while not producing any bands of the caliber of the Beatles or the Rolling Stones, overall, the movement was no less successful than the earlier generation of British rock. This carried over to the record charts. 1983 saw unprecedented success for British acts on American radio. In retrospect, it is not surprising. These English artists realized that how they looked could be as important as how they sounded and that MTV videos were the future of promoting their music. Although many of the British bands of this era were one-hit wonders, some had great success, and a few continue with careers reaching nearly 40 years in length. One such band to emerge from England in the 1980s was Duran Duran.

Duran Duran

Duran Duran was the perfect band for the video age on MTV. The five members were referred to as "The Fab Five," not so much for musical similarities with the Beatles (the Fab Four) as for their popularity with their female teenage fans. Their success and lengthy career (40 years as of 2018) gives the band the greatest legacy of any British MTV-friendly band. Their videos showcasing exotic locations and the good-looking members of the band (at times with slightly feminine makeup) had the same effect that the slightly long-haired Beatles had nearly 20 years earlier. The slightly androgynous look became big on MTV in the 1980s. Duran Duran's success in the United States will forever be linked to MTV, even though the band was still creating new music in 2019. Listen to two songs from the band, one from the height of their meteoric MTV rise in 1982 ("Hungry Like The Wolf") and one recorded in 2015 ("Pressure Off").

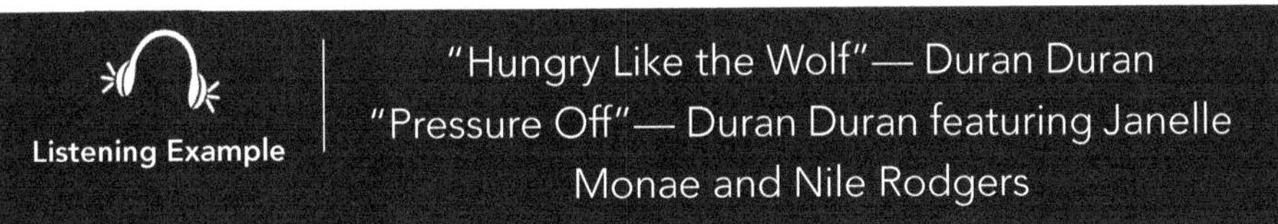

Culture Club

Some British artists used the androgynous look for shock value, and some used it as a political statement to shine a spotlight on gender stereotypes. Culture Club was successful at using cross-dressing for both purposes. In 1984, cross-dressing was not a practice that was as socially acceptable as it is today. Boy George, the lead singer of Culture Club, often wore dresses and feminine makeup. The group's name was created from its eclectic mix of members: "a gay Irishman as a lead singer, a black British bassist, a blond Englishman on guitar, and a Jewish drummer" ("Mira Parkes" n.d.). This type of integration was rare, and the band wanted to capitalize on it. MTV became the perfect place to do so. There was shock value, particularly in America, where alternative lifestyles were still out of the public eye. Any video on MTV that shocked people was the perfect promotion for both a band and the network, and Culture Club was shocking in 1984. Changes in societal norms occur over time with the introduction and very gradual acceptance of new ideas and practices, and MTV is credited with creating an environment where these new ideas were displayed.

FIGURE 7.5

Eurythmics

Another British artist who pushed the boundaries of societal norms was Annie Lennox of Eurythmics. Eurythmics were a pop duo composed of lead singer Lennox and keyboardist and multi-instrumentalist Dave Stewart. Lennox often dressed in what was stereotypically male attire and sported a crew cut hairstyle to poke fun at societal norms. The duo's synthesizer-based music and unusual videos became regular viewing on MTV. Watch the video for "Sweet Dreams (Are Made of This)," and pay particular attention to the synthesized heavy sound and the unusual combination of Lennox's look and the contrast of technology versus the roaming cows that inhabit the video.

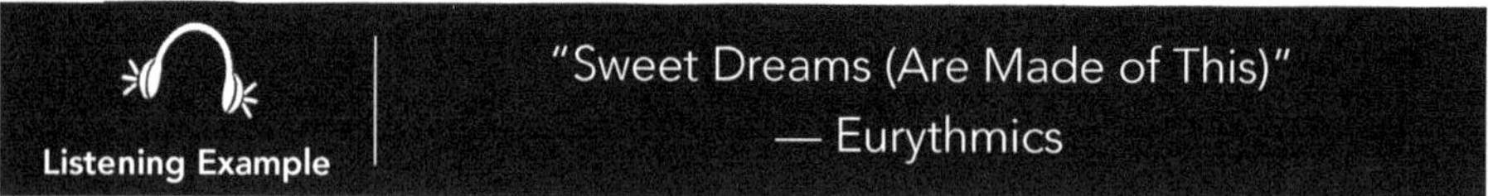

The Police

The Police, a trio formed in London in 1977, were one of the first new wave bands to achieve mainstream success. Punk, reggae, disco, and jazz influenced the Police. Lead singer, songwriter, and bassist Sting (born Gordon Sumner in 1951), guitarist Andy Summers (born 1942), and American drummer Stewart Copeland (born 1952) created a fusion of all of the sounds mentioned above. Their success predates MTV, and their final studio album, *Synchronicity*, was released in 1983. It sold more than eight million copies in the United States alone, and they have sold more than 75 million records worldwide ("Biography" n.d.). Their 1978 song "Roxanne" shows elements of punk and reggae, yet their sound was also influenced by mainstream rock and roll.

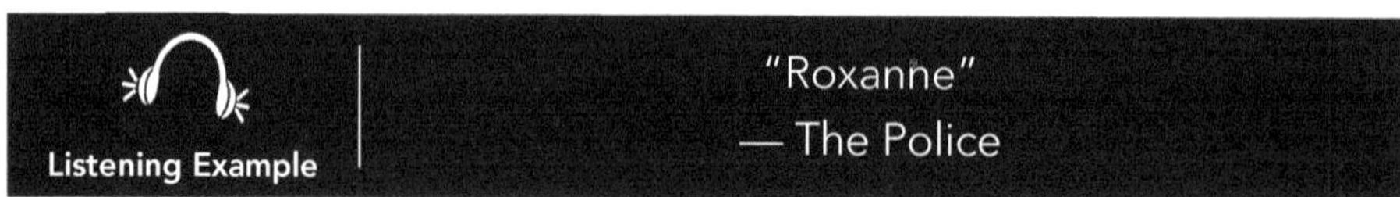

American New Wave

While American new wave took a back seat to its British counterpart and to the mainstream dance pop artists discussed previously, the B-52s, the Cars, and Devo had success, showing just how broad-based the new wave sound could be. The B-52s featured a garage band sound with retro influences from the 1950s and 1960s. Their best-known songs include "Rock Lobster" and "Love Shack." Devo featured science fiction themes, odd-metered songs, and a heavy synthesized sound. While never mainstream or incredibly popular, they have to this day maintained a strong cult following. They did chart on *Billboard* in 1980 with the song "Whip It," the video of which was played heavily on MTV in 1981. The most commercially successful of the American new wave bands was the Cars.

The Cars

The Cars formed in Boston, Massachusetts, in 1976 but became known later in the decade and into the 1980s for combining 1970s punk, guitar-driven music, and the new danceable, synthesizer-driven sound of the 1980s. Their most successful album, 1984's *Heartbeat City,* contained the major hits "You Might Think," which won them Video of the Year from MTV in 1984, "Drive" (their most successful single), "Magic," and "Hello Again." The band broke up in 1988 and reunited briefly in 2010. They were inducted into the Rock and Roll Hall of Fame in 2018.

The Hair Bands

There needs to be differentiation between heavy metal and the music of the hair bands of the 1980s and beyond. Although the music did have a similar audience of teenage boys and young men, the attitude and look were quite different. The hair bands were perfect for MTV. The long and often big hairstyles and makeup, paired with hard partying and the scantily clad women in the music videos, were the perfect combination for the teenage male. Gone was the anger of 1970s heavy metal and in was the glam rock influence, soaring tenor vocals, and eye candy necessary for great television. Several bands became big during this time, including Motley Crue, Poison, Twisted Sister, and Def Leppard. Other bands that had existed previously in the 1970s also fit well into this category, including Van Halen and Kiss from the United States and Scorpions from Germany. The most success garnered by any of the bands was enjoyed by New Jersey's Bon Jovi.

Bon Jovi

The band was formed in 1983 in Sayreville, New Jersey, by singer and songwriter Jon Bon Jovi (born 1962). Since that time, the band has had one of the top-selling songs of the 1980s in "Livin' on a Prayer," released 13 studio albums, sold more than 100 million records, and performed live for more than 34 million people (Coscarelli 2017). In 2005, they released *Have a Nice Day*, a country music–influenced album. The song "Who Says You Can't Go Home" won a Grammy Award and is the first number one single by a rock band on the country charts ("Bon Jovi" n.d.). The song was released in three versions, including a mainstream rock version, a country duet with Jennifer Nettles of country band Sugarland, and an adult contemporary version. Bon Jovi's popularity continues well into their fourth decade on the charts, which is a rare occurrence in rock music.

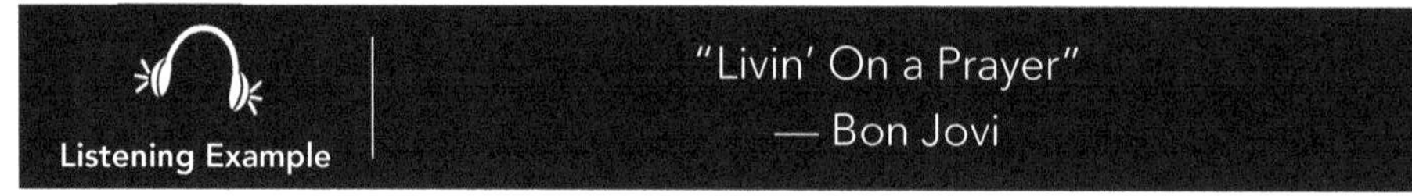

Guns N' Roses

One other very successful hair band of the 1980s was Guns N' Roses. The band began in 1985 in Los Angeles. Their first album, *Appetite for Destruction*, sold more than 30 million copies and produced three hit singles: "Welcome to the Jungle," "Paradise City," and "Sweet Child o' Mine" (Weiderhorn 2019). While Guns N' Roses was often categorized as a hair band, they had an energy reminiscent of earlier heavy metal and garnered fans from both subgenres. They served as a middle-ground band, somewhere between the glam of Motley Crue and the aggressive speed metal of Metallica.

Heavy Metal and Metallica

Metallica was one of the most commercially successful heavy metal bands of the 1980s, formed in 1981 in Los Angeles by vocalist James Hetfield and drummer Lars Ulrich. While hair bands were incredibly radio friendly, the darker tones of Metallica and other metal bands were less successful on radio, even though they received heavy rotation on MTV. Metallica had a base of fans who saw past the pop sensibilities of hair band rock, believing it was uninspired and weak. Metallica's fans wanted a more aggressive sound. The band's third album, *Master of Puppets,* released in 1986, is considered a staple of 1980s heavy metal. The album's political statements, rare in metal music at the time, made *Puppets* the first thrash metal album to earn platinum status, and the record was deemed "culturally, historically, and aesthetically significant" enough to be preserved in the Library of Congress (Hartmann 2016). Listen to the aggressive sound of "Master of Puppets" from the 1986 album. The song is about drug use and is sung to the abuser from the drug's point of view.

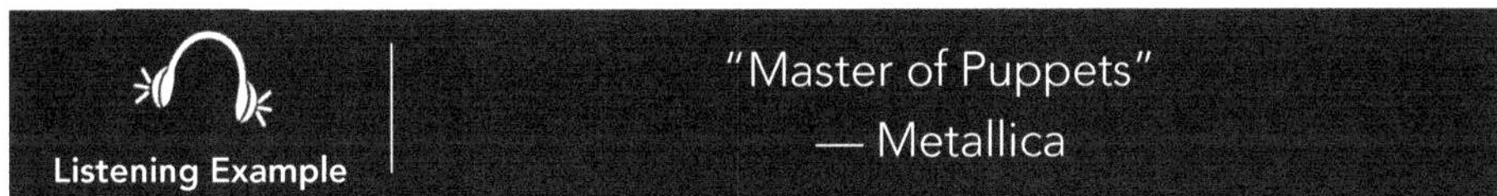

AC/DC

One of the most underrated bands in rock history is AC/DC. Though often considered a heavy metal band, they consider themselves "just a rock and roll band, nothing more, nothing less" ("AC/DC" n.d.). Brothers Angus (born 1955) and Malcolm (1953–2017) Young formed the Australian band in Sydney in 1973. They had success in the 1970s with vocalist Bon Scott (1946–1980) but achieved even greater fame with the addition of vocalist Brian Johnson (born 1947) after Scott's death from alcohol poisoning. The first album with Johnson, 1980's *Back in Black,* was recorded as a memorial to Scott. The album went on to sell 50 million copies, making it one of the best-selling albums in history. The band has sold more than 200 million records (RIAA 2019) and was elected into the Rock and Roll Hall of Fame in 2003. The band continues but has recently dealt with adversity, as Malcolm Young died in 2017 after a battle with dementia, lead singer Brian Johnson has had to stop singing due to hearing loss, and bassist Cliff Williams retired. For a while in 2016, Axl Rose sang lead vocals, though it was rumored in 2018 that Johnson and drummer Phil Rudd were rejoining Angus

Young in the studio. Listen to "Hells Bells" from *Back in Black*. The tolling of the bell we hear is in reference to the recent death of Scott.

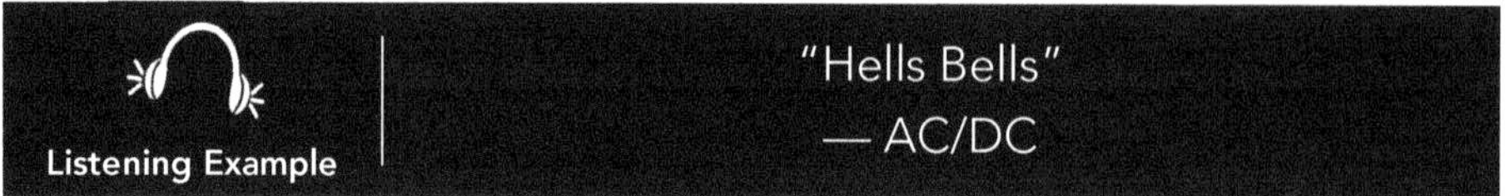

The 1980s Singer-Songwriters

The 1980s, though heavily dominated by MTV's glam, British artists, and hair bands, still had singer-songwriters who had success on the charts. Billy Joel, Elton John, and others had continued success in the 1980s (see Chapter 5, "Singer-Songwriters"). This chapter will focus on just two of the most successful singer-songwriters of the decade: Bruce Springsteen and John (Cougar) Mellencamp.

Bruce Springsteen

Bruce Springsteen (born 1949), known for his work with the E Street Band, is a native of Freehold, New Jersey, and his music is strongly associated with his home state. Springsteen is best known for his two biggest albums, 1975's *Born to Run* and 1984's *Born in the USA*. Springsteen is known for his blue-collar poetry, often creating characters in his songs who are dealing with struggles in their daily lives. On *Born to Run*, Springsteen wanted to create a new version of the Wall of Sound popularized by Phil Spector in the 1960s. His backing band provided the engine for this sound, and the album became Springsteen's first big hit. In 1984, Springsteen released *Born in the USA*, one of the most successful albums of the 1980s. The album has sold more than 30 million copies and had seven Top 10 singles (Forde 2012). The album is a combination of dark lyric content, often about the things that Springsteen believed to be wrong in the United States, paired with energetic, powerful instrumentals. While MTV was showing us videos of Michael Jackson, Prince, and Culture Club, they also showed Springsteen. Often dressed in jeans and a white T-shirt, Springsteen, perceived as "the guy next door," defied the 1980s glam/unapproachable rock

FIGURE 7.6 Bruce Springsteen

star persona. He is also known for his live concerts, at times running longer than three hours. He continues to tour and create albums. "Born to Run," from the album of the same name, deals with young people yearning to escape what they perceive to be a bleak future, and "My Hometown," from *Born in the USA,* deals with the struggle of small towns to exist. This song is from the perspective of an older married man and his concern for his family.

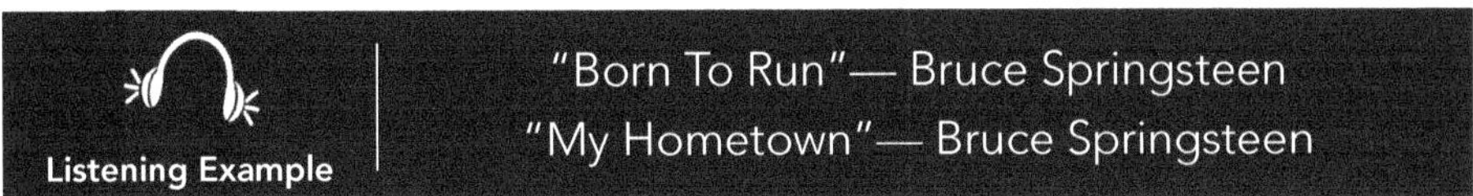

John Mellencamp

John Mellencamp (born 1951) is a singer-songwriter from Indiana. His style of songwriting is sometimes called "heartland rock," as his music was often reflective of his Midwest upbringing. While Mellencamp is a rock and roller, he also uses acoustic instruments, combining electric guitars with fiddles and accordions. Mellencamp is one of the founding members of Farm Aid, a benefit concert started in 1985 and continued each year since to assist struggling farmers. Since 1985, it has raised more than $50 million for family farms ("Annual Report" 2018). The first listening example, "Jack and Diane," is from his 1982 album *American Fool.* At the time, Mellencamp was going by the name John Cougar. This is a song about growing up in the heartland and dealing with the joys of youth and the unsure future of what adulthood may bring. In "Rain on the Scarecrow," from the 1985 album *Scarecrow,* Mellencamp addresses the death of the American family farm, as the era was rife with bank foreclosures. While some referred to this style of music as "roots rock," the popularity of Mellencamp's music was far greater than any subgenre classification would suggest.

College Rock

The sound of college rock represented a hybrid of punk and new wave styles with the added influence of folk music. The term "college rock" was both a style and a description of how the music became popular. In the late 1970s and into the 1980s, most college and university radio stations were student-run, nonprofit entities that did not have wide listening bases. They were not attempting to make a profit, so their song list did not need to satisfy a particular commercial base. As there were plenty of commercial radio stations, and college stations had no desire (or ability) to compete with those stations, many of the DJs programmed music that was not available on mainstream radio. One band that went on to mainstream success but began as a college rock mainstay was R.E.M.

R.E.M.

R.E.M., composed of singer Michael Stipe, guitarist Peter Buck, bassist Mike Mills, and drummer Bill Berry, formed in Athens, Georgia, in 1980. They went on to gradual success in the 1980s through constant touring and college radio airplay. Much of the live concerts were at colleges and universities along the East Coast of the United States. Their first single, "Radio Free Europe," was released independently on Hib-Tone records in 1981. Throughout the 1980s, R.E.M.'s music became more political, a reaction to the conservativism that was reflected in the Reagan presidency. This new liberal message hit big with college students but still failed to break into mainstream radio. R.E.M. rejected the synthesizer-heavy songs of the day, favoring electric and acoustic guitars.

R.E.M. first had mainstream success with the 1987 album *Document* and the song "The One I Love." It would be their first Top 20 song in the United States and the United Kingdom. Their greatest success would come in 1991 with "Losing My Religion," one of the most successful singles of the 1990s. The video was in heavy rotation on MTV, and the song was a mainstream radio hit. The band was elected into the Rock and Roll Hall of Fame in 2007 and broke up in 2011 (Hilton 2011). They are often cited as one of the biggest influences on grunge musicians. Kurt Cobain of Nirvana said, "I don't know how that band does what they do. God, they're the greatest. They've dealt with their success like saints, and they keep delivering great music" (Buchanan 2012). Other great bands of the 1990s, including Radiohead and Pearl Jam, list R.E.M. as major influences. The song "The One I Love" was often thought of as a love song, but lyricist and singer Stipe later

FIGURE 7.7 R.E.M.

commented that it was a song about "using people over and over again." "Losing My Religion" is a song based around a mandolin groove. It is about obsessive love, but the term "losing my religion" is a Southern U.S. colloquialism referring to someone getting angry and swearing.

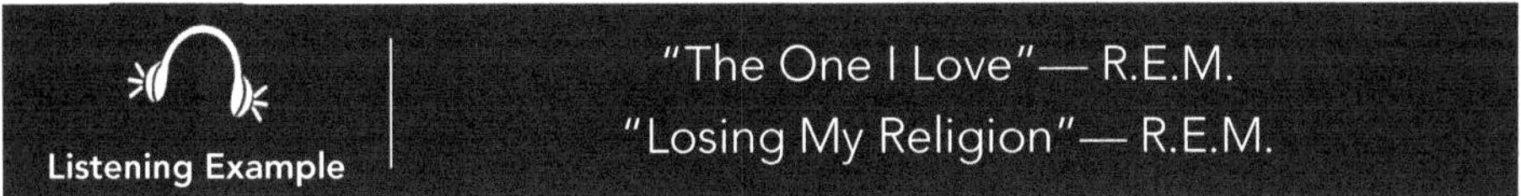

U2

U2 was formed in Dublin, Ireland, in 1976. By 1983, with their first successful singles, "Sunday Bloody Sunday" and "Pride (In the Name of Love)," they had become known for their socially conscious lyrics, often delving into political and spiritual themes. Like R.E.M., they avoided the cliché guitar solos and synthesizers many groups were using at the time. Though initially rooted in punk, U2 developed throughout the 1980s utilizing electronic dance and new wave styles. They have sold more than 170 million albums worldwide, have won 22 Grammy awards (more than any other band), and were inducted into the Rock and Roll Hall of Fame in 2005 (Mason 2015). The band, including vocalist Bono, guitarist the Edge, bassist Adam Clayton, and drummer Larry Mullen Jr., created some of the most socially conscious rock of the 1980s, including 1984's "Pride (In the Name of Love)." The song, written about the U.S. civil rights struggle of the 1960s and the life of Dr. Martin Luther King Jr., became the first big hit by U2 on MTV and their first Top 40 single in the United States.

By 1987, their music had become more introspective, exemplified by their U.S. number one hit "I Still Haven't Found What I'm Looking For." A song about the desire for spiritual fulfillment, it was praised by critics, and lead singer Bono was lauded as a poet in the vein of Bob Dylan. The band continues to perform and lead lives of social activism, including raising money for famine relief, the fight to end HIV/AIDS, and even a benefit to help musicians who lost their instruments in Hurricane Katrina.

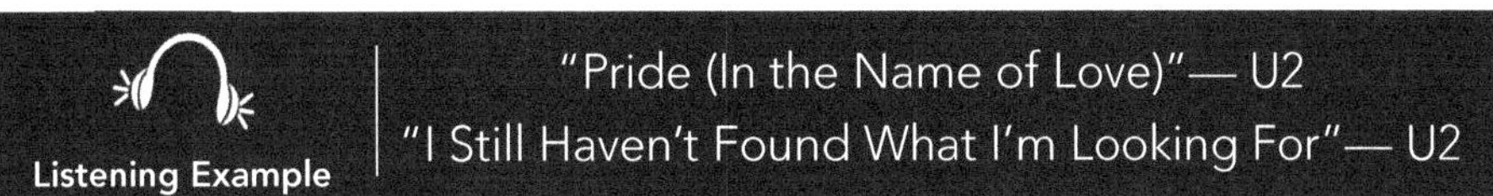

Rap and Hip Hop

Rap music developed in the 1970s within a broader culture called hip hop. The hip hop culture included rapping, scratching records, break dancing, and graffiti art. While hip hop has often been used as a synonym for rap music, this is incorrect, as hip hop does not require rapping. "Hip hop" is best used to define the culture as a whole rather than any particular element of that culture. The rhythmic rhyming of rapping can be traced back to African American disc jockeys from the 1940s and 1950s who often introduced songs or identified their stations with clever rhymes. While this did exist in African American culture, the origins of hip hop and rap can be traced to the island of Jamaica.

DJ Kool Herc

DJ Kool Herc (born 1955), a Jamaican immigrant, began teaching teenagers the art of hip hop deejaying in the Bronx borough of New York City. In Jamaica, DJs often would talk in rhyme over the prerecorded dance grooves at outdoor parties. Once in the United States, Kool Herc taught his protégés the art of using two turntables to mix different rhythmic breaks or to extend one break. He ended up calling the dancers at his shows "break boys" and "break girls." Their dance forms developed at Herc's parties and, by the early 1980s, were called "breakdancing" by the media.

One of Herc's students would move rap and hip hop out of the street and into the public realm. Afrika Bambaataa (born 1957) utilized this new dance music and culture as a way to keep competing gang members from violence. Bambaataa is given credit as one of the creators of hip hop culture, eventually spreading it through his Universal Zulu Nation organization. He would eventually add electronic sounds, based on his appreciation of the music of experimental German group Kraftwerk, to create what he referred to as "electrofunk" (Palladev 2017). His album *Planet Rock* reflected a new development in hip hop. This new style moved rap and hip hop away from the stripped-down, simplistic sound to a more mainstream style of dance music.

Sugar Hill Gang

One of the first rap recordings to gain any mainstream success was "Rapper's Delight," recorded by the Sugar Hill Gang in 1979. This song was a boast (the bragging of the rapper) about friends and family by the three rappers on the record. It was light-hearted in nature and reflected the party atmosphere of early raps. It sampled the disco hit "Good Times" by the band Chic.

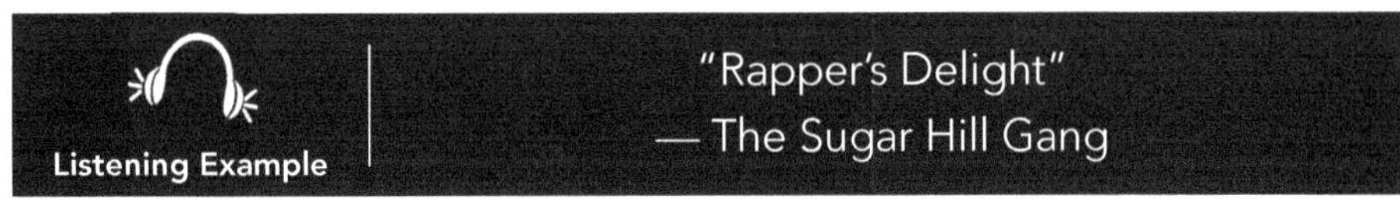

Grandmaster Flash

Grandmaster Flash (Joseph Saddler, born 1958) was a protégé of DJ Kool Herc. In 2007, he became the first hip hop artist inducted into the Rock and Roll Hall of Fame. He is one of the great early innovators in scratching records and mixing sounds. His group, the Furious Five, is credited with creating one of the first rap records that addressed social issues. "The Message," featuring Melle Mel and released in 1982, chronicled life in the inner-city ghetto.

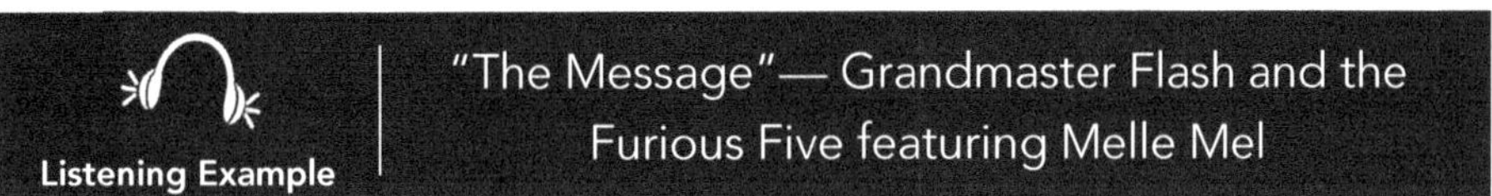

Run-D.M.C.

The first rap album to break through to a wide audience was 1986's *Raising Hell* by Run-D.M.C. It sold three million copies and was the first rap album to receive regular airplay on MTV. A big part of that acceptance was the inclusion of "Walk This Way," a cover of Aerosmith's 1975 heavy metal song. Their producer, Rick Rubin (cofounder of Def Jam Recordings), thought that including a cover song would be a great idea. Like many other peripheral styles of music, adding a more familiar sound can bring a genre to a new audience. Run-D.M.C. is considered a major contributor to the gradual integration of rap and mainstream rock. The MTV video, starring both Run-D.M.C. and Steven Tyler and Joe Perry of Aerosmith, was a huge hit, and many white teenagers first became familiar with rap music through the song and its exposure on MTV.

FIGURE 7.8 Run-D.M.C.

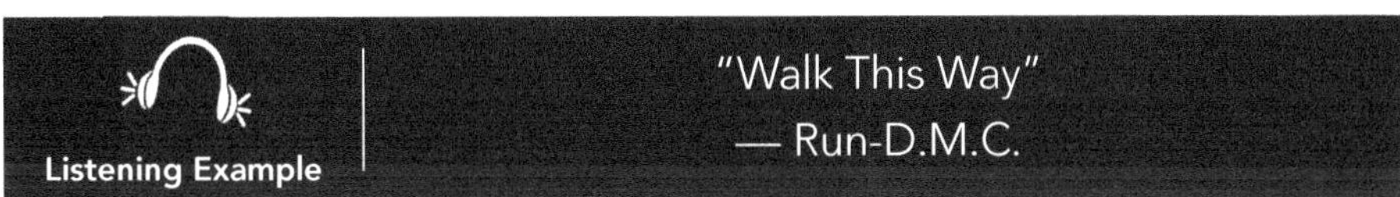

The Beastie Boys

Another rap group that would bridge the racial gap in music was the Beastie Boys. They formed in 1979 out of a love for punk rock but moved their sound to rap by 1983. The three upper-middle-class white teens from New York City (Michael "Mike D" Diamond, Adam "MCA" Yauch, and Adam "Ad-Rock" Horovitz) hired Rick Rubin to DJ some of their concerts but immediately began using him as a producer when they signed to his new record label, Def Jam. In 1986, they released *Licensed to Ill* to critical and commercial success. It was the first rap album to top the *Billboard* album charts and sell more than 10 million copies (Caufield 2012). It sampled from mainstream rock artists (Led Zeppelin), punk bands (the Clash), and other rappers. The song "(You Gotta) Fight for Your Right (To Party!)" became a teen anthem and brought African American and white kids together at concerts in a way not previously seen. The Beastie Boys became one of the targets of the PMRC for their lyrical content, and their live shows became fodder for the press. Rap music and its norms were new and threatening to white audiences unfamiliar with the origins of the music.

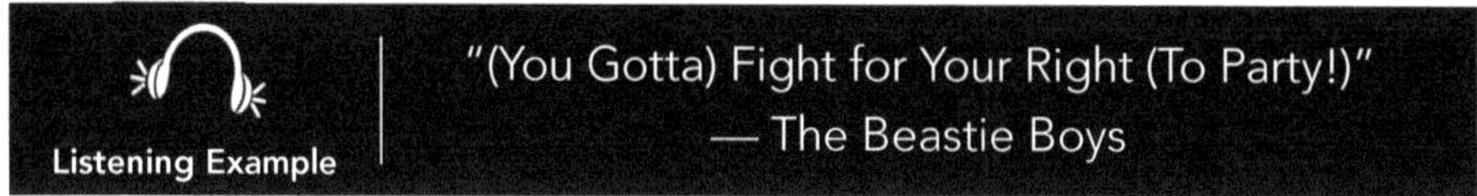

Public Enemy

Public Enemy, formed in New York in 1986, was known for their political music and criticism of the way African Americans were viewed by mainstream America. Their music was based on the idea that the police and local and federal governments perceived every African American as a public enemy. Musically, Public Enemy was known for their dense sound, sampling tracks from jazz and funk. The overlapping samples made the sound busier than most rap music had been up to that point. Public Enemy became the group that led rap music from the beginnings of party music through its adolescence of social consciousness to an era when political statements could become the basis for rap music. While never as popular or mainstream as Run-D.M.C. or the Beastie Boys, Public Enemy would become one of the most critically praised rap groups of the 1980s and 1990s.

FIGURE 7.9 Public Enemy

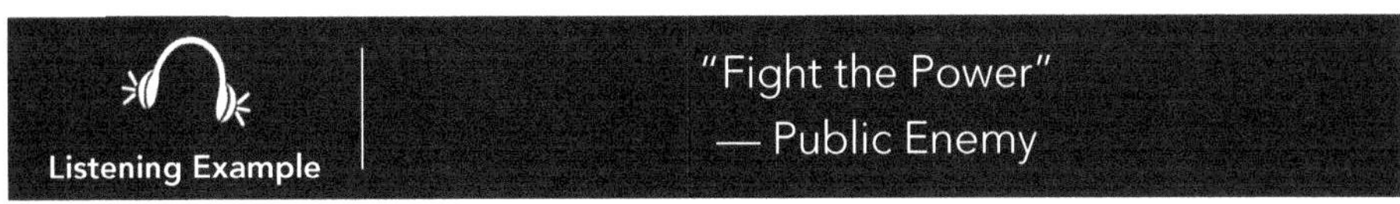

Throughout the 1980s and 1990s, rap music would continue to expand its reach. With most styles of music, the first decade is often homogenous. Once that initial period ends, we see a branching out of sounds and styles. Subgenres of rap and hip hop would become prevalent in the late 1980s and beyond. The new styles that reflected these changes included gangsta rap, which reflected a lifestyle mirroring gang membership, the promotion of violence and crime, profanity, and the sexual objectification of women. The antipolice lyrics offered by Los Angeles–based N.W.A. (Niggaz Wit Attitudes) caused MTV to ban their videos and the FBI to warn them of possible prosecution. Their 1988 album *Straight Outta Compton* is considered the beginning of gangsta rap.

At the same time, other artists would create rap from a very different point of view. DJ Jazzy Jeff (Jeff Townes) and rapper the Fresh Prince (Will Smith) formed a duo in West Philadelphia, creating music that was geared toward a pop audience. Their first hit, "Parents Just Don't Understand," included a funny MTV video and won the very first Grammy Award for best rap performance. The humor and absence of profanity offered an easy entry point for fans who were not ready for or interested in the gritty lyrics of N.W.A.. Another style of rap came from Long Island's De La Soul, known for their unusual sampling and experimental sounds. Their 1989 album *3 Feet High and Rising* is considered to be a masterpiece of rap. Their subject matter covered suburban life and love and sampled Steely Dan and Hall & Oates. Queen Latifah (born Dana Owens in 1970) became a pioneer in feminist rap, dealing with issues important to African American women, including relationship problems and domestic violence. Her music was a reaction to the sexism rampant in rap music at that time. She has continued to perform as a more traditional singer, actor, and producer.

The music industry greatly expanded in the 1980s. With the addition of MTV and cable television, the ways in which we would be entertained would change radically. Music dominated by synthesizers would become big, continuing the dance music of the previous decade. Michael Jackson and Madonna would dominate the record charts. Rap music would grow from its infancy to include a wide variety of sounds and performers. Albums sold in greater numbers than ever before, and music became bigger, utilizing greater instrumentation and more complex sounds. Rock music was bigger than ever, but the move into the 1990s would bring about great change that would upset the music industry's status quo and how music was created, recorded, marketed, and disseminated.

References

"AC/DC." Rocknet Radio. Accessed July 24, 2019. https://rocknetradio.ml/artist/ac-dc/.

"Biography." The Police. https://www.thepolice.com/biography.

"Bon Jovi: Charts & Awards—*Billboard* Albums." AllMusic. Accessed November 10, 2018. https://www.allmusic.com/artist/bon-jovi-mn0000069534/awards.

Buchanan, Brett. "Kurt Cobain's Daughter Reveals Bizarre Michael Stipe Video." Alternative Nation, May 29, 2019. https://www.alternativenation.net/kurt-cobain-daughter-reveals-bizarre-michael-stipe-video/.

Caufield, Keith. "Beastie Boys—Chart History." *Billboard*, May 4, 2012. https://www.billboard.com/articles/news/489107/beastie-boys-blazed-billboard-chart-history.

Coscarelli, Joe. "Bon Jovi Leads 2018 Rock & Roll Hall of Fame Inductees: 'It's About Time'." *New York Times*, December 13, 2017. https://www.nytimes.com/2017/12/13/arts/music/rock-roll-hall-fame-bon-jovi-nina-simone-cars.html.

Farm Aid. "Annual Report." Accessed October 15, 2018. https://www.farmaid.org/about-us/annual-report/.

Forde, Ian. "Bruce Springsteen Still Shows Who's Boss." *Irish Examiner*, July 13, 2013. https://www.irishexaminer.com/lifestyle/artsfilmtv/music/bruce-springsteen-still-shows-whos-boss-200576.html.

Grein, Paul. "Remembering Michael Jacksons Record-Setting Music Career." Grammy, May 15, 2017. https://www.grammy.com/grammys/news/remembering-michael-jacksons-record-setting-music-career.

Hamill, Laura. "The Best-Selling Female Artists of All Time." Decluttr, September 8, 2018. https://www.decluttr.com/blog/2018/08/09/the-best-selling-female-artists-of-all-time/.

Hartmann, Graham. "Metallica's *Master of Puppets* Selected for Preservation by the Library of Congress." Loudwire, March 23, 2016. https://loudwire.com/metallica-master-of-puppets-preservation-u-s-library-of-congress/.

Hilton, Robin. "R.E.M. Calls It A Day, Announces Breakup." NPR, September 21, 2011. https://www.npr.org/sections/allsongs/2011/09/21/140670548/r-e-m-calls-it-a-day-announce-breakup.

Huey, Steve. "The Jackson 5: Biography & History." Allmusic. Accessed November 28, 2018. https://www.allmusic.com/artist/the-jackson-5-mn0000083013/biographyAllMusic.

Kaufman, Gil. "The Michael Jackson Estates Billion-Dollar Turnaround: From $500 Million in Debt to $500 Million in Cash." *Billboard*, March 15, 2016. https://www.billboard.com/articles/business/7262698/michael-jackson-estate-billion-dollar-turnaround-sony-atv.

Mason, Anthony. "U2: What They're Still Looking For." CBS News, May 24, 2015. https://www.cbsnews.com/news/u2-what-theyre-still-looking-for.

"Michael Jackson's Best-Selling Studio Albums." *The Telegraph*, June 26, 2009. https://www.telegraph.co.uk/culture/music/michael-jackson/5648176/Michael-Jacksons-best-selling-studio-albums.html.

"Mira Parkes Speak with Mikey Craig." The Soul Survivors Magazine. Accessed November 18, 2018. http://btpubs.co.uk/publication/?i=516603&article_id=3155634&view=articleBrowser&ver=html5#{"issue_id":516603,"view":"articleBrowser","article_id":"3155634"}.

Palladev, George. "Afrika Bambaataa + Kraftwerk = Planet Rock, Electrofunk & Techno. Story Behind Legendary Rip-Off." Medium, July 30, 2017. https://medium.com/12edit/afrikaa-bambaataa-kraftwerk-planet-rock-879769d440f4.

"Prince Awards and Nominations." Princevault. Accessed November 18, 2018. https://www.princevault.com/index.php?title=Awards_Won.

RIAA. "Gold & Platinum." Accessed November 16, 2019. https://www.riaa.com/gold-platinum/?tab_active=awards_by_artist#search_section.

United States Senate. "Record Labeling: Hearing Before the Committee on Commerce, Science, and Transportation." United States Senate, Ninety-Ninth Congress, First Session on Contents of Music and the Lyrics of Records, 1985. Accessed December 1, 2018. https://babel.hathitrust.org/cgi/pt?id=mdp.39015011009050&view=1up&seq=5.

Unterberger, Andrew, and Ed Christman. "How Michael Jackson's 'Bad Became the First Album to Notch Five *Billboard* Hot 100 No. 1s." *Billboard*, August 31, 2017. https://www.billboard.com/articles/columns/pop/7948954/michael-jackson-bad-hot-100-five-number-one-hits.

Weiderhorn, Jon. "32 Year Ago: Guns N' Roses Releases *Appetite for Destruction*." Loudwire, July 21, 2019. https://loudwire.com/guns-n-roses-appetite-for-destruction-album-anniversary/.

Figure Credits

IMG. 7.1: Source: https://en.wikipedia.org/wiki/File:Parental_Advistory_Logo_(old).png.

Fig. 7.1: Source: https://commons.wikimedia.org/wiki/File:MTV_Logo_2010.svg.

& PEACE
IN
WEST & EAST
Tes
West

CHAPTER

8

The 1990s

Historical Context for the Decade

The 1990s brought great changes throughout the world. The fall of the Berlin Wall in 1989 ended the separation of East and West Germany, divided at the end of World War II. The Berlin Wall became a physical and philosophical divide between capitalist Western Europe and Soviet Union–dominated Eastern Europe. President Ronald Reagan's famous speech at the Berlin Wall in June 1987 reflected the shift in politics within the Soviet Union. Soviet Premier Mikhail Gorbachev was seeking greater cooperation with the West. Reagan's speech included the line: "General Secretary Gorbachev, if you seek peace, if you seek prosperity for the Soviet Union and Eastern Europe, if you seek liberalization, come here to this gate. Mr. Gorbachev, open this gate. Mr. Gorbachev, tear down this wall!" (Rafferty n.d.). Within the next couple of years, the Soviet Union itself would break apart into many smaller countries. The Cold War, which had dominated American national security since the end of World War II and had American schoolchildren practicing nuclear bomb drills, would end. Although it would eventually be replaced with a new fear, a non-state-sponsored form of terrorism, this marked a fundamental shift in the political hierarchy of the world.

The George H. W. Bush (Reagan's successor) presidency of 1989–1993 would be followed by the two-term presidency of Bill Clinton (1993–2001). Pressure from around the world would lead to an end of the practice of apartheid (separation of races) in South Africa. The Internet would become commercially viable in the 1990s, and cell phones would change the way we communicate. MTV would begin to add programming that would move away from the music video, incorporating scripted and reality television shows. By the end of the 1990s, MTV ran an average of eight hours of music videos per day. That number has continued to shrink to about three hours per day in 2016 ("The Fall Of 'TRL'" 2008). The audience was changing, and MTV needed to change with that audience. By the end of the decade, Napster would allow users to share digital copies of music free of charge, changing the way we consumed music forever.

Music is a reflection of society as a whole, and music would reflect the above changes and be changed itself by the events of history. The 1990s brought a new era in rock and roll. While some of the artists and bands from the 1980s continued to have success (e.g., Bon Jovi, Van Halen, Metallica), the popular music charts were changing to reflect the continued broadening of pop music. Although always somewhat broad in scope, the very definition of what rock was would change in the 1990s. Could rock and roll include rap and hip hop? Could it include country music? These changes would forever alter the way record companies would market music.

Is it important to remember that popular music is music that is mass-produced, disseminated, and consumed by a large segment of the population during any given period or era. The term was never meant to define a style of music. The recording industry, however, has always used the term "pop" to describe a certain style of music geared to a certain audience. This would become increasingly difficult for record companies in the 1990s and beyond.

Women dominated the record charts in the 1990s in a way not seen previously. Although the girl groups of the early 1960s had great success, the female artists of the 1990s would top almost every category for record sales and overall popularity. A new "girl power" movement occurred in music, empowering girls and women and leading the way to what would later become the "Me Too" movement. The pop music charts, previously ruled by mainstream rock acts, would now also include country music. Like the domination by female artists, country music had a place in rock and roll, but what had previously been an occasional crossover hit by someone like Kenny Rogers in the 1970s or 1980s would become the norm in the 1990s. By the end of the decade and into the 2000s, the entire industry would change to adapt to the wide-open, diverse listening audiences around the world. Like the Berlin Wall, the walls of the charts would fall, and the recording industry's ability to dictate our listening habits would begin to lose its dominant power. One of the last major genres to have great independent success on the charts in the old system of creating hits was grunge.

Grunge

Grunge was a music style influenced by heavy metal, punk, and alternative rock. It emerged in the Pacific Northwest in the late 1980s. Seattle, Washington, became the musical center of the grunge sound. Grunge, like many music styles, was a reaction to the complex music created in the 1980s. That era of synthesized dance music, highly orchestrated pop, and glam-centered heavy metal was ready for a reaction from a younger audience. As mentioned earlier in this text, music is cyclical and will always build up in instrumentation and complexity over a period of years or decades. The reaction, however, will be swift and will always take music back to the simplest common cores of rock—the guitar, voice, and drums. Grunge music most often included distorted guitar sounds, a heavy bass line, loud drums, and a vocalist. Although this was also the recipe for heavy metal and punk in previous generations, grunge would differ in its approach and attitude. The lyrics of grunge were often angst-filled, lacking the bravado and anger of heavy metal and punk, instead focusing on alienation and apathy. Grunge was less about railing against authority and more about feeling confined by society as a whole. While grunge did not dominate the charts to the same degree that many other subgenres did in the 1990s, and most of the bands were gone before the end of the decade, it would go on to influence many styles that did continue into the new millennium.

The musical direction of grunge came from the melding of up-tempo punk with the slower heavy sounds of 1970s heavy metal. One way grunge is often described is that the songs contain reflective and introspective, quiet verses combined with louder, angrier metal choruses. This stereotype, however, does not describe all grunge music. The term "grunge" is used in three ways to describe the subculture. First, it describes how the musicians looked, often wearing flannel shirts and having long, unkempt hair. It also describes the distorted guitar sound, and finally, it describes the attitude of apathy that came through in many of the songs. Unlike most previous guitar rock, grunge often did not live and die by the guitar solo. Rather, many grunge musicians created a more ensemble-based sound, working off grooves and avoiding the virtuosity of the solo. Two of the biggest bands to emerge with this sound from the Seattle area were Nirvana and Pearl Jam.

Nirvana

Comprising vocalist and guitarist Kurt Cobain (1967–1994), bassist Krist Novoselic (born 1965), and drummer Dave Grohl (born 1969), Nirvana hit it big with their 1991 album *Nevermind* and their first single "Smells Like Teen Spirit." Cobain quickly became the spokesperson for this new subculture and the voice of the new generation known as Generation X. His cynical, disaffected attitude reflected the dissatisfaction and confusion this generation often felt. Cobain was not comfortable with his role as spokesperson and his newfound fame. Cobain suffered from heroin addiction and depression, and he committed suicide in 1994, effectively ending the career of the band. The song "Lithium" from *Nevermind* is a great example of grunge. The disaffected lyrics of the quiet verses are met with a sudden wail of guitars in the chorus, taking the songs from introspection to forceful extroversion.

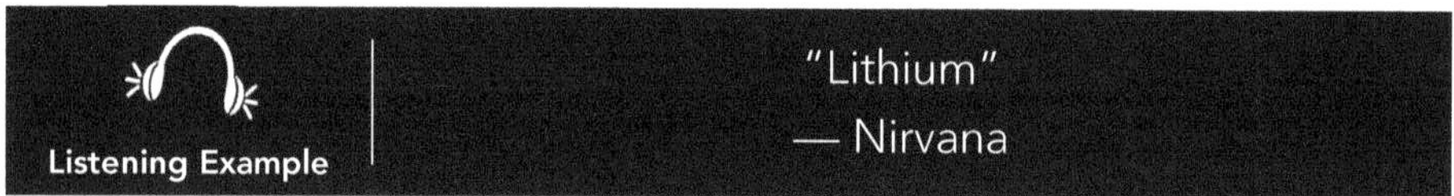

Pearl Jam

Pearl Jam was formed in Seattle, Washington, in 1990 by vocalist Eddie Vedder, lead guitarist Mike McCready, rhythm guitarist Stone Gossard, and bassist Jeff Ament. Their most current drummer is Matt Cameron. Pearl Jam, unlike Nirvana, has had a long career as a band with great chart success. They have sold more than 85 million records worldwide (RIAA 2018). Eddie Vedder's voice became the most recognizable and often imitated voice in all of rock music from the 1990s. In 1991, they recorded their debut album *Ten*. The hit singles "Evenflow," "Jeremy," and "Alive" were all representative of the dark material on the album, dealing with suicide, loneliness, and even homelessness. The lyrics for "Jeremy" were created from a true story about a student who ended his life in front of his classmates.

Country Music and Its Assimilation into Rock

Country music has always influenced rock and roll. In the early 1950s, Hank Williams (1923–1953) had unprecedented success on the *Billboard* country and western charts, scoring 35 Top 10 singles from 1947–1953. While country and western music (as it was then called) was quite different than the country music that would dominate the charts in the 1990s, Williams, considered one of the greatest artists of the 20th century, would influence many rock artists, including Elvis Presley, Jerry Lee Lewis, the Rolling Stones, and the Beatles. His influence is considered so important to rock and roll that he was inducted into the Rock and Roll Hall of Fame in 1987. Country music would continue to influence rock and roll through the rockabilly music of Sun Records in the 1950s. Country music had a much greater influence on Chuck Berry than did the blues or gospel. The great confusion that occurred when Presley and Berry first hit the scene in 1956 was due to the country music sound in Berry's "Maybelline" and the hybrid country and blues sound Presley created.

The true assimilation of country and rock would begin with Kenny Rogers in the 1970s and early 1980s. His songs "Lady" (written by Lionel Richie of the Commodores) and "Islands in the Stream" (written by Barry Gibb of the Bee Gees) were both mainstream pop hits. Many of his more traditional country hits were also incredibly pop radio friendly. "Islands in the Stream" topped the *Billboard* Hot 100 as well as the *Billboard* country and adult contemporary charts. This success began to break down barriers. The ability of country songs to cross over to the pop charts would continue through the 1980s but would reach its peak in the 1990s, beginning with Garth Brooks.

Garth Brooks

Garth Brooks (born 1962) became hugely popular in the 1990s based on his ability to integrate country music and rock and roll. Having sold more than 170 million records worldwide, Brooks is the best-selling solo artist in the United States, with only the Beatles having sold more records (Betts 2015). He won the American Music Award for best solo artist of the 1990s. Though Brooks decided to record country music early in his career, he also listed pop singer-songwriters Dan Fogelberg, James Taylor, Billy Joel, and Bruce Springsteen as his favorite musicians. One of Brooks's biggest hits was "Shameless," a cover of a 1986 Billy Joel recording. Brooks even sang a duet with Kiss on a re-recording of their hit "Hard Luck Woman." Like Rogers before him, Brooks borrowed heavily from the mainstream rock world, and the effect on both the country and pop charts was staggering. Brooks's success opened the eyes of many rock fans who had previously ignored

FIGURE 8.1 Garth Brooks

or been resistant to country music. Throughout this text, previously limited styles of music have joined the mainstream due to adopting elements from a more popular form. For the first time, album sales in the 1990s would be full of these crossover artists. The lines became blurred. Was it country? Was it rock? The answer to both questions was yes.

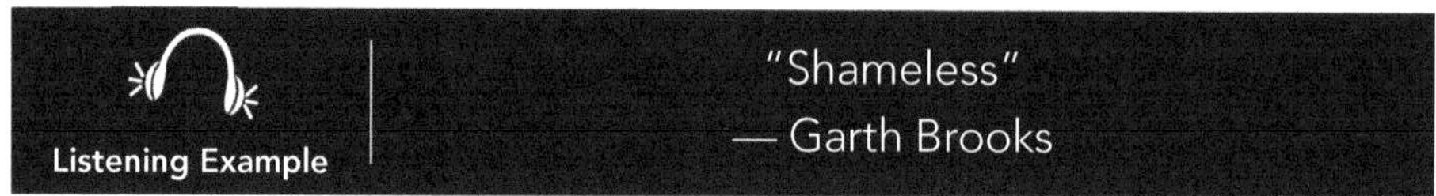

Many other artists had great success in 1990s country music, including Alan Jackson, George Strait, and Brooks & Dunn. Many female country artists had platinum albums in the 1990s, including Reba McEntire, LeAnn Rimes, Mary Chapin Carpenter, and Faith Hill. Shania Twain, however, became the biggest-selling female country artist of the decade and the biggest crossover success.

Shania Twain

Shania Twain (born 1965) is a Canadian singer who is the best-selling female artist in country music history. She has sold more than 100 million records and is the only female artist to have three consecutive albums achieve diamond status (10 million units sold; Pruett n.d.) Her 1997 album *Come on Over* is the highest-selling album by any female artist ever, moving more than 40 million copies. "Man! I Feel Like a Woman" became a girl power anthem, representative of the new female empowerment movement that began in the decade. "You're Still the One" became one of the biggest love songs of the decade and one of the most popular wedding songs of the past 20 years.

The success of Shania Twain would be representative of the domination of the pop charts by women. While this movement was indicative of the beginnings of a female empowerment movement that would continue through the "Me Too" movement 20 years later, the success of female artists would also help to advance women's rights moving forward. The success on the record charts of women in the 1990s would represent the decade with the greatest record sales overall, and female artists would dominate mainstream rock, contemporary rhythm and blues (R&B), singer-songwriters, and adult contemporary charts. The greatest-selling mainstream rock album of the decade was by Canadian singer Alanis Morissette.

Notable Female Singer-Songwriters and Solo Artists of the 1990s

Alanis Morissette

Alanis Morissette (born 1974) released two dance pop albums in the early 1990s but achieved fame with *Jagged Little Pill*, released in 1995. The album, labeled alt-rock or grunge, has sold more than 33 million copies worldwide (Barclay, Jack, and Schneider 2011). The angst and aggression fit perfectly at a time when grunge was beginning to wane and other female successes in music tended toward R&B and country. It won five Grammy Awards in 1995, including Album of the Year ("38th Grammy Awards" n.d.) The song "You Oughta Know" is an angry song directed at a former lover who has someone new. Its raw sexual lyrics were in tune with the new norms developing in feminism. Morissette's look and the aggressive sound of the album appealed to women who no longer identified with the packaged pop stars of the past.

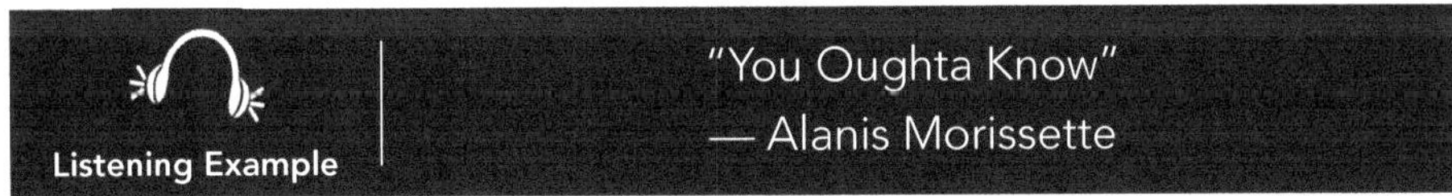

Morissette's success would be mirrored throughout pop music and the girl power movement of the 1990s. One British pop group that adopted the term "girl power" would have great success in the decade.

The Spice Girls

The Spice Girls formed in 1994, and their first single, "Wannabe," reached number one in 37 countries in 1996 ("Hall of Fame—Spice Girls!" n.d.) Their debut album, *Spice*, is the biggest-selling album by a female group in pop history. The nicknames of the five members of the group (Posh, Ginger, Baby, Sporty, and Scary) became iconic during the decade. The message of empowerment for preteens, teens, and young women moved female equality forward in the decade and created an easy entrance into feminism for young girls and women. The song "Wannabe" sells this message of female solidarity.

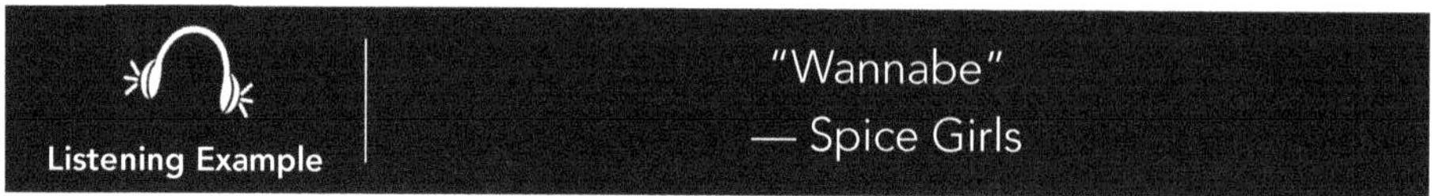

The success of female artists would not be limited to any one style of music. The singer-songwriter had a resurgence in the 1990s, and the most notable of these were female artists. Sarah McLachlan, another Canadian singer-songwriter, would have great success, singing emotional ballads and cofounding Lilith Fair in 1997. Her album of that year, *Surfacing,* included the hit song "Angel," dedicated to those who died from drug overdoses. It became an international hit, and she became one of the feminist leaders of music. Lilith Fair, a concert tour in the late 1990s, was all female and promoted feminist causes. It began as a reaction to the male-dominated music industry, from record companies to radio stations that refused to play more than one female-created song in a row. The tour from 1997 to 1999 became one of the highest-grossing tours of each of those summers, featuring Suzanne Vega, Paula Cole, Indigo Girls, and Sheryl Crow (Freydkin 1998). Crow's 1994 song "All I Wanna Do" became a smash hit, and her album *Tuesday Night Music Club* went on to sell more than seven million copies. In 1995, the album won Crow three Grammy Awards, for record of the year, best new artist, and best female vocal performance (Recording Academy n.d.). Other female singer-songwriters would have great success in the decade, including Nora Jones, Jewel, Tori Amos, and Fiona Apple.

Celine Dion

Dion (born 1968) was born in French-speaking Quebec, Canada, and released a series of successful French-language albums during her teen years in Canada. She began releasing English-language records in the early 1990s. Her 1996 album *Falling Into You* and her 1997 album *Let's Talk About Love* were both certified diamond in the United States. She is the best-selling Canadian artist of all time and has sold more than 250 million records around the world ("Celine Dion" 2019). Her song "My Heart Will Go On" from the soundtrack of the movie *Titanic* is one of the most popular singles of the decade.

Whitney Houston

Whitney Houston (1963–2012) is considered one of the greatest female voices of the 20th century and is in the Guinness Book of World records as the most awarded female artist of all time (Sony Music Entertainment n.d.). She was one of three female voices of the contemporary R&B scene that became most recognizable and had the greatest success in the 1990s.

Houston's success began in the mid-1980s, when she had seven consecutive number one singles from 1985 to 1988. Her success continued in the 1990s with her acting debut in the romantic drama *The Bodyguard*. The soundtrack to the film, for which Houston recorded seven songs, is one of the best-selling soundtrack albums of all time. "I Will Always Love You," recorded for the soundtrack, became the best-selling single by a woman in music history and the fifth-best-selling single of all time (Kaufman 2012). Houston's gospel-infused style came naturally. Her mother (Cissy Houston) is a well-known gospel musician. Her cousin is pop singer Dionne Warwick, and her godmother is Darlene Love. Her phenomenal voice and model-like looks made her videos perfect for MTV and her music popular with almost all audiences. In the 2000s, her career began to suffer, and there were rumors of drug use. Unfortunately, she passed away in 2012 from a heart attack brought on by drug use. Her performances are considered some of the greatest of the 20th century.

FIGURE 8.2 Whitney Houston

Listening Example | "I Will Always Love You" — Whitney Houston

Mariah Carey

Another great voice from the decade is Mariah Carey. Carey (born 1970) became the voice of the 1990s, selling more records than any other artist during that decade. Her albums dominated the charts in the 1990s, and she has sold in excess of 200 million records worldwide. She has had 18 number one singles in the United States, more than any other solo artist ("Mariah Carey" 2017). She is the third-best-selling female artist in U.S. history, trailing only Madonna and Barbra Streisand. In "Someday," you can hear the great range of Carey's voice.

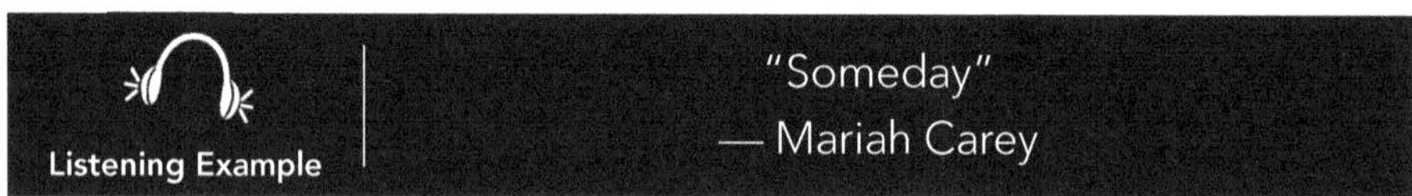

Janet Jackson

The Jackson family, known for the careers of the Jackson 5 and later, Michael Jackson, also produced a great female artist. Janet Jackson (born 1966), the youngest child of the Jackson family, began her career as an actress in the 1970s and early 1980s before her rise to fame as a singer with the 1986 album *Control*. Jackson's success continued and increased in the 1990s. As her lyrics matured, so did her popularity, and she became a role model for teenage girls across the country. Her 1990s albums were more provocative, and her videos and live tours brought changes in choreography and fashion not seen since her older brother had dominated the 1980s. Her famous performance at the Super Bowl XXXVIII halftime show with Justin Timberlake was controversial, as their choreography involved the famous "wardrobe malfunction." Her next album's sales suffered from the backlash to the Super Bowl performance. Although not having the success of Whitney Houston or Mariah Carey in the 1990s, Jackson's career has been more even, and she has continued to release new songs and albums into the 21st century and toured as recently as 2018.

FIGURE 8.3 Janet on Unbreakable Tour

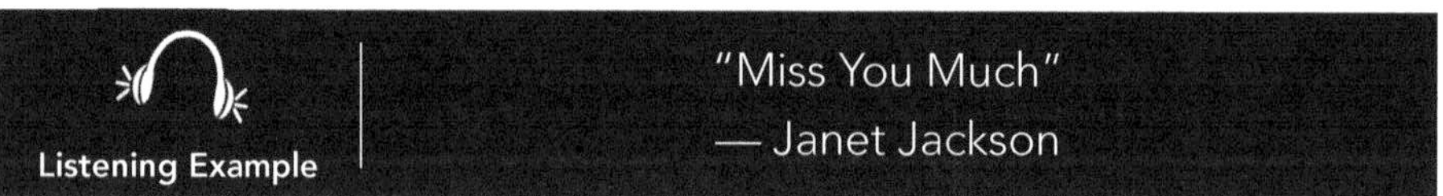

Boy Bands

FIGURE 8.4 Backstreet Boys

Although women were incredibly dominant in the music scene of the 1990s, "boy bands" also were important. Backstreet Boys was formed in Orlando, Florida, in 1993. The prefab construction of the group brought critical scorn, but the fans loved the band. Backstreet Boys, much like the Spice Girls and New Kids on the Block, was formed in response to an open call for auditions in a newspaper. Lou Pearlman named the group after an outdoor market in Orlando. They toured throughout the next two years before receiving a record contract. The group first recorded in Sweden and had success in Europe before releasing their debut album, *Backstreet Boys,* in 1996. Their first single reached number one in Germany. It took another year for the group to break through in the United States. Once it did, its rise was meteoric. In 1997, "Quit Playing Games with My Heart" became a number two hit in the United States. The third album by the group, 1999's *Millennium*, entered the charts at number one and sold more than one million copies in its first week. The album became the best-selling album of 1999 (Lynch 2016). Backstreet Boys would become the most popular boy band in U.S. history and has continued to tour and release records well into the 21st century. In 2011, New Kids on the Block and Backstreet Boys co-headlined a tour. Lou Pearlman would form another group, NSYNC, in 1996. While they only continued until 2002, they sold more than 30 million records. One of the band members, Justin Timberlake, went on to become one of the best-selling music artists of the 2000s.

Rap and Hip Hop in the 1990s

By the 1990s, rap had begun to undergo changes, as will happen to any music form after a decade of success. The wider varieties of rap from the late 1980s still rarely received much airplay, even though *Yo! MTV Raps* became one of MTV's highest-rated shows.

The show ran from 1988 until 1995 but was hugely popular from 1989 through 1992. As rap evolved, one of the new stories of the genre centered on the battle between East Coast and West Coast rap. While West Coast rap, based out of Los Angeles, included the gangsta rap of Dr. Dre (formerly of N.W.A.), Snoop Doggy Dogg, and Tupac Shakur, the New York City–based East Coast rap was represented by Notorious B.I.G., Nas, and De La Soul. West Coast rap was based around the violence in the community and was often negative toward the way the police dealt with that violence and the citizens they protected. The rivalry between East and West Coast rap became more than a war of words. Within one year, both Tupac Shakur and Notorious B.I.G. were murdered. Neither killer had been caught by 2018, and some believed the deaths were a product of the rivalry. Rap and hip hop would continue to change throughout the 1990s, leading toward the success of Eminem and Gnarls Barkley in the 2000s.

Many other styles of music from the 1990s came into existence by fusing two established subgenres. Rap and metal music could be combined (Cypress Hill), and pop and punk could work well together (Green Day). Progressive rock continued with the success of Radiohead. Punk and reggae styles would once again come together with the Mighty Mighty Bosstones, No Doubt, and Sublime all having success with the ska-punk style. Hootie and the Blowfish would have one of the biggest albums of the decade with *Cracked Rear View,* capitalizing on the ever-present need for roots/mainstream rock in the tradition of John Mellencamp and Tom Petty. Metallica continued its prominence with its 1990 self-titled album. House and techno dance music gained prominence during the 1990s, and newer forms like rave and trip hop would continue to evolve. Hip hop and soul influences, under the banner of neo-soul, combined on albums by Lauryn Hill and Erykah Badu. *The Miseducation of Lauryn Hill* (1998) sold 19 million copies worldwide and won Hill five Grammy Awards (Rosenberg 2017).

It is impossible to cover every nuance of the musical changes that occurred in the 1990s. While country and a dominance by female artists became two of the biggest stories about 1990s music, moving forward toward the new millennium in rock and roll caused the field to grow, and the divisions between subgenres of rock continued to become more cloudy. The ability to create, market, and consume music with less influence from large record companies would lead to a vast number of choices too great to consume. Our ability to purchase music on our cell phones without ever leaving our homes would completely change how the music industry would operate. As we approached the new millennium, everything would change, but great rock and roll would continue.

References

"38th Grammy Awards." Rock on the Net. Accessed December 7, 2018. http://www.rockonthenet.com/archive/1996/grammys.htm.

Barclay, Michael, Ian A. D. Jack, and Jason Schneider. *Have Not Been the Same: The Canrock Renaissance 1985–1995*, 10th anniversary ed. ECW Press, 2011.

Betts, Stephen L. "Garth Brooks Surpasses Elvis Presley in Album Sales … Again." *Rolling Stone*, January 13, 2015. https://www.rollingstone.com/music/music-country/garth-brooks-surpasses-elvis-presley-in-album-sales-again-79447/.

"Celine Dion." Canadian Tire Center. Accessed July 24, 2019. http://www.canadiantirecentre.com/event/celine-dion/.

"Fall of 'TRL' and the Rise of Internet Video, The." NPR, November 12, 2008. https://www.npr.org/templates/story/story.php?storyId=96869060.

Freydkin, Donna. "Lilith Fair: Lovely, Lively and Long Overdue." CNN, July 28, 1998. http://www.cnn.com/SHOWBIZ/Music/9807/28/lilith.fair/.

"Hall of Fame—Spice Girls!" Upbeat Radio. Accessed December 5, 2018. https://upbeatradio.net/v3/News.Article?article=869.

Kaufman, Gil. "Whitney Houston's Musical Legacy, By The Numbers." MTV Networks, February 12, 2012. http://www.mtv.com/news/1679039/whitney-houston-musical-legacy/.

Lynch, John. "The Biggest Hit Album the Year You Were Born." *Business Insider*, January 26, 2016. https://www.businessinsider.com/best-selling-albums-by-year-2016-6.

"Mariah Carey." Rock Mafia. Last modified 2017. http://rockmafia.com/mariah-carey/.

Pruett, David B. "Shania Twain." Grove Music Online. https://www.oxfordmusiconline.com/grovemusic/abstract/10.1093/gmo/9781561592630.001.0001/omo-9781561592630-e-1002258563?_start=1&pos=1&q=shania%20twain&search=quick#firsthit.

Rafferty, John P. "Mr. Gorbachev, Tear Down This Wall!: Reagan's Berlin Speech." *Encyclopaedia Britannica*. Accessed December 6, 2018. https://www.britannica.com/story/mr-gorbachev-tear-down-this-wall-reagans-berlin-speech.

Recording Academy. "Sheryl Crow." Grammy.com. Accessed December 4, 2018. https://www.grammy.com/grammys/artists/sheryl-crow.

RIAA. "Gold and Platinum." Accessed December 5, 2018. https://www.riaa.com/gold-platinum/?tab_active=top_tallies&ttt=TAA#search_section.

Rosenberg, Sari. "November 14, 1998: Lauryn Hill's Doo Wop (That Thing)' Debuted at No. 1." Lifetime, November 14, 2017. https://www.mylifetime.com/she-did-that/november-14-1998-lauryn-hills-doo-wop-that-thing-debuted-at-no-1.

Sony Music Entertainment. "Whitney Houston." Accessed July 24, 2019. https://www.whitneyhouston.com/awards/.

Figure Credits

IMG. 8.1: Copyright © by Lear 21 (CC-BY-SA 3.0) at https://commons.wikimedia.org/wiki/File:West_and_East_Germans_at_the_Brandenburg_Gate_in_1989.jpg.

Fig. 8.1: Copyright © by John Mathew Smith and www.celebrity-photos.com (CC BY-SA 2.0) at https://commons.wikimedia.org/wiki/File:Garth_Brooks_1.jpg.

Fig. 8.2: Source: https://commons.wikimedia.org/wiki/File:Whitney_Houston_Welcome_Home_Heroes_1_cropped.jpg.

Fig. 8.3: Copyright © by Rich Esteban (CC BY-SA 4.0) at https://commons.wikimedia.org/wiki/File:JanetJacksonUnbreakableTourSanFran2015.jpg.

Fig. 8.4: Copyright © by Krystaleen (CC BY-SA 3.0) at https://commons.wikimedia.org/wiki/File:BSB_Old_Navy_Performance.jpg.

CHAPTER

9 The 2000s

Historical Context for the Decade

Advances in technology meant the decade that began the new millennium greatly changed how we create and consume rock music. The record industry changed in every possible way, from the ways artists composed music, to the ways music was marketed and distributed, to the ways music was purchased, to even the forms of the music itself.

In 2000, George W. Bush was elected president of the United States. On September 11, 2001, terrorists hijacked four jetliners and crashed three of them into buildings, two in New York City at the World Trade Center Towers and one into the Pentagon building in Washington, D.C.. The fourth plane was intended to fly into the U.S. Capitol building but instead crashed into a field in southwest Pennsylvania when passengers attempted to regain control of the plane. This terrorist attack on U.S. soil was unprecedented and changed the way the United States would conduct security. The attack also changed the entertainment industry. Movie content was often altered if the film involved an airplane crash or had images of the World Trade Center. Songs that were critical of the government or the police were removed or altered by several bands on new albums released in the days and weeks after the attacks. While the U.S. government imposed no such censorship, public sentiment would not have accepted criticism at the time. Songs that expressed patriotism, such as "God Bless the U.S.A." by Lee Greenwood and the national anthem as performed by Whitney Houston, were played in heavy rotation on radio stations.

FIGURE 9.1

The historic election of Barack Obama, the first African American to hold the office of president, occurred in 2008. This election in many ways mirrored the changing face of American society. Minority groups such as African Americans and Hispanic Americans increased in both population and power in the United States political system. American society, always cautious when dealing with change, became increasingly accepting of many new diverse points of view while simultaneously becoming less accepting of Arab Americans, who were mislabeled as terrorists due to the 9/11 attacks. During the decade, we lost many important musicians from rock and roll, including George Harrison from the Beatles (2001), Ray Charles (2004), and Michael Jackson (2009).

Technology in the New Millennium

New technology dominated the new millennium and changed the music industry. By the beginning of the new millennium, record sales peaked, and the record industry quickly began to lose money as album sales plummeted. In fact, the record industry would lose over 50% of its earnings by 2010 (Goldman 2010). The perfect storm responsible for this recession in the industry was new technology that enabled digital downloading.

In 1999, Napster, created by college freshman Shawn Fanning, was released for the first time, allowing users to share music by downloading mp3s. By 2001, Napster had 80 million users (Gowan 2002). Apple's iTunes followed in 2001. While these early sites existed to allow users to share files free of charge, lawsuits would eventually force the sites to collect licensing fees from users, either in the form of a subscription fee or a per-song and/or album fee. Though the ways we listened to music had changed over the years (e.g., LP, cassette, CD), the ability to download one song directly to a computer forced change in the music industry. While record companies chose to blame their losses on illegal downloading and sharing of digitized music, the problem was far more complex. The new technology allowed access to so much music that lengthy trends or dominant genres in music became things of the past. This led to difficulties in marketing new music. In addition, the record companies could no longer rely on profits generated by album sales. Album sales had provided most of the profits for record companies, and the companies could no longer rely on selling albums in the same quantities. They needed to find a way to grab some of the profits from these online music platforms, but they focused first on litigation, forcing Napster to go out of business in 2002. By that point, though, several other similar programs existed, and the industry could not stop the new trend. The old order, with record companies controlling every aspect of the creation, production, and distribution of music, was ending. Artists could now record their own music on computer programs (such as Pro Tools) that produced a quality sound not possible in the past without paying for expensive recording studio time. The artist could burn and create artwork for his or her own CDs or bypass the physical form completely for a digital mp3 release. The artist could advertise the music and stream live performances online. While this do-it-yourself style could sometimes lead to a record company contract, at other times it allowed performers to direct their own careers. Indeed, the combination of new technologies, the Internet, search platforms such as Google, and social media platforms, including YouTube, enabled musicians to create, market, and distribute their music without the assistance of a record company. By the end of the decade, Justin Bieber would become incredibly popular by releasing videos on YouTube himself.

From 1999 to 2003, the music industry saw a loss of 25% in sales. By 2010, that loss grew to over 50% (Goldman 2010). Once digital music was easily available and an iPod could store large numbers of songs, users preferred to buy single songs rather than purchase entire albums of material. While the technology has changed, it is interesting to note the pattern that emerged. At rock and roll's beginning, single songs on 45 rpm records outsold albums until 1968. Album sales outsold singles until 2005, when digital downloads surpassed album sales (Vincent 2015). By the 2000s, MTV, which fueled the great success of the recording industry in the 1980s and 1990s, had switched much of its programming to non-musical entertainment and relegated music videos to small blocks of programming time. The Internet and social media also provided the public with a new form of entertainment. Because of listeners' ability to create their own self-programmed radio and find almost any recording on YouTube, the need to purchase music became less vital. Record companies initially were very reactionary to these changes, condemning the new technology rather than collaborating with it. Finally, and most crucially, the teenagers whose disposable income had fueled the record industry since the beginning of rock and roll in the 1950s found new outlets for that income, including cell phones and video games. By the end of the decade, many of the traditional recording studios and record stores, such as Sam Goody and Tower Records, could no longer stay in business. Many record companies failed. What this failure meant, and continues to mean, for consumers, however, is an unlimited choice of music that is accessible 24 hours a day, seven days a week.

Another new addition to the technology of the decade would be the more widespread use of Auto-Tune. Though originally developed to correct the pitch of a singer who was out of tune, it has become a sound effect used by musicians for its unique sound. The use of the technology as a sound effect first became popular with the song "Believe" by Cher in 1998. It has since become one of the go-to special effects for musicians, though some, particularly mainstream, rock bands have derided it for making most pop music sound the same and acting as a sort of Photoshop for the human voice. Love it or hate it, though, Auto-Tune has become so ubiquitous that most professional rock recordings are now using the technology.

The domination of rock and roll radio would also suffer with the changes in the new millennium. Teens in the 2000s listened to far less commercial FM radio, preferring to use Spotify or Pandora, which allow individuals to customize their listening experience. Sirius satellite radio includes stations that focus on only one artist or one narrow subgenre. These new technologies and new ways of listening to music have created smaller and smaller niches in music, rejecting the dominant genres propagated and promoted by powerful record companies in the past.

The Institutional Pop Star Remade for the New Age

During the first decade of the 2000s, several pop stars began their careers due to success on television. This was not a new phenomenon, as we can go back to the 1960s, when the Monkees became a prefabricated rock band for a TV show through open casting calls. Some of the media institutions best known for creating the ready-made pop star of the 2000s were *American Idol*, the Walt Disney Company, and Nickelodeon. The television show *American Idol,* which debuted in 2002, allowed those sitting at home to vote for a specific singer, giving viewers a role in creating the next pop star. Carrie Underwood, Kelly Clarkson, and Adam Lambert all have careers based on their success on *American Idol.* Media conglomerates Disney and Nickelodeon became responsible for creating many pop stars of the decade, including Justin Timberlake, Britney Spears, Christina Aguilera, Miley Cyrus, and Ariana Grande. The television shows these singers starred in as teenagers moved them toward careers as pop music royalty in the 2000s and beyond.

Kelly Clarkson

FIGURE 9.2

One of the most successful artists to emerge from *American Idol* was Kelly Clarkson (born 1982). After winning the inaugural season of *American Idol* in 2002, her single "A Moment Like This" became the biggest-selling single in the U.S. that year. She won two Grammy Awards for her 2004 album *Breakaway* (Recording Academy 2017). One of the singles from that album, "Since U Been Gone," reached number two on the *Billboard* Hot 100 and was listed by *Rolling Stone* magazine as one of the 500 best songs of all time (*Rolling Stone* 2011). It continues the trend of female empowerment songs that first became prominent in the previous decade.

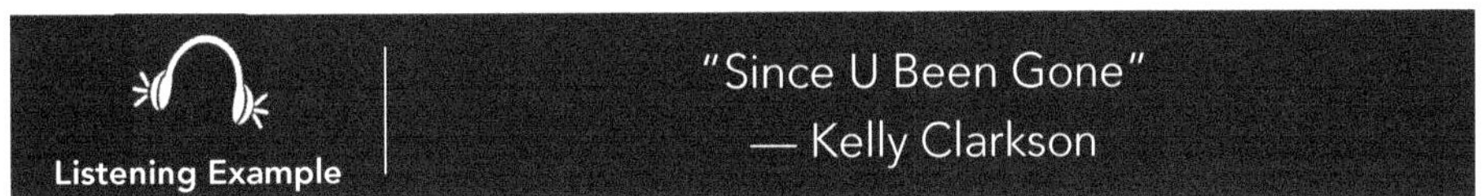

While most *American Idol* winners had fleeting success on the pop charts, Clarkson's fame has continued, and she scored 11 Top 10 songs through 2016. In 2016, she became a children's author, and in 2017, she joined the reality TV show *The Voice* as a judge and voice coach. She is set to begin hosting her own daytime talk show in the fall of 2019 (Hibberd 2018).

Justin Timberlake

FIGURE 9.3

Media giant Disney also introduced many artists who would become popular in the 2000s. Justin Timberlake (born 1981) began his career on *The All New Mickey Mouse Club* and later became even better known as one of the singers in NSYNC, one of the most popular boy bands in the late 1990s. His greatest success would be as a solo artist. He won two Grammy Awards for his debut album *Justified* in 2002, but his worldwide fame would occur with the release of his second album, 2006's *FutureSex/LoveSounds*. It debuted at number one on the *Billboard* album charts and contained three number one singles. This album, critically praised for the songwriting that blended multiple music genres, would influence many other artists. Since he was a singer emerging from a boy band in the '90s, Timberlake's music was initially maligned, but his brilliance as a songwriter, singer, and dancer made him one of the most successful artists of the new millennium. During the height of his career in 2008, he took a four-year break from music to concentrate on acting and had several starring roles in major movies. He has sold over 32 million albums and 56 million singles throughout the world ("Justin Timberlake Returning" 2019).

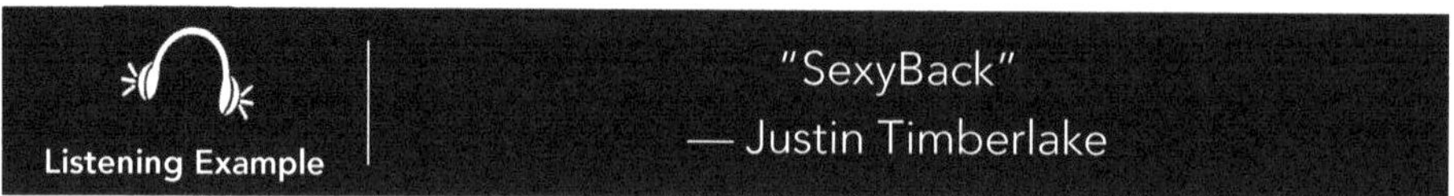

Britney Spears

FIGURE 9.4

Another alumna of the *All New Mickey Mouse Club* was Britney Spears (born 1981). Her first two albums, 1999's *Baby One More Time and* 2000's *Oops! ... I Did It Again,* made her the most successful teen artist of all time. At a time when MTV's success was waning, her videos became enormously popular. She has sold over 150 million albums worldwide and was the best-selling female artist of the 2000s in the United States (Aniftos 2017). Her best-selling single was 1999's "Baby One More Time," a mainstream pop hit with a video that mixed her teen image with up-front sexuality. By the middle of the decade, her sound had evolved to include R&B and electronica. Her success opened up the charts to many more teen pop stars in the 2000s.

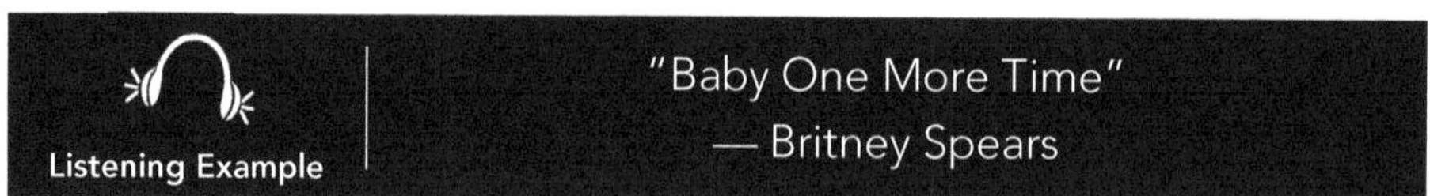

Christina Aguilera

Christina Aguilera (born 1980) was also an alum of *The All New Mickey Mouse Club.* She grew up in a suburb of Pittsburgh, Pennsylvania, and became a local celebrity at age 8 singing the national anthem at local professional baseball and hockey games.

At the age of 10, she was a semifinalist on the national television show *Star Search*. She joined the cast of *The All New Mickey Mouse Club* in 1993. This led to her recording the theme song to the Disney movie *Mulan*, "Reflection," which brought her to the attention of RCA Records. Her first album, released in 1999, went to number one on the *Billboard* album chart and sold over 14 million copies worldwide. Riding the wave of teen pop in the late '90s, her first single, "Genie in a Bottle," went to number one in over 20 countries. She was recognized by *Billboard* as one of the top female artists of all time (Zellner 2018). Her 2003 album *Stripped* is another great example of the wave of girl power–themed music, promoting self-esteem, gender equality, and sexual liberation. Her single "Beautiful" is considered an anthem for the LGBTQ community. Subsequent albums have showed off her vocal range, which includes pop, blues, jazz, and Latin-based forms. Aguilera cites Whitney Houston and R&B singer Etta James as her main influences.

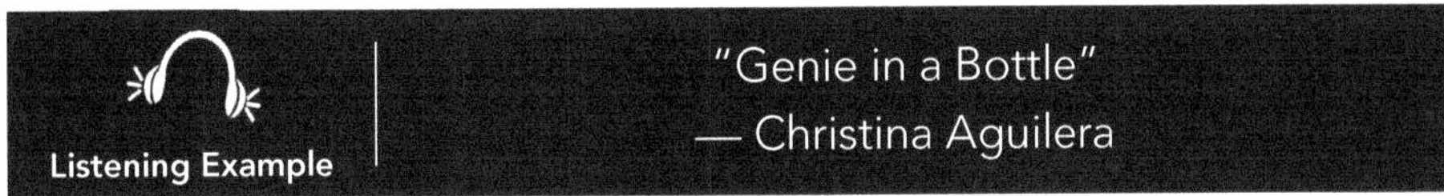

Mainstream Rock in the 2000s

One of the great things about rock and roll is that its musicians will always borrow from one another, and the widespread use of the Internet moved the blending of rock styles to a new high in the 2000s. While descriptive labels such as post-grunge, nu metal, emo, and pop punk were used to describe rock styles in the 2000s, the listener/consumer always should remember that these terms rarely describe what we hear and are used primarily as marketing tools by the industry. The music industry has always believed that if you can brand it, you can sell it. Rather than divide mainstream rock into many subgenres, we will study four bands that had great success during the decade, though some of the bands had begun their careers a decade earlier.

Foo Fighters

Foo Fighters were originally a one-man band formed in Seattle, Washington, in 1994 by former Nirvana drummer Dave Grohl following Nirvana's dissolution in the wake of front man Kurt Cobain's suicide. Grohl had been writing songs on guitar during his time in Nirvana but was intimidated by his respect for Cobain's songs. He eventually formed a band, switching to guitar and vocals full-time. The band included

Chris Shifflet on lead guitar, Taylor Hawkins on drums, and former Nirvana road guitarist Pat Smear. Though their first album was released in 1995, their greatest success came at the end of the decade and leading into the 21st century. While their sound is often referred to as post-grunge, that label may be dictated as much or more by the history of the band members than by the actual music the band produces. Foo Fighters continues to record albums well into the second decade of the 2000s.

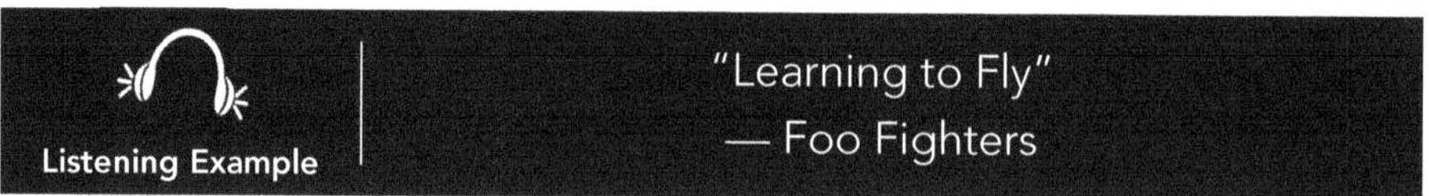

Nickelback

Nickelback is a Canadian rock band formed in 1995. They have sold over 50 million albums worldwide and are ranked as one of the most successful rock acts of the decade by *Billboard* ("Nickelback Named Group" 2009). The band includes singer/guitarist Chad Kroeger, keyboardist Ryan Peake, bassist Mike Kroeger, and drummer Daniel Adair. Their album *Silver Side Up* was released on September 11, 2001, and their best-known song, "How You Remind Me," topped the mainstream, modern, and pop charts, becoming the biggest single of 2002. While the band remained very successful through the remainder of the decade and beyond, their style of rock became one that people would love to hate, considering it too pop oriented. In 2013, *Rolling Stone* magazine readers named Nickelback as the second-worst band of the 1990s, so it should be noted that a band's success and critical appeal do not always seem to coincide (*Rolling Stone* 2013).

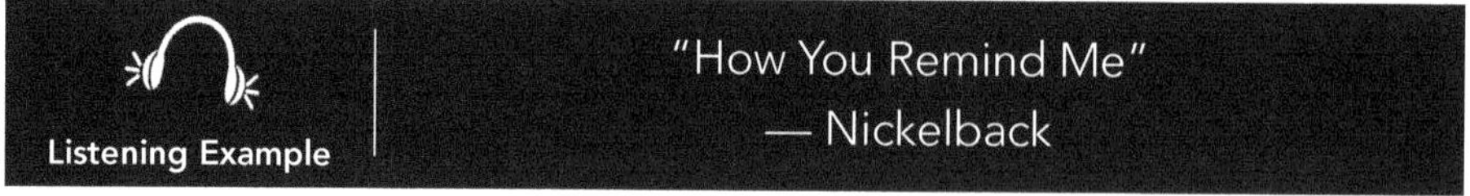

Green Day

Green Day, formed in Berkeley, California, in 1986, originally helped to bring punk rock to the mainstream in a way that never occurred during its original 1970s incarnation. Singer Billie Jo Armstrong, bassist Mike Dirnt, and drummer Tre Cool first achieved success with *Dookie* in 1994. Subsequent releases, though well received, failed to match that success. In 2004, the concept album *American Idiot*, a rock opera, gained a new following among younger fans. The album told the story of a character named Jesus of Suburbia. It represented the disillusionment with the Iraq felt by many younger people and was a direct protest of the George W. Bush presidency and the perception of war as a tool used by greedy corporations to achieve economic success. The album included five singles: "Wake Me Up When September Ends," "Boulevard of Broken Dreams," "Holiday," "American Idiot," and "Jesus of Suburbia." *American Idiot* won the Grammy Award for best rock album in 2005 and has sold over 16 million copies worldwide (Recording Academy 2015). A Broadway show was created based around the concept album, and plans exist for a movie.

FIGURE 9.5

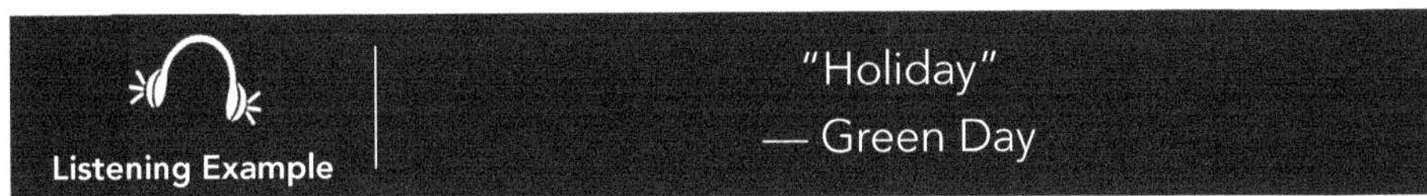

While bands like Green Day fused elements of '70s punk with the pop of the 1990s and 2000s, others were influenced by the grunge movement of the 1990s. While punk first influenced emo, the popular incarnation was more directly a descendant of the grunge attitude of punk-driven music, with a greater use of emotional expression, often citing insecurity, introversion, misanthropy, and, at times, depression. One of the first bands to have great success with this style of music was Jimmy Eat World. Their 2001 release *Bleed American*, later changed to *Jimmy Eat World* following the 2001 World Trade Center attacks, became the first album by an emo band to have great success, selling over two million copies (Payne 2016). The song "The Middle" is about dealing with feeling left out but offers hope that others are feeling the same way.

Other bands had success with similar styles in the 2000s, including Fall Out Boy, Death Cab for Cutie, and Dashboard Confessional. While the subgenre seemed to wane by the end of the decade, there has always been and will always be angst-driven rock for every new generation.

R&B for the New Century

As we read in Chapter 8, R&B, particularly R&B created by female singers, had great popularity in the 1990s as Whitney Houston, Mariah Carey, and many other singers moved the music to mainstream pop status. This trend continued in the 2000s. While Mariah Carey continued her success, new artists Destiny's Child (and later Beyoncé), Alicia Keys, Mary J. Blige, and British singer Amy Winehouse would satisfy the need for soulful singing that never goes out of style.

Destiny's Child

FIGURE 9.6

The song "Survivor" by Destiny's Child also continued the trend of female empowerment that dominated the 1990s. Destiny's Child was formed in 1997 in Houston, Texas. The most popular and final lineup of the group included Beyoncé Knowles, Kelly Rowland, and Michelle Williams. Though the group was only popular for seven years prior to their breakup in 2005, they are considered one of the most successful musical trios of all time, having sold over 60 million records (*Billboard* 2019). Beyoncé would go on to dominate the charts in the late 2000s and through the following decade.

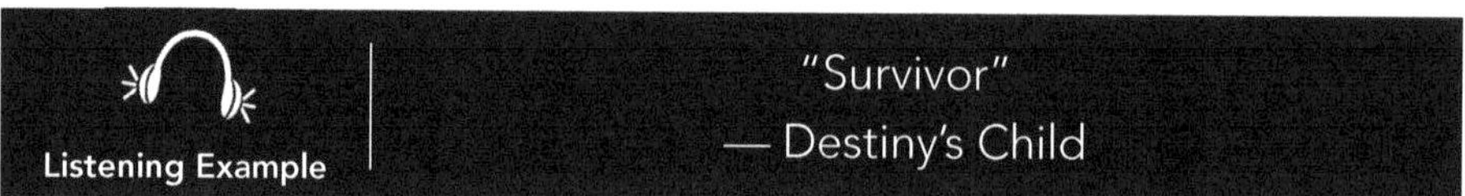

Alicia Keys

Alicia Keys (born 1981) is a classically trained pianist who began composing at the age of 12 and was signed to a major record label at 15. Her gospel-influenced debut album, *Songs in A Minor*, released in 2001 (Martens 2001), earned her five Grammy Awards and sold over 12 million copies (Recording Academy 2019). During her career, she has sold over 30 million albums and was considered one of the greatest R&B artists of the 2000s. She is also a humanitarian, having founded a nonprofit to fight HIV/AIDS.

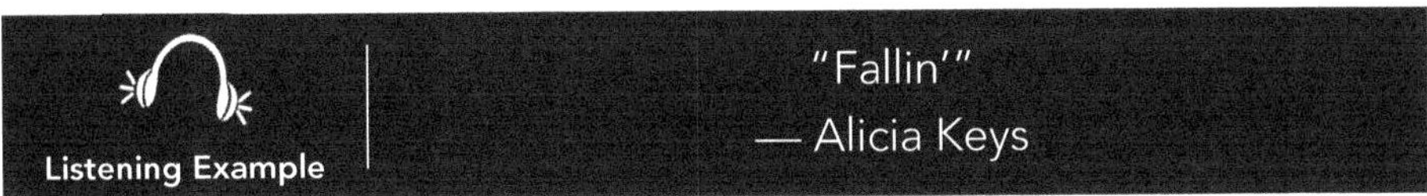

Amy Winehouse

Amy Winehouse (1983–2011) was a British singer and songwriter best known for her alto voice that incorporated soul, rhythm and blues, and jazz. Her second album, *Back to Black*, released in 2006, won five Grammy Awards in 2008, the most ever won by a British woman. The awards included Album of the Year, Record of the Year, and Best New Artist (Leeds 2008). Her short career was marred by poor stage performances due to her struggles with drug and alcohol addiction, bulimia, depression, and performance anxiety. Her last project involved singing a duet with jazz vocalist Tony Bennett. He described her as "a really great jazz singer, a true jazz singer" (*The Daily Show* 2011). Many artists who followed have named her as a great influence on their work. These include Lady Gaga, Bruno Mars, Ellie Goulding, and Sam Smith.

FIGURE 9.7

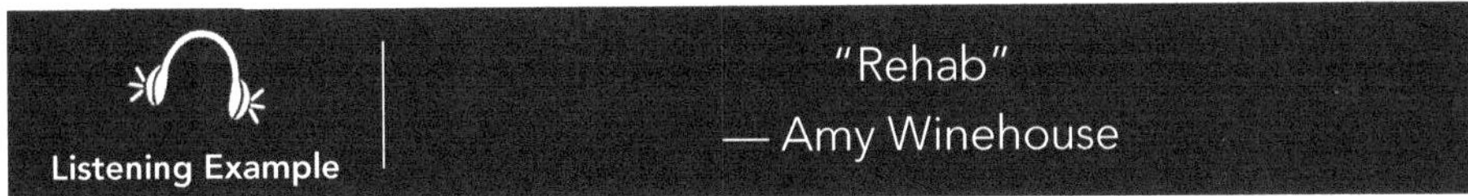

Rap and Hip Hop

Rap and hip hop, like many other music styles in the 2000s, saw a sharp decline in sales. This was in part due to the new varied ways that music was consumed in the decade, including through illegal downloads. Rap, like all other forms of popular music, was now competing with an exploding variety of new music styles, blending new influences and diluting the more mainstream homogenous forms of the past. However, several important changes and new musicians emerged in the new decade to keep rap and hip hop moving forward.

Eminem

Detroit, Michigan native Eminem (born Marshall Mathers in 1972) began his career in the 1990s but became world-renowned once he signed to Dr. Dre's Aftermath

FIGURE 9.8

Entertainment. Dr. Dre produced his 2000 release *The Marshall Mathers LP* and 2002's *The Eminem Show.* Eminem is one of the most celebrated rap artists of all time, having garnered 15 Grammy Awards and an Academy Award for Best Original Song in 2002 for "Lose Yourself," from the semi-autobiographical film *8 Mile* ("Eminem Is Our 2013 Global Icon!" 2013). In the U.S., Eminem was the best-selling artist of the 2000s and has sold over 100 million records worldwide ("Eminem" n.d.). While he has struggled against criticism for lyrics that were considered misogynistic, racist, and sexist, his success would be unparalleled in the new millennium.

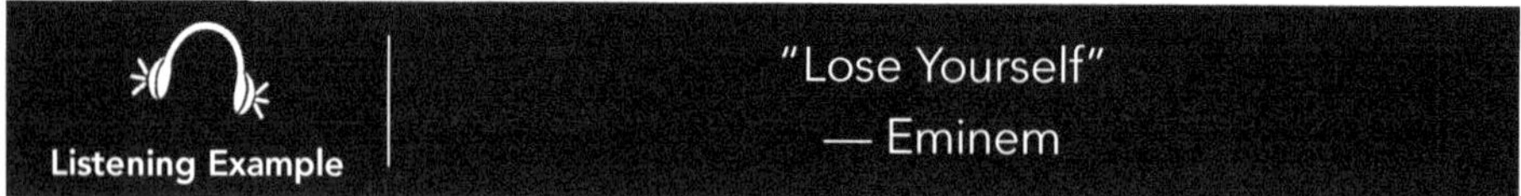

Kanye West

One American rap artist made his mark well beyond the music industry. Kanye West (born 1977) did not have the stereotypical childhood of many other rap artists. His mother was a college professor who raised Kanye in the suburbs of Chicago, with a brief stay in China when West was 10 years old. He graduated from high school and attended Chicago State University but dropped out when it began to interfere with his music career. West produced songs for other artists but wanted to get his own career as a rapper off the ground. His big break occurred by chance. After a near-fatal car accident, he focused more on writing his own raps and released *The College Dropout* in 2004. The album is consistently ranked as one of the greatest hip hop albums of all time. He was nominated for 10 Grammy Awards (Montgomery 2004). West is a great example of how hip hop has diversified. His musical styles are vast, incorporating soul, indie rock, punk, gospel, and a host of other musical styles. His lyric content is far more diverse than much of rap's earlier output. In a savvy business move, West has diversified into the world of fashion, and his empire continues to grow. He is also known for his publicity stunts, including a controversy at the 2009

MTV Video Music Awards, when West, unhappy that Beyoncé did not win the award for best female video, took the microphone from winner Taylor Swift and protested on live television. His personal life continues to make headlines because of his marriage to reality television star Kim Kardashian. While always in the news, West is credited with broadening the base of hip hop music, erasing stereotypes and going against the grain for his social and political views.

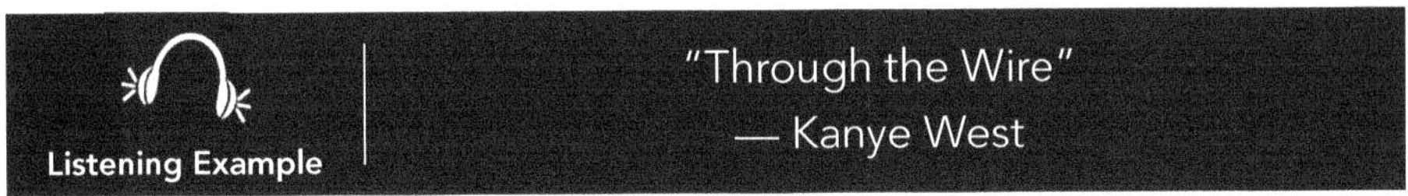

Jay-Z

Jay-Z, born Shawn Carter in 1969, is one of the most acclaimed rap artists of all time, having won 22 Grammy Awards and placing 14 number one albums on the *Billboard* 200 chart list (Kreps 2017). His success as a rapper has been equaled by his success as a businessperson. Jay-Z was raised in Brooklyn, NY, and sold crack cocaine as a teenager. He cocreated Roc-A-Fella Records in 1995 after having not received a recording contract. His album *The Blueprint* was released on September 11, 2001, and is considered so culturally significant that the Library of Congress has preserved it in the National Recording Registry. His business empire is unprecedented in music. He started his own clothing line in 2003, is part owner of the Brooklyn Nets NBA team, owns a chain of upscale sports bars, and is a real estate mogul. His successful image, which goes far beyond rap, has become a new model for musicians in the exploding media world of the 21st century. He has been married to singer Beyoncé since 2008.

Popular music styles have always borrowed from other popular music styles. This blending of styles keeps music fresh and acknowledges great work from musicians in other genres and subgenres. Two styles that became popular during the 2000s were crunk and numetal.

Crunk

Crunk is a subgenre of hip hop that developed in the southern United States, particularly in Memphis, Tennessee, and Atlanta, Georgia. The style borrowed heavily from the electronic dance music prevalent in African American clubs. While utilizing a drum machine, heavy bass sounds, and a synth-based ostinato, the rapper is usually repeating a call-and-response pattern. This music is meant to be danced to, creating an almost hypnotic effect on the dancers. Atlanta's Lil Jon is considered to be the most popular crunk artist. His song "Get Low," from his 2002 album *Kings of Crunk*, is considered to be the song that brought crunk to the mainstream.

Nu Metal

Nu metal combines heavy metal music with elements of other forms, including hip hop, funk, and grunge. While some rap acts of the 1980s were known for scratching metal albums and '90s hip hop sampled metal, by the mid-'90s, metal groups were incorporating rap vocals into their heavy metal music. This style peaked with Linkin Park's *Hybrid Theory* album in 2000. The album has sold over 11 million records and remains the best-selling rock album of the 21st century (Kristobak n.d.). Lead vocalist Chester Bennington (1976–2017) provided the more melodic singing, while Mike Shinoda (born 1977) provided a more rap-like delivery.

Country Music

As we read in Chapter 8, country music became mainstream pop in terms of record sales, and country music artists enjoyed greater crossover appeal in the 1990s. By the next decade, country music was expanding its hold on popular music, growing in its diversity. During the 2000s, we saw hit country songs that responded variously to the September 11th attacks. "Courtesy of the Red, White, and Blue (Angry American)" by Toby Keith supported military response to the attacks, while other country artists blasted President George W. Bush. Country music in the 2000s also began changing the subject matter previously based on rural living to include sun, surf, sand, and frozen drinks. This style, which had its origins in the 1970s with Jimmy Buffett, was known as "gulf and western." Alan Jackson teamed up with Parrothead king Buffett on "It's Five O'Clock Somewhere" in 2003, which kicked off this new country music trend of celebrating the sun, surf, and sand. Country music still boasted songs that celebrated traditional country music subject matter, such as Gretchen Wilson's celebration of the so-called "redneck" lifestyle in the song "Redneck Woman," while updating them with the themes of female empowerment seen in other genres as well. The 2000s also saw the beginning of a career that would dominate both the pop and country charts in the following years—that of Taylor Swift. Darius Rucker, African American lead singer of 1990s folk rock band Hootie and the Blowfish, would become one of the most famous country singers of the 2000s. His number one hit in 2008 would become the first country number one song by an African American in 25 years (Guerra 2009).

Listening Example

"Redneck Woman"— Gretchen Wilson
"It's Five O'Clock Somewhere"
— Alan Jackson w/Jimmy Buffett

Moving Forward to the New Decade

The diverse sounds in country music were indicative of the new digital age, which had a profound impact on popular music. Music fans could no longer be easily categorized with terms as simple as rock, country, pop, rap, or metal, as new production, distribution, and consumption methods completely changed the process from composition to our buying habits as fans. While this chapter introduced many artists and styles that were born of this new reality, the subgenres become too numerous to adequately cover. The sheer expanse of music availability has given us greater choices, so much so that no one style dominates for any length of time. The old faithful styles of rock, pop, and country have now cross-pollinated, ending the days of easily categorizing music. The new decade will bring about even greater diversity and greater influence from technology than observed in the 2000s.

References

"500 Greatest Songs of All Time." *Rolling Stone*. https://www.rollingstone.com/music/music-lists/500-greatest-songs-of-all-time-151127/kelly-clarkson-since-u-been-gone-2-154502/. Accessed June 19, 2019.

Aniftos, Rania. "Britney Spears to Receive First-Ever Icon Award at 2017 Radio Disney Music Awards." *Billboard*, April 5, 2017.

"Billboard Music Award for Top Female Artist." Wikipedia. https://en.wikipedia.org/wiki/Billboard_Music_Award_for_Top_Female_Artist. Accessed June 19, 2019.

"Billboard's Greatest Trios of All Time." *Billboard*, April 30, 2008.

Daily Show, The. Tony Bennett appearance on *The Daily Show*, September 29, 2011.

"Eminem." Shady Records. https://shadyrecords.com/artist/eminem-2/.

"Eminem Is Our 2013 Global Icon!" MTVEMA. http://www.mtvema.com/news/9vdqcz/eminem-is-our-2013-global-icon Retrieved June 18 2019.

Goldman, David. "Music's Lost Decade: Sales Cut in Half." CNN Money, February 3, 2010. https://money.cnn.com/2010/02/02/news/companies/napster_music_industry/

Gowan, Michael. "Requiem for Napster." *PC World*, May 18, 2002. Accessed July 13, 2013.

Guerra, Joey. "Darius Rucker Thrilled to Be Living His Dream." *Houston Chronicle*, March 13, 2009. https://www.chron.com/entertainment/music/article/Darius-Rucker-thrilled-to-be-living-his-dream-1737141.php.

Hibberd, James. "Kelly Clarkson Officially Launching a Daytime Talk Show." *Entertainment Weekly*, September 19, 2018.

"Justin Timberlake Returning to Lake Tahoe for American Century Championship." *Tahoe Daily Tribune*, June 20, 2019. https://www.tahoedailytribune.com/news/justin-timberlake-returning-to-lake-tahoe-for-american-century-championship/.

Kreps, Daniel. "Jay-Z Claims 14th Number One LP with '4:44'." *Rolling Stone*, July 16, 2017. https://www.rollingstone.com/music/music-news/on-the-charts-jay-z-claims-14th-number-one-lp-with-444-197938/ .

Kristobak, Ryan. "Looking Back at Linkin Park's 'Hybrid Theory,' the Best-Selling Debut of the 21st Century." Culture Trip. Accessed June 2, 2019. https://theculturetrip.com/north-america/usa/california/articles/looking-back-at-linkin-parks-hybrid-theory-the-best-selling-debut-of-the-21st-century/.

Leeds, Jeff. "Amy Winehouse Wins Big at Grammy Awards." *New York Times*, February 11, 2008. https://www.nytimes.com/2008/02/11/arts/music/11gram.html.

Martens, Todd. "Keys' Debut Tops the Billboard 200." *Billboard*, July 5, 2001.

Montgomery, James. "Kanye Scores 10 Grammy Nominations; Usher and Alicia Keys Land Eight." MTV News. http://www.mtv.com/news/1494569/kanye-scores-10-grammy-nominations-usher-and-alicia-keys-land-eight/ 2004.

"Nickelback Named Group Of the Decade by *Billboard*." *Toronto Star*, December 15, 2009. Accessed March 28, 2012. https://www.thestar.com/entertainment/music/2009/12/15/nickelback_named_group_of_the_decade_by_billboard.html.

Payne, Chris. "2016 Showdown: Battle of the Pop-Punk Veterans." *Billboard*, September 30, 2016.

"Readers' Poll: The Ten Worst Bands of the 1990s." *Rolling Stone*, May 9, 2013. https://www.rollingstone.com/music/music-lists/readers-poll-the-ten-worst-bands-of-the-nineties-13654/2-nickelback-241032/.

Recording Academy. "Kelly Clarkson." Grammy.com. https://www.grammy.com/grammys/artists/kelly-clarkson.

Recording Academy. "2004 Grammy Award Winners." Grammy.com. Accessed January 22, 2015. http://awardsandwinners.com/category/grammy-awards/2004/

Vincent, James. "Digital Music Revenue Overtakes CD Sales for the First Time Globally." The Verge, April 15, 2015. https://www.theverge.com/2015/4/15/8419567/digital-physical-music-sales-overtake-globally.

Figure Credits

IMG. 9.1: Copyright © by Michael Foran (CC BY 2.0) at https://commons.wikimedia.org/wiki/File:WTC_smoking_on_9-11.jpeg.

Fig. 9.1: Source: https://commons.wikimedia.org/wiki/File:President_Barack_Obama.jpg.

Fig. 9.2: Copyright © by jeaneeem (CC BY 2.0) at https://commons.wikimedia.org/wiki/File:Kelly_Clarkson_in_Canberra,_2005_(3).jpg.

Fig. 9.3: Copyright © by Gage Skidmore (CC BY-SA 2.0) at https://commons.wikimedia.org/wiki/File:Justin_Timberlake_by_Gage_Skidmore_2.jpg.

Fig. 9.4: Source: https://commons.wikimedia.org/wiki/File:Britney_Spears.jpg.

Fig. 9.5: Copyright © by Daniel D'Auria (CC BY-SA 2.0) at https://commons.wikimedia.org/wiki/File:Greenday2010.jpg.

Fig. 9.6: Copyright © by Pete Sekesan (CC BY 2.0) at https://commons.wikimedia.org/wiki/File:Destiny_Child_at_Super_Bowl_XLVII_halftime_show.jpg.

Fig. 9.7: Copyright © by Rama (CC BY-SA 2.0 FR) at https://commons.wikimedia.org/wiki/File:Amy_Winehouse_f4962007_crop.jpg.

Fig. 9.8: Copyright © by Mika-photography (CC BY-SA 3.0) at https://commons.wikimedia.org/wiki/File:Eminem-01-mika.jpg.

DONT
TREAD ON
#METOO
I CAN
WEAR WHAT
I WANT TO
BOY
BYE
RESIST

CHAPTER

10

The 2010s and Beyond

Historical Context for the Decade

The 2010s became a decade of political controversy, natural disasters, and social change. In 2010, the Deepwater Horizon oil platform in the Gulf of Mexico exploded, causing the worst oil spill and man-made disaster in U.S. history. In 2012, Hurricane Sandy ravaged the New Jersey-New York coastline, causing 70 billion dollars in damage. Five years later, Hurricanes Harvey and Maria were even more destructive in Houston and Puerto Rico, respectively. That same year, Barack Obama easily won a second term as president of the United States. However, four years later, billionaire businessman and television personality Donald Trump would defeat former Secretary of State Hillary Clinton to succeed Obama in a controversial election in which Secretary Clinton won the popular vote. Many women considered Trump's victory a defeat for women. This and many other events of the decade would bring about greater social change.

Throughout the decade, incidents involving the sexual harassment of women, police brutality against African Americans, and violence against the LGBTQ community raised anger and highlighted the need for widespread change. In 2014 and 2015, the treatment of African Americans suspected of having committed crimes was protested through rioting in Ferguson, Missouri, and Baltimore, Maryland, following the questionable deaths of unarmed African Americans during police investigations. The following year, a terrorist attack at a nightclub frequented by LGBTQ persons in Orlando, Florida, killed 50 people. In 2017, the #MeToo movement became a national headline following sexual abuse allegations against Hollywood power broker Harvey Weinstein. These incidents all served to bring about a new form of activism, pushing the United States to focus more attention on these long-fought struggles. In 2016, this new activism was one of the reasons Bob Dylan became the first popular musician to receive the Nobel Prize in Literature (Ellis-Peterson and Flood 2016).

The decade beginning in 2010 heralded new changes in music technology and new opportunities for the creation, distribution, and consumption of music. Musicians could now create music using software that allowed them to bypass the traditional recording studio. The distribution of music shifted to be primarily digital, with most consumers obtaining their music through digital streaming services such as Spotify and Apple Music and à la carte stores, including Apple iTunes. Some artists made exclusive releases through only one of these services, creating greater competition. Listening to music became more convenient through new and even smaller storage and listening devices, building upon the personal computer with tablet computers, smartphones, and even smartwatches. As humans could now portably access almost any information on demand, radio listening took a back seat to streaming services. These changes increased the scope of the popular styles of music available, broadening the base of popular music while focusing less on any one style.

Hip Hop Overtakes Rock in Popularity

After four decades of growth, hip hop officially became more popular than mainstream rock in the United States. Artists such as Drake, Kendrick Lamar, Chance the Rapper, and Childish Gambino were new artists who had great success in the 2010s. They were joined by artists who had success in previous decades, such as Kanye West, Eminem, and Jay-Z. With each new decade following their initial mainstream success in the 1980s, rap and hip hop continued to expand their sound and audiences, crossing racial, geographic, and socioeconomic barriers. With the emergence of streaming services, hip hop experienced growth, while some other forms of music lost some popularity as the accessibility of greater numbers of genres and subgenres occurred.

Drake

FIGURE 10.1

Aubrey Drake Graham (Drake) (born 1986) is a Canadian actor and rapper who first gained fame on the teen drama television series *Degrassi: The Next Generation.* He independently released recordings until he was signed by Lil Wayne's production company in 2009. Drake's success in the 2010s is unmatched. His albums released in the decade all became platinum-selling, and he owns the record for the most time spent on the Hot 100 charts, at 431 consecutive weeks (Anderson 2017). He also has the highest digital singles sales of any artist. He has won many Juno (the equivalent of the Canadian Grammy) Awards, American Music Awards, and four Grammy Awards.

Childish Gambino

FIGURE 10.2

Childish Gambino (born Donald Glover, Jr., in 1983) is an American rapper, actor, and comedian. He began his career in 2006 as a writer for the television comedy *30 Rock* but went on to star onscreen in the television comedy *Community,* and he created and starred in the FX series *Atlanta.* His song "This Is America" won four Grammy Awards at the 2019 ceremony (Yglesias 2019). The song is indicative of the political environment of the decade, addressing gun violence and racism.

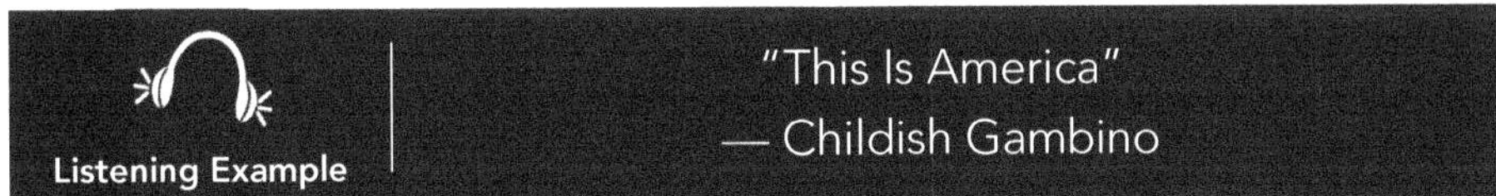

Mainstream Rock Isn't Mainstream Anymore ...

What is mainstream rock as we move farther into the new millennium? We know rock is no longer the most consumed music, so using the term "mainstream" or "pop" is problematic. The hybrid nature of music from the 1990s and continuing through the next two decades made categorizing music more difficult, requiring new terms to brand music. As more of these brands existed, they became more specific, overlapping the styles these new terms were meant to differentiate. The term "pop," for example, which should have been used to describe the music most popular and consumed at any given time, was always corrupted, as it was often used to describe a particular genre of music that described the audience rather than the music itself. As rap and hip hop became the most consumed music, the term "pop" should have been applied to those styles of music; however, artists and fans of that music would protest against this label, as the most current perception of "pop" music is very different from rap and hip hop.

Musicians with past success who continued to rock the 2010s included AC/DC, Green Day, Metallica, and David Bowie, whose greatest success in the decade occurred in 2016 just before his death. Bands that had their initial success in the decade included Imagine Dragons, Avenged Sevenfold, Train, and Maroon 5.

Imagine Dragons

FIGURE 10.3

Imagine Dragons, formed in Provo, Utah, first had success once they moved to Las Vegas, Nevada. In 2012, they released *Night Visions.* The album was an instant success, achieving Top 10 status in over a dozen countries. The album's biggest single, "Radioactive," became the largest-selling rock single of 2013. It was the most streamed song on Spotify in the U.S. in 2013 (Lopez 2013), was nominated for two Grammy Awards, and won for Best Rock Performance (Recording Academy n.d.). A second single from the album, "Demons," also became one of rock's biggest downloads since the beginning of the digital download age.

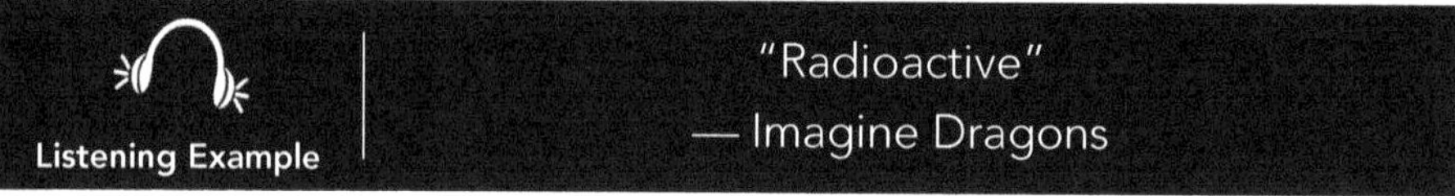

Greta Van Fleet

Another mainstream rock band to have success in the second half of the decade was Greta Van Fleet. The band was formed in Michigan in 2012 by brothers Josh, Jake, and Sam Kiszka with friend Danny Wagner added as the drummer in 2013. They scored a huge hit in 2017 with the first song they ever wrote together, "Highway Tune."

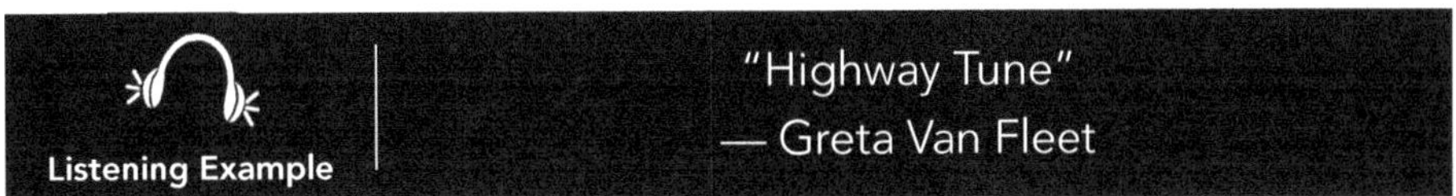

The success of these bands as well as those who began their careers earlier but continued to have success in the decade shows that mainstream rock would continue to be a force, even as the new technology gave access to so much music that no one style would dominate. Another reason rock would lose its status as the most popular music during the decade was that the rock category itself was delineated, subdivided into genres that are more specific in an attempt to highlight every musical difference to counter the effect of the vast choices of the digital streaming age. Bon Iver and Mumford & Sons are bands that became known under the indie folk band label that continued the success of rock in the 2010s.

Bon Iver

Bon Iver, the touring group for indie musician Justin Vernon, released its first record, *For Emma, Forever Ago,* in February of 2008. It followed nearly two years of work during which Vernon became seriously ill, had his previous band split up, and went through the end of a relationship. He decided to move to a cabin in the woods of Wisconsin for solitude. The song demos he made were originally self-released, but he eventually signed with Jagjaguwar, a small independent label. The simply recorded songs quickly became the go-to music for television shows such as *One Tree Hill* and *House.* Critical acclaim followed from *Rolling Stone*, *Pitchfork*, and other publications. Greater success would follow with his 2011 album, *Bon Iver, Bon Iver.* For this album, Vernon brought in several other musicians to "change the musical scene of the record." This album was critically acclaimed, with *Pitchfork* awarding it best album of 2011 (Petrusich 2011). It won the Grammy Award for Best Alternative Album of the year, and Bon Iver was awarded Best New Artist. The song "Holocene" was awarded Song of the Year and Record of the Year (Recording Academy n.d.).

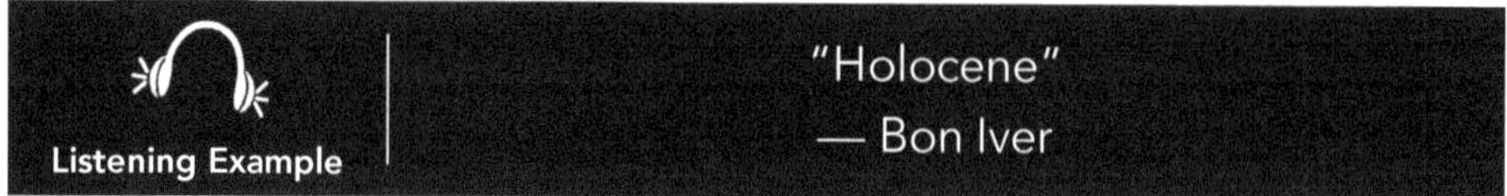

Mumford & Sons

Mumford & Sons, formed in London, England, in 2008, are classified as folk rock. They play acoustic instruments in the bluegrass and folk tradition, including banjo, mandolin, and acoustic bass violin. The band consists of Marcus Mumford, Ben Lovett, Winston Marshall, and Ted Dwane. The name for the band was chosen because it sounded like an old business name. The sound of Mumford & Sons weaves together bluegrass, rock, and country and is a great example of the true expansive nature of the music industry in the 2010s. Their second studio album, *Babel*, was released in 2012 and debuted at number one on the *Billboard* charts in both the U.S. and U.K., selling over one million units in the first week (Caufield 2012). It also won the Grammy Award for Album of the Year in 2013 (Huffpost 2013).

FIGURE 10.4

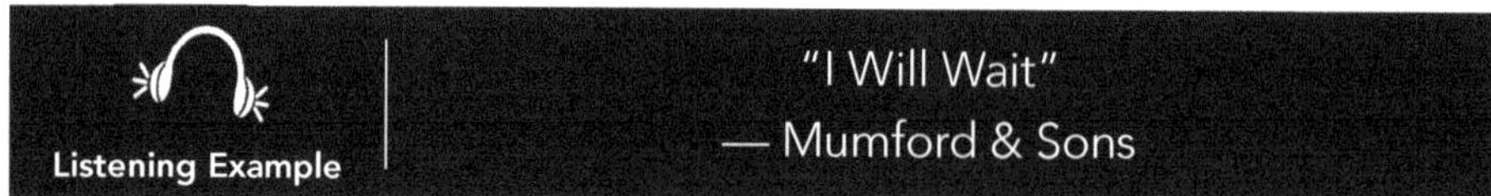

Singer-Songwriters in the New Decade

The singer-songwriters had a resurgence in the 2010s, continuing the tradition in music for introspective, intimate songs. While the singer-songwriters have lost some ground in popularity due to the greater scope of available music, Adele, Ed Sheeran, Sam Smith, Jack Johnson, Sara Bareilles, and Meghan Trainor have had great success in the decade.

Sara Bareilles

Sara Bareilles (born 1979) first achieved success in 2007 with the single "Love Song," which sold over 3 million copies (Grein 2014). Prior to that, she was a leader in the a capella choir at UCLA, her alma mater. Her greatest success occurred in 2013 when she released her Grammy-nominated album *The Blessed Unrest* with the hit single "Brave." Bareilles, along with Jack Antonoff of the band Fun., wrote the song as a message to a friend who was having difficulty coming out as gay. "Brave" became a new civil rights anthem during a decade when the struggle for equal rights for women and the LGBTQ community took center stage. Bareilles also composed the score for the Broadway musical *Waitress*, which opened in 2015 and was nominated for a Tony Award the following year (Broadway World 2016). Her career since that time has included acting on Broadway and television and writing an autobiography called *Sounds Like Me: My Life (So Far) in Song*.

Ed Sheeran

Another musician who helped to shape the music of the 2010s is British-born singer-songwriter Ed Sheeran (born 1991). His debut album was enormously successful in the U.K. in 2011. His second release, *X* (pronounced "multiply"), reached number one in the United States and U.K. and was one of the best-selling albums in the world in 2015. He received the British equivalent of the Grammy, the Brit award, for the album and won the 2016 Grammy Award for Song of the Year for the single "Thinking Out Loud" (*Los Angeles Times* 2015). He has also written songs for Taylor Swift, One Direction, and Justin Bieber.

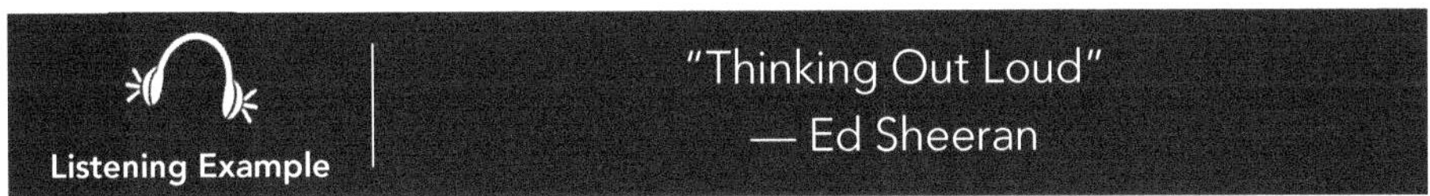

Adele

Adele has had the greatest success of any singer-songwriter of the 2000s and the greatest success of any musician in the 2010s. Adele Adkins (born 1988) is an English

FIGURE 10.5

singer-songwriter who first became successful following the release of her debut album *19* in 2008. While *19* achieved multiplatinum status, her follow-up album, *21*, released in 2011, broke many records. It was the best-selling album in the world in 2011 and 2012, selling over 31 million copies (Serjeant 2016). *21* provided three number one singles: "Rolling in the Deep," "Someone Like You," and "Set Fire to the Rain." It won six Grammy Awards in 2012, which tied a record (Recording Academy n.d.). She released her next album, *25*, in 2015. It became the best-selling album of that year, and its first single, "Hello," was the first song to sell over one million digital copies in its first week (Trust 2015). The song "Rolling in the Deep" from 2011's *21* is a blues and gospel-inspired pop hit from the point of view of an ex-lover.

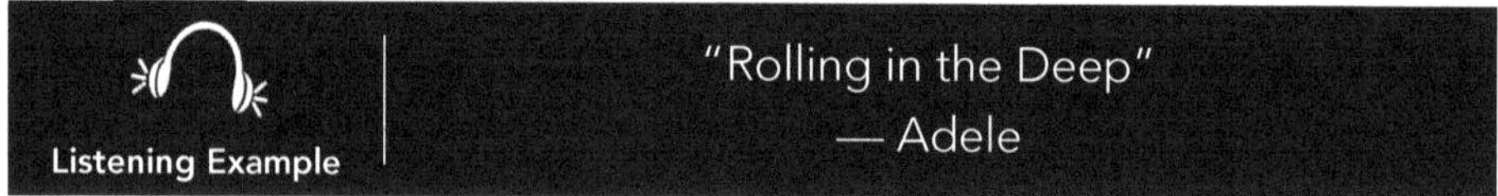

Teen Pop Gets Socially Aware …

While music evolves with each new generation, the most popular music of most of the rock and roll era has been geared toward younger teenagers. While the music may be called rock and roll, bubblegum rock, teen pop, or just pop, the young teen population has always been a force in driving record sales. As was observed in the 2000s, teen pop has a devoted audience, sometimes achieved through the teen pop television machines of Disney or Nickelodeon. While it has been common to call any music consumed by teenagers pop, pop (short for popular) should be used not to describe a style or music. Rather, it should only be used as a descriptive term, naming any music style that at any given time is most consumed. However, when the term "pop" is used in modern terms, it is best to add the term "teen." Prior to the 1990s, teen pop ignored most social or political messages. With the new emphasis on female empowerment in the new millennium, however, many artists are creating music geared toward empowering teen girls. This trend became even more popular in the 2010s with the success of Katy Perry and Lady Gaga.

Katy Perry

Katy Perry (born Katheryn Hudson 1984) broke into the scene in 2008. Her 2010 album *Teenage Dream* became the first album by a female in history to have five number one songs (Trust 2011). The album borrows heavily from European dance music, which was influenced by the rise in hip hop music over the past decade. The song "Firework" is a teen anthem of self-respect and empowerment. Like many other female artists of the 2000s, Perry wrote and performed music to inspire young women. Her 2013 album *Prism* included another self-empowerment anthem, "Roar."

FIGURE 10.6

Lady Gaga

Lady Gaga (born Stefani Germanotta in 1986) was known early in her career for over-the-top costumes and publicity stunts, which at times overshadowed her great songwriting and performing. She grew up in New York City and, after time as a songwriter, released her debut album, 2008's *The Fame*, followed by the EP *The Fame Monster* in 2009. While both of these albums were successful, 2011's *Born This Way* debuted at number one on the *Billboard* charts and sold over one million copies in the first week of release (Martens 2011). The lead single, "Born This Way," became an anthem of the decade, joining a plethora of songs that empowered women, racial minorities, and the LGBTQ community. In 2014, she collaborated with jazz singer Tony Bennett to create the jazz album *Cheek to Cheek*, which was highly acclaimed and served to change her image from a performer known for her shocking costumes to one in which her vocal talents took center stage. She also began acting in TV's *American Horror Story*. In 2018, she starred in the remake of the film *A Star is Born*, writing the music for the film and performing it live with actor Bradley Cooper. She was awarded an Oscar for Best Original Song for a Movie Soundtrack and was nominated for Best Actress in a Film. In 2012, she created the Born This Way Foundation as a philanthropic organization dedicated to youth empowerment and equal rights for LGBTQ citizens.

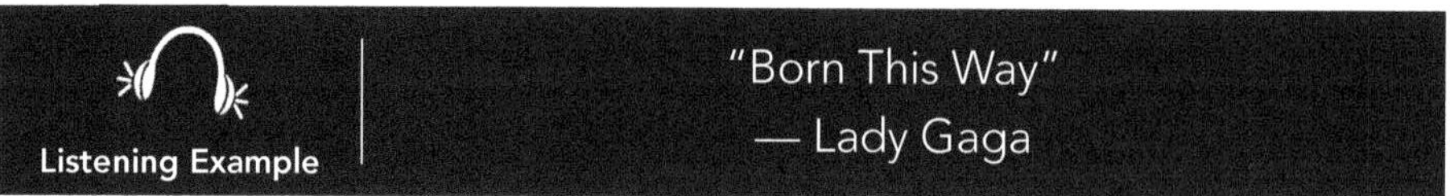

One Direction and the Continued Success of The Pre-Fab Boy Bands

Though often looked upon with disdain by many rock fans, there is a long tradition of prefabricated pop boy bands in rock. While the Beatles may occasionally be referred to as "the original boy band," that is an incorrect label. They were a rock band, as they came together on their own, played instruments, and wrote most of their own songs. The term "boy band" really refers to the "prefabricated" boy bands that began with the Monkees in 1966, a group that was formed through a long audition process rather than the more organic process by which most bands are formed—thus the term "pre-fab." Other boy bands have dominated the charts throughout the decades, including New Kids on the Block, NSYNC, and Backstreet Boys. As there will always be teen girls as music fans, there will always be boy bands. The biggest "pre-fab" group of the 2010s is One Direction.

When Niall Horan, Liam Payne, Louis Tomlinson, Zayn Malik, and Harry Styles competed on the British version of the TV music competition *The X Factor* in 2010, all were eliminated in the early rounds but were encouraged by judge Simon Cowell to form a group. They did not win the competition but instantly became popular in Great Britain. Their first album, *Up All Night*, released in 2012, became the first debut album by any British artist to debut at number one on the *Billboard* Hot 100 chart. They are also the only band to have their first four albums debut at number one on the *Billboard* Hot 200 chart (Caufield 2014). These are records not equaled by the Monkees or any other boy band—or, incidentally, the Beatles.

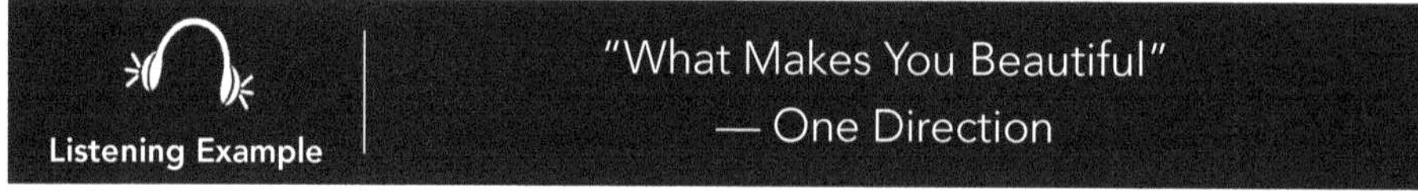

Country Music, the Crossover of Taylor Swift, and the Ascension of Chris Stapleton

In Chapters 8 and 9, we discussed the evolution of country music, moving away from sounds that are more traditional for that genre and incorporating sounds typically found in mainstream rock and pop. In the 2010s, country music continued to evolve.

Taylor Swift

Taylor Swift (born 1989) became the most successful artist of the new millennium. Raised in Pennsylvania, her family moved to Nashville, Tennessee, when she was 14 to support Swift's search for fame in country music. Her crossover into pop music began in earnest with her second album, *Fearless*, released in 2008. The album won four Grammy Awards and was the best-selling album in the U.S. in 2009 (Caufield 2010). The album had crossover hits with "You Belong to Me" and "Love Story." This trend in her music continued through to her fifth album, *1989*, released in 2014. The album charted three number one pop singles. Swift's often autobiographical lyrics about the trials of growing up, falling in love, making mistakes, and being vulnerable hit home with teenage girls and young women. With the release of *Reputation* in late 2017, Swift's transformation from country to crossover artist to pop artist became complete. The release of the first single off the album, "Look What You Made Me Do," is categorized as electropop. The transformation of Swift is evident when listening to 2008's "Love Story" and 2018's "Look What You Made Me Do."

FIGURE 10.7

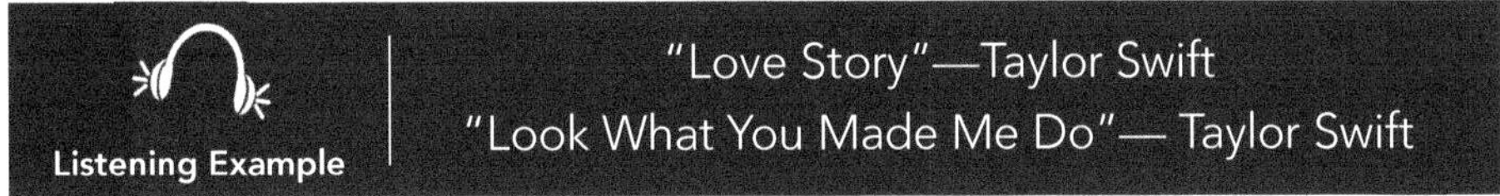

Country music, while at times moving toward pop and adding the influence of "gulf and western," still retained elements of simple storytelling based on blue-collar lives for which it had been known in previous decades. One example of this continued tradition is in the music of Chris Stapleton. Stapleton (born 1978) grew up in Kentucky the son of a coal miner. He worked as a songwriter in Nashville, first forming a bluegrass band and then a Southern rock band. His debut album, *Traveller,* was released in 2015 to great critical acclaim. It was the highest-selling country album of 2016 (Casey 2017) and included the hit song "Traveller."

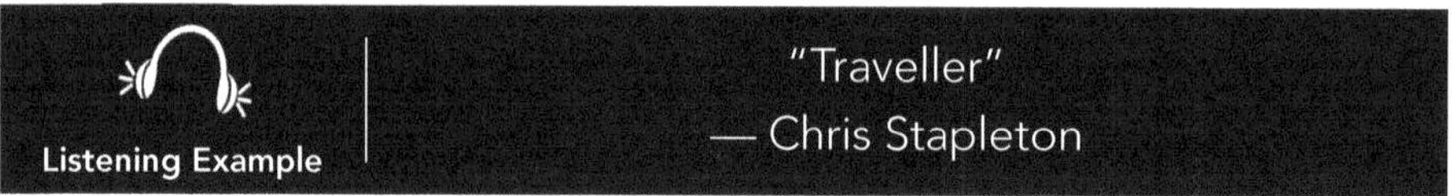

Rhythm and Blues in the 2010s

While R&B, like all pop music styles during this decade, became less prominent due to the broader range of popular music available to consumers, the style continued to have prominent artists. R&B performers adopted elements from electropop and EDM (electronic dance music) styles, bringing their music toward greater pop success. Rihanna has had more number one singles than any other female artist, and very few artists have enjoyed the popularity of Beyoncé during the 2010s.

Rihanna

FIGURE 10.8

Rihanna (born Robyn Rihanna Fenty in 1988) is from the Caribbean island of Barbados. She has been active in the music business since 2005, and her career in the 2010s has mirrored the fusion of music styles that has represented the decade. This incorporation of styles has served her well as an international star. Her combination of pop, dance, Caribbean, and R&B styles was successful in pulling in fans of all of those styles. In addition, Rihanna owns a fashion business and is a humanitarian and political ambassador for her native Barbados. Her 2016 album *Anti* included the hit single "Needed Me."

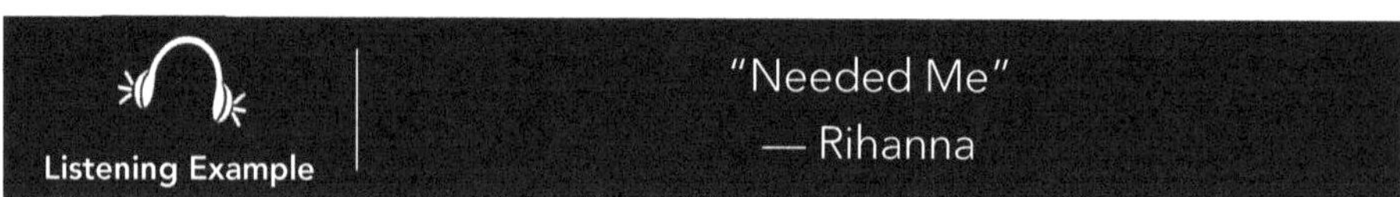

Beyoncé

Beyoncé has become one of the best-known entertainers of the new millennium. Born Beyoncé Knowles in 1981, she rose to fame in the late 1990s as leader of the R&B group Destiny's Child (see Chapter 9). In 2016, she released the album *Lemonade*, which received universal acclaim. In the 2010s, she is the most celebrated, highest-earning, and most awarded singer. Nominated for nine Grammys for *Lemonade,* she became the first female artist to have all 12 tracks from one album chart at the same time on the *Billboard* Hot 100 chart (Mendizabal 2016). The first single, "Formation," is a song promoting African American empowerment and pride. It is considered an anthem for the #BlackLivesMatter movement and considered by many rock critics to be the best song of 2016.

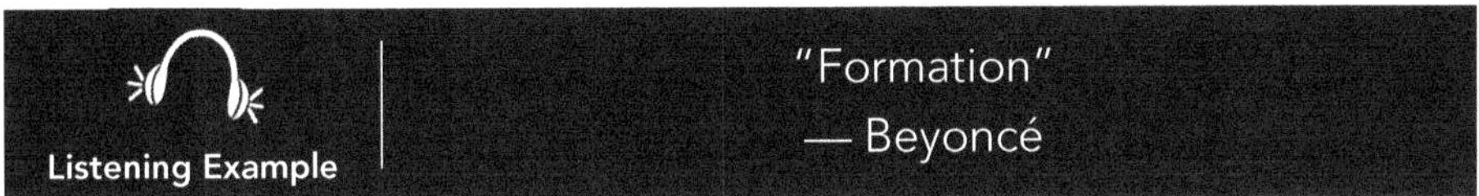

Many other great R&B artists significantly contributed to the decade, including Bruno Mars, John Legend, Frank Ocean, The Weeknd, and Alicia Keys. There was also continued success for artists whose careers began earlier, including Janet Jackson and Mariah Carey. Sadly, we lost one of the greatest singers of the 20th century when Whitney Houston passed away in 2012. Contemporary R&B music will continue to be successful, as it has always been the root of all of our popular music. The African American–based music rooted in the blues and gospel styles will always be a dominant factor in contemporary music. No matter how many styles might exist, they will all borrow from rhythm and blues.

Heavy Metal

While the heavy metal genre has been dominated by bands of great longevity such as Metallica, Anthrax, Slayer, and Megadeth, newer heavy metal bands also saw success in the 2010s. These bands often combined elements of the thrash metal bands listed above that had great success in the '80s and '90s with the alternative and progressive metal bands that followed grunge into the later 1990s (Jane's Addiction, Soundgarden, and Alice in Chains). The result is a diversity of sound not previously seen in metal music.

FIGURE 10.9 Avenged Sevenfold

Avenged Sevenfold, from Huntington Beach, California, and formed in 1999, achieved their greatest success in the 2010s. They began adding elements of progressive metal into their music throughout the decade, culminating in 2016's release of *The Stage*. In the song "The Stage," you will hear elements of symphonic progressive rock wrapped in the heavy drums and metal guitar riffs.

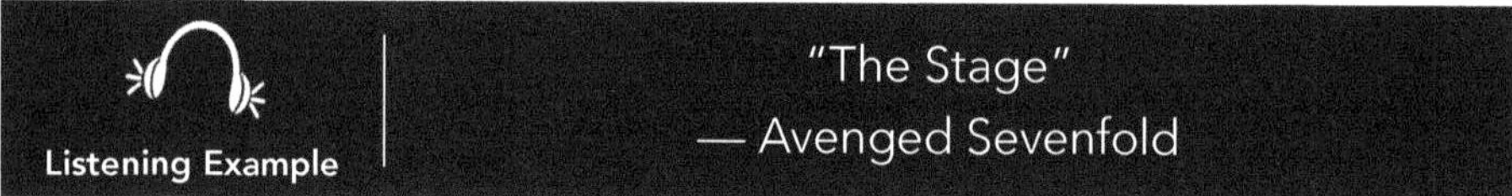

"The Stage"
— Avenged Sevenfold

EDM (Electronic Dance Music)

FIGURE 10.10 Skrillex

EDM continues the long tradition of dance music created for clubs. Following the decline of disco in the early 1980s, other styles such as Detroit techno and house dominated club dance music. Once raves became big in the 1990s, American record companies began using "EDM" as an umbrella term for most new dance music. Many other music styles contributed to EDM, including hip hop, Jamaican dub, electro funk, '80s synth pop, and the experimental synthesized music of German group Kraftwerk. What emerged is an amalgamation of dance music, borrowing the best ideas from many sources to create a super-dance form. The DJs who perform and mix EDM have become famous in the same way that hip hop DJs did in the 1980s and '90s. With the exception of disco in the mid-1970s, the American public had never readily taken to dance music, as it seemed impersonal, especially electronic dance music. The breakthrough in the United States came in the mid-2000s when EDM DJs began collaborating with more mainstream musicians. Once this breakthrough occurred, U.S. consumers had less of a problem with not seeing a musician perform on a traditional instrument. As with previous dance music, the audience became the show. Two of the greatest EDM artists of the decade are Avicii (1989–2018) and Skrillex (born 1988).

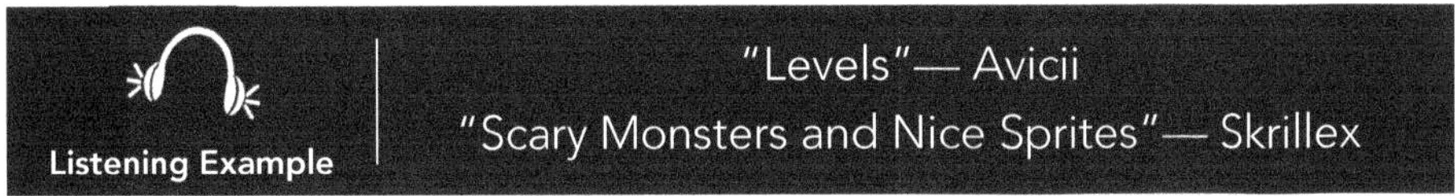

K-Pop

K-pop, which originated in South Korea in the 1990s, has become increasingly popular in the United States during the 2010s. While having some relationship to traditional Korean culture, K-pop utilizes much of the influence of Western music, including rock, pop, hip hop, dance, gospel, and country music. Like hip hop in the U.S., K-pop is more than just a style of music; it represents a subculture including fashion and dance styles. It grew out of the influence of Western rock and roll, which slowly began influencing South Korea following the end of World War II and increased following the Korean War. The Beatles became a huge hit in South Korea in the 1960s, inspiring many Koreans to form rock bands. These bands copied Western rock and roll but through the life and listening experiences of Korean teens. This new style entered into the musical palette in the early 2000s but became well known with the success of "Gangnam Style" by K-pop artist Psy. The song, first released on YouTube, has been viewed over three billion times since its release in 2012 (Herman 2017). By the end of that year, the song had hit number one in over 30 countries, exposing new people to the music who had never heard of K-pop before. Once this occurred, *Billboard* magazine began an online column dedicated to K-pop, and iTunes has its own K-pop chart. This new influence of music previously absent from most Western rock will continue to add ingredients to an already complicated musical recipe as we move forward.

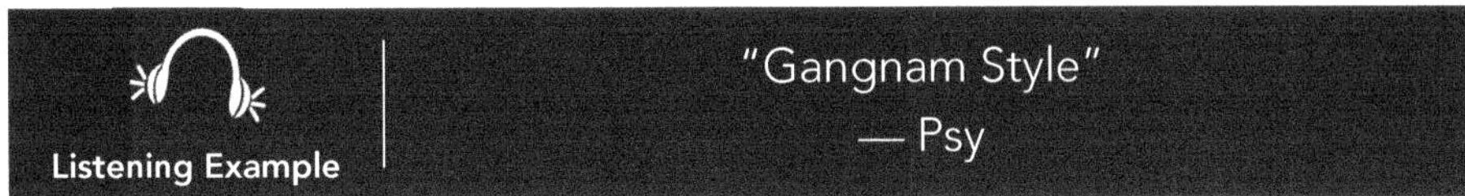

A Brief Epilogue

Throughout much of its brief history, rock music followed an easily chartable pattern. A young generation became infatuated with a certain sound. To cash in on the fad, record companies did their best to recreate that sound as quickly as possible. The style steadily rose in popularity, adapted new sounds, and grew increasingly more complex. That complexity was then rejected by a younger generation in favor of a

FIGURE 10.11

more simple sound. Wash, rinse, repeat. Things were predictable. Our choices seemed immense, yet not to the degree that we could not conceive of the possibilities. The system worked. Radio liked it, record companies liked it, and we liked it. Once the Internet and the digital age hit, rock went down a different one-way road with no possibility of turning around. The consumer now has access to so many music styles: unlimited and thus inconceivable choice. Because of the immensity of possibilities, rock and roll and all of its subgenres will never dominate society the way it did in the past. Generations of kids were identified by what they listened to while teenagers. This is not meant to sound like an epitaph, though; rock has not died. Rather, it has gone supernova. It has expanded and permeated into every possible audible art form. As our world continues to grow closer, so does our music. Nothing lives in a bubble. Everything is influenced by everything and will influence everything. While the musical path is not quite as clear as it once was, the possibilities are now endless, remarkable, and continually moving forward.

References

"2016 Tony Awards Nominations—*Hamilton* Breaks Record with 16! And the Nominees Are …". Broadway World, May 3, 2016. https://www.broadwayworld.com/article/2016-Tony-Awards-Nominations-And-the-Nominees-Are-20160503.

Anderson, Trevor. "Drake Isn't on the *Billboard* Hot 100 for the First Time Since 2009." *Billboard*, August 15, 2017. https://www.billboard.com/articles/columns/chart-beat/7905015/drake-hot-100-record-431-weeks-2009.

Casey, Jim. "The 10 Best-Selling Country Albums of 2016 Include Blake Shelton, Keith Urban & Carrie Underwood—But Who's No. 1?" Nash Country Daily, January 10, 2017. http://www.nashcountrydaily.com/2017/01/10/the-10-best-selling-country-albums-of-2016-include-blake-shelton-keith-urban-carrie-underwood-but-whos-no-1/. Retrieved June 13, 2019.

Caulfield, Keith. "Taylor Swift Edges Susan Boyle For 2009's Top Selling Album." *Billboard*, January 6, 2010. https://www.billboard.com/articles/news/960801/taylor-swift-edges-susan-boyle-for-2009s-top-selling-album.

———. "Mumford & Sons' 'Babel' Scores Biggest Debut of Year, Bows at No. 1 on *Billboard* 200 Chart." *Billboard*, October 2, 2012. https://www.billboard.com/articles/news/474818/mumford-sons-babel-scores-biggest-debut-of-year-bows-at-no-1-on-billboard-200Billboard.

———. "One Direction's Four Makes Historic No.1 Debut on *Billboard* 200 Chart." *Billboard*, November 26, 2013. https://www.billboard.com/articles/columns/chart-beat/6327789/one-direction-four-no-1-debut-billboard-200.

Ellis-Peterson, Hannah and Alison Flood. "Bob Dylan Wins Nobel Prize in Literature." *The Guardian*, October 13, 2016. https://www.theguardian.com/books/2016/oct/13/bob-dylan-wins-2016-nobel-prize-in-literature.

"Grammys 2015: Complete List of Winners and Nominees." *Los Angeles Times*, February 8, 2015. https://www.latimes.com/entertainment/music/la-et-ms-grammys-2015-nominees-winners-list-story.html.

Grein, Paul. "Chart Watch: Pharrell Steps Up." Yahoo! Entertainment, April 30th, 2014. https://www.yahoo.com/entertainment/blogs/chart-watch/chart-watch--pharrell-steps-up-004435636.html.

Herman, Tamar. "Psy Thanks Fans for Gangnam Style Reaching 3 Billion Views on YouTube." *Billboard*, November 26, 2017. https://www.billboard.com/articles/columns/k-town/8046953/psy-gangnam-style-youtube-3-billion-views.

Lopez, Korina. "Spotify Reveals 2013's Most-Streamed Artists." *USA Today*, December 14, 2013. www.usatoday.com/story/life/music/2013/12/03/spotify-reveals-2013-most-streamed-artists/3810405/.

Martens, Todd. "Lady Gaga Tops the 1 Million Mark in First-Week Album Sales." *Los Angeles Times* music blog, June 1, 2011. https://latimesblogs.latimes.com/music_blog/2011/06/lady-gaga-tops-the-1million-mark-in-first-week-album-sales.html.

Mendizabal, Amaya. "All 12 of Beyoncé's Lemonade Tracks Debut on Hot 100." *Billboard*, May 2, 2016. https://www.billboard.com/articles/columns/chart-beat/7350443/beyonce-lemonade-tracks-debut-hot-100.

"Mumford & Sons, 'Babel,' Album of the Year Grammy Winner, Bests Jack White, Frank Ocean, Fun., the Black Keys." Huffpost, February 10th, 2013. https://www.huffpost.com/entry/mumford-and-sons-babel-album-of-the-year_n_2654390.

Petrusich, Amanda. "The Top 50 Albums of 2011." Pitchfork, December 15th, 2011. https://pitchfork.com/features/lists-and-guides/8727-the-top-50-albums-of-2011/?page=5.

Recording Academy. "Adele." Grammy.com. https://www.grammy.com/grammys/artists/adele.

———. "Bon Iver." Grammy.com. Accessed June 9, 2019. https://www.grammy.com/grammys/artists/bon-iver.

———. "Imagine Dragons." Grammy.com. Accessed June 8, 2019. https://www.grammy.com/grammys/artists/imagine-dragons.

Serjeant, Jill. "Adele Says She Battled Depression Before and After Son's Birth." Reuters, October 31, 2016. https://www.reuters.com/article/us-people-adele-idUSKBN12V20I.

Trust, Gary. "Katy Perry Makes Hot 100 History: Ties Michael Jackson's Record." *Billboard*, August 17, 2011. https://www.billboard.com/articles/news/467879/katy-perry-makes-hot-100-history-ties-michael-jacksons-record.

———. "Adele Says 'Hello' to No. 1 Hot 100 Debut; First Song to Sell 1 Million Downloads in a Week." *Billboard*, November 2, 2015. https://www.billboard.com/articles/columns/chart-beat/6746355/adele-hello-no-1-hot-100-debut-one-million-downloads-week.

Yglesias, Ana. "Childish Gambino Wins Record of the Year For 'This Is America.'" Recording Academy, Feb 10, 2019. https://www.grammy.com/grammys/news/childish-gambino-wins-record-year-america-2019-grammys.

Figure Credits

IMG. 10.1: Source: https://commons.wikimedia.org/wiki/File:Donald_Trump_official_portrait.jpg.

IMG. 10.2: Copyright © by Rob Kall (CC BY 2.0) at https://commons.wikimedia.org/wiki/File:-womensmarch2018_Philly_Philadelphia_-MeToo_(25934196348).jpg.

Fig. 10.1: Copyright © by The Come Up Show (CC BY 2.0) at https://commons.wikimedia.org/wiki/File:Drake_at_the_Velvet_Underground_-_2017_(35986086223)_(cropped).jpg.

Fig. 10.2: Source: https://commons.wikimedia.org/wiki/File:Donald_Glover_TIFF_2015.jpg.

Fig. 10.3: Copyright © by Drew de F Fawkes (CC BY 2.0) at https://commons.wikimedia.org/wiki/File:Imagine_Dragons,_Roundhouse,_London_(35390234536).jpg.

Fig. 10.4: Copyright © by Lich Stefan Schäfer (CC BY-SA 4.0) at https://commons.wikimedia.org/wiki/File:MS2015.jpg.

Fig. 10.5: Copyright © by Kristopher Harris (CC BY 2.0) at https://commons.wikimedia.org/wiki/File:Adele_%27Adele_Live_2016%27_-_Nashville_DSC04637_(30373924806).jpg.

Fig. 10.6: Copyright © by Huntley Paton (CC BY-SA 2.0) at https://commons.wikimedia.org/wiki/File:Katy_Perry_-_Super_Bowl_XLIX_Halftime_02.jpg.

Fig. 10.7: Copyright © by GabboT (CC BY-SA 2.0) at https://commons.wikimedia.org/wiki/File:Taylor_Swift_092_(18118778038).jpg.

Fig. 10.8: Source: https://commons.wikimedia.org/wiki/File:Rihanna_concert_in_Washington_DC_(2).jpg.

Fig. 10.9: Copyright © by Mickthompso7 (CC BY-SA 4.0) at https://commons.wikimedia.org/wiki/File:Ax7-photos-extralarge_1308870662183.jpg.

Fig. 10.10: Copyright © by Weekly Dig (CC BY 2.0) at https://commons.wikimedia.org/wiki/File:Skrillex.jpg.

Fig. 10.11: Copyright © 2010 Depositphotos/SergeyNivens.

Index

B

C

D

G

J

M

N

O

P

Q

R

S

T

U

V

W

X

Y

Z